Critical Essays on Toni Morrison

Nellie Y. McKay

G. K. Hall & Co. • Boston, Massachusetts

Library of Congress Cataloging in Publication Data

McKay, Nellie Y.

  Critical essays on Toni Morrison.

  (Critical essays on American literature)
  Includes index.
  1. Morrison, Toni—Criticism and interpretation.
I. Title II. Series.
PS3563.08749Z76 1988   813'.54   87-34989
ISBN 0-8161-8884-X (alk. paper)

This publication is printed on permanent durable acid-free paper
MANUFACTURED IN THE UNITED STATES OF AMERICA

CRITICAL ESSAYS ON AMERICAN LITERATURE

This series seeks to anthologize the most important criticism on a wide variety of topics and writers in American Literature. Our readers will find in various volumes not only a generous selection of reprinted articles and reviews but original essays, bibliographies, manuscript sections, and other materials brought to public attention for the first time. This collection of reviews and essays traces the critical reputation of Toni Morrison, one of the most important writers in America. The introduction by Nellie Y. McKay gives an overview of Morrison's career and critical reactions to it. Included are reviews of all Morrison's books, two major interviews, and articles on *The Bluest Eye*, *Sula*, *Song of Solomon*, and *Tar Baby*, along with a section of essays on general topics. Among the authors of reprinted essays are Ruby Dee, Robert G. O'Meally, Gerry Brenner, Eleanor W. Traylor, and Genevieve Fabre. There are also nine original essays commissioned specifically for publication in this volume, new studies by Michael Awkward, Trudier Harris, Deborah E. McDowell, Robert Grant, Kathleen O'Shaughnessy, Craig H. Werner, Carolyn Denard, Margaret B. Wilkerson, and Anne Adams. We are confident that this book will make a permanent and significant contribution to American literary study.

James Nagel, GENERAL EDITOR

Northeastern University

For Warner Berthoff and Robert Kiely
teachers and friends

and

for Connie and Preston Williams
family by love and choice

and

for Joyce and Don Scott
enduring friends

CONTENTS

INTRODUCTION

Toni Morrison has said:

> I am not *like* James Joyce; I am not *like* Thomas Hardy; I am not *like* Faulkner. I am not *like* in that sense. . . . My effort is to be *like* something that has probably only been fully expressed in [black] music. . . . Writing novels is a way to encompass this—this something.[1]

This "something," she tells us, is the "quality of hunger and disturbance [in the spirituals and in jazz] that never ends." Emotional closure, she thinks, is not compatible with the black artistic sensibility. "Jazz always keeps you on the edge," she notes. "There is no final chord. . . . a long chord, but no final chord."[2] Her explanation of the affinity between her writing and black music defines her sense of tradition. "For a long time, the art form that was healing for Black people," she tells us, "was music. That music is no longer *exclusively* ours; . . . it is the mode of contemporary music everywhere. So another form has to take that place."[3] She suggests that the African-American novel is that form. The black writer, she believes, can bring something unique—approximating the profound depths of black music—to fiction: "an ineffable quality . . . that is curiously black."[4] That essence of ancient, authentic blackness in her work separates her from the "greats" of modernism with whom she is so often compared, and makes her kin to poets like Langston Hughes and "The Negro Speaks of Rivers."[5] But how do we account for it? "Where does the first line of any novel—like any journey—actually begin?"[6] The second question, asked of Morrison by Gloria Naylor, herself a well-acclaimed novelist, is, in fact, a probe of traditions. Responding to her own inquiry, Naylor cites the much-quoted opening line of Morrison's first novel, *The Bluest Eye*: "Quiet as it's kept, there were no marigolds in the fall of 1941."[7] "That sentence," she observed, "was the product of a thousand tributaries before it would ultimately swell with an existence of its own, flowing off to become yet another source to unaccountable possibilities," including Naylor's own works.[8] But whence did it come? From what black source and how? Morrison claims to have read almost no novels by black male or female writers until after she began to publish. Yet, her early books resonate with

1

echoes of the black aesthetic tradition, proof, she says, of her inherent connectedness to the ineffable qualities of blackness.[9] And, she insists, black writers have ancestors, not "just parents, . . . [but] timeless people whose relationships to the characters are benevolent, instructive, and protective, . . . [and who] provide a certain kind of wisdom" to them.[10] But if Morrison claims the black aesthetic in place of modernism, and if, as Michael Awkward and others in this collection insist, the black male tradition often presented "roadblocks" for black female writers, then within that latter tradition she claims a black women's "tradition . . . [a] world as perceived by black women at certain times . . . however they treat it, and whatever they select out of it to record."[11] Writing out of both the black and black women's traditions, her novels are a rejection of white patriarchal modernism, and are radical revisions of the race and male-centered Afro-American literary tradition, and aim to liberate the latter from the social realism into which it has long been mired.

Since that first line of her first book, Toni Morrison has published three additional novels, and another is expected.[12] When the new book appears, she will become the first black American woman to have five novels to her credit, an achievement gained by only a few black male writers. But in spite of her distinctive accomplishments, many tributaries connect Morrison to the black female tradition in writing. Quiet as it's kept, the long prose form (as Morrison likes to call her work, because this description differentiates it from the short story),[13] believed by most people to have been slow in developing as a mode of writing among black women, has been widely appropriated by them. Between 1859, when Harriet Wilson's *Our Nig* appeared, and 1964, at least fifty-nine such works by black women went into print.[14] That number has probably doubled since 1964. During the Harlem Renaissance of the 1920s and early 1930s, Jessie Fauset was the only black author to publish three novels. Within this tradition, Morrison says that, as an individual black woman novelist, she works on "one facet of a prism [that] has millions of sides . . . and then you read [another] book [by] a black woman who has this sensibility and this power and this talent and she's over there writing about that side of this huge sort of diamond . . . I claim this little part."[15] She shares another special link in this chain of tradition with Fauset, who, while she was literary editor of the *Crisis*, "discovered" the most significant Harlem Renaissance writers and published their first works in that journal.[16] As senior editor at Random House, Morrison brought several black writers, including Angela Davis, Toni Cade Bambara, Henry Dumas, and Gayl Jones to that publisher's lists. Her interest in promoting black writers, as was Fauset's, was her desire to participate in the development of a canon in black literature in which writers "can get down to the craft of writing . . . [as] black people talking to black people."[17]

Morrison, a woman of many talents, comes from a long line of hard-working, industrious black people who actively fought racial oppression and inferior social and economic status. Fleeing poverty of mind and body and searching for better educational opportunities for their children, her maternal grandparents left Alabama and traveled by way of Kentucky to Ohio early in this century. Her father, a Georgian by birth, also fled that state's hostile racial climate and settled in Ohio. The second of four children, Morrison, born Chloe Anthony Wofford, grew up in Lorain, Ohio, during the Great Depression. Even then she learned that neither race, class, nor gender precluded opposition to inhumane conditions. When her family was forced to accept public aid, Morrison's mother, in great indignation, wrote a letter to Franklin D. Roosevelt protesting the bug-ridden meal that welfare recipients were given.[18] But Morrison's childhood world was not primarily dominated by black responses to white oppression. In fact, in Lorain, where everyone was poor, neighborhoods were less rigidly segregated than in many parts of the country, and overt racial hostility was not prevalent. Memorable are her recollections of the richness of black lore, black music, black myths, and the cultural rituals of her family and community. Her grandfather played the violin, her mother sang in the choir and decoded dream symbols, and there were signs, visitations, and ways of knowing that transcended concrete reality. Storytelling, especially of ghost stories, was shared activity for the men and women in her family. As a teenager, Morrison read the European literary masters—English, Russian, and French.

Morrison attended Howard University, where she changed her name to Toni, and received an undergraduate degree in English. Then she earned a master's degree from Cornell University. Her thesis was on Faulkner and Virginia Woolf. In 1957, as an instructor in English, she returned to Howard from Texas Southern University where she had gone on her first teaching appointment. At Howard, she began to write, but little came of it there. It took marriage, two sons, a divorce, an eighteen-month return to Lorain, an editing job at the textbook subsidiary of Random House in Syracuse, and writing at night after the children were asleep (to combat the loneliness she felt then and there) to bring her efforts to full bloom. In 1970, *The Bluest Eye* appeared from Holt, Rinehart, and Winston. By this time Morrison had moved to an editorial position at Random House in New York City.

The Novels and Their Readers

The Bluest Eye makes one of the most powerful attacks yet on the relationship between Western standards of female beauty and the psychological oppression of black women. But Pecola Breedlove's predicament, as the young black girl who feels that blackness condemns her to ugliness and lovelessness, is not only a problem for black girls and women. Morrison makes this clear in an exposé of the "ugliness" of black poverty, powerlessness, and loss of positive self-concept in this poignant, haunting, poetic narrative. *The Bluest Eye* was not an instant literary success, and it was out of print by 1974. Its reincarnation, however, has been triumphant. Initially, it had few black reviewers; although its notices appeared in important organs: the library journals, the *New York Times Book Review*, the *New Yorker*, *Newsweek*, *Black World*, *CLA Journal*, and *Freedomways* among them, and it brought Toni Morrison to public notice. In its wake, her name appeared frequently in magazine articles in which she commented on black life and women's issues, and according to critic Susan Blake, in one year she wrote twenty-eight reviews for the *New York Times*.[19]

Sula, her second book, which Morrison calls a novel about black women's friendships, and about good and evil, appeared in 1973. *Sula* not only breaks with popular stereotypes of black women in western literature, but creates one of the few black women heroines to deliberately embrace the role of a pariah. Although not universally liked, *Sula* had a wider reception than *The Bluest Eye*, and brought Morrison national recognition. Black women and men were widely represented among its critics, with black women identifying most often with the issues that it raised. *Redbook* excerpted it, and the Book-of-the-Month Club offered it as an alternate selection. In 1975 it was nominated for the National Book Award in Fiction. Still, in the middle of the 1970s, Morrison's name and books were not household words in the conventional dwelling place of significant American writers and contemporary American literature. And most readers had negative responses to this book. Black journalist Margo Jefferson, writing in *Ms.*, was an exception. She recognized the complexity of the characters in both of Morrison's early books and called them "rich, confident . . . [and] filled with pleasure and pain."[20]

Song of Solomon, published in 1977, changed Toni Morrison's public reputation from aspiring novelist to outstanding American writer. It was the most extensively reviewed of her books but the one black women are most critical of. This was also her first novel with a male hero, and a questing one at that, a theme readily recognizable in Anglo-European literature. The power of the novel, however, is in Morrison's use of black mythology and the strength of its elements of black culture. The *New York Times Book Review* gave the book front page space; it was named a Book-of-the-Month Club selection, the first by a black writer to receive such attention since Richard Wright's *Native Son* in 1940.[21] In 1978 Morrison won the National Book Critics Circle Award and the American Academy and Institute of Arts and Letters Award for this novel. A year later, *Song of Solomon* was a paperback best-seller with 570,000 copies in print. Other accolades also came to her. She was featured on a PBS series, "Writers in America," appointed to President Carter's National Council of the Arts, and elected to the American Academy and Institute of Arts and Letters.

Tar Baby, a modern version of the many-versioned folk tale, was published in 1981, and Toni Morrison was featured on the cover of *Newsweek*. Never before had this happened to a black American woman writer, and, as the author herself smilingly quipped, to a "gray-haired middle-aged" one at that.[22] Unlike her previous books, this one is set in the French West Indies, outside of the predominantly black community and outside of the borders and protections of life in the United States. It was also her first book with white people as central actors. A month after its release, *Tar Baby* was on the *New York Times* best-seller list, where it remained for four months.[23] Her appearances to promote the book included a European tour. Toni Morrison, black woman writer, had put Lorain, Ohio, on the literary map, raised the currency of black women writers in American literature, and was an American writer of international fame.

No doubt there were several reasons, unrelated to the literary merits of the works, that account for the limited, mixed and/or unfavorable attention that greeted *The Bluest Eye* and *Sula* during the first half of the 1970s. Perhaps the most compelling is that the majority of the early readers who reviewed these books were white Americans who were uncomfortable with Morrison's characterizations—with the unvarnished portrayals of black women's lives in a society where race and gender oppressed them constantly; where the weak or innocent were doubly oppressed; where those who stayed at home and behaved "well" did not inherit the earth; and black women pariahs "went down" like "mighty oaks." How does a white critic respond to a book about a young black girl who goes mad in quest of blue eyes when Ruby Dee, a hardy, worldly wise black woman, can only say ". . . *The Bluest Eye* . . . my heart hurts. It's all I can do not to lie down and cry";[24] and another asks a black audience, "How many Pecolas did you help create today?"[25] White critics praised Morrison's writing—her precise poetic prose, her vision, her perceptions of black pain, and the ways in which she constructed narrative—but, as Jerry Bryant noted, Pecola Breedlove and Eva and Sula Peace bear no resemblances to the stereotypes of black women that populate our national literature. "Most of us," he wrote, "have been conditioned to expect something else in black characters, especially black female characters. . . . We do not expect to see a fierceness bordering on the demonic."[26] On a more negative note, Sara Blackburn, in a *New York Times* review of *Sula*, noted condescendingly that the rise of the women's movement probably gave *The Bluest Eye* an audience, and an uncritical one, since middle-class white women were anxious to acknowledge the existence of poor black women. But *Sula* was just too much for Blackburn, who did not conceal her antipathy toward the work. It was narrowly conceived, she complained, and praised the art but dismissed the materials from which that came. "Toni Morrison," she wrote, "is far too talented to remain only a marvelous recorder of the black side of provincial American life,"[27] and she advised Morrison to "address a riskier contemporary American reality . . . and take her place among the most serious, important, and talented American novelists."[28] *The Bluest Eye* and *Sula* disturb readers in disquieting ways.

On the other hand, *Song of Solomon* and *Tar Baby*, brilliant novels in their own right, are considerably less confusing, threatening, or intimidating for white readers than the earlier books. Even with its focus on black history and myth, *Song of Solomon* embraces the comfortable, familiar Anglo-Western theme of the young man in search of himself. Pecola Breedlove and Eva and Sula Peace force reader confrontations with an unsettling concrete reality of pain and suffering, while Pilate, the most significant woman in *Song of Solomon*, is larger than life, a mythic figure, transcending time and place and the abilities of mere mortals. The characters in this book offer literary reassurance rather than literary agitation. Even the Seven Days, with their potential threat of unbridled racial violence, can be explained and understood. Critic Earl Frederick's response to *Song of Solomon* illustrates. Writing in the *Nation* and commenting on the often-heard white complaint that black literature is not universal, he observed: "If there is any hope that a current black author can achieve, to the satisfaction of whites, not just an adequate but an irrefutable mix of black form and human content . . . then it must rest with Toni Morrison."[29] White Americans identified with Morrison's third novel on another level too: they had more empathy for a book "driven by men."[30] The conventional literary audience responded to *Tar Baby* in a similar tone. Jadine, the Sorbonne-educated high-fashion Paris model, and Ondine Childs, her old-fashioned, conservative aunt, are drastically unlike familiar stereotypes of black women in white Western literature, but they are equally unlike Eva and Sula Peace. Sidney Childs is the epitome of the faithful retainer—the much-wished-for reliable black man. Even Son, primitive, exotic, and frightening when he appears, is harmless in his relationship to white people, once the reader takes his measure. These are not disturbing characters, except perhaps inasmuch as they represent the worst fears of white racists: that black people have aspirations and a sense of self beyond basic instincts of survival. Linda Hill called *Tar Baby* "an enchanting journey into a world seldom seen by black or white readers. . . . [a] complex, mystifying, paradoxical black *and* white world. . . . [with] phrases like music and painting—chords, melodies, scales, and tones. . . . [Morrison] entertains, jokes, teases, promises, fulfills."[31] These two novels gave many white readers themes and patterns with which they could identify. Their "black texts" were often unrecognized.

Critical Essays on Toni Morrison

This volume is the first of its kind to appear on this author and the first in this series on a black woman writer.[32] Now a major figure for the teaching, writing, and research on contemporary American literature, Morrison's place here is richly deserved. Her novels are widely read and discussed in classrooms across the country in courses in Afro-American Studies, American literature, and Women's Studies. Enormous changes in the critical perceptions of her writings and of her importance to American and Women's literature have occurred since 1970, most notably demonstrated by the inclusion of the complete text of *The Bluest Eye* in the Norton Anthology of Women's Literature. Unquestionably, Toni Morrison has entered the canon.

Another proof of Morrison's status in the academy is in the rapidly growing body of critical attention that her work is enjoying. As one of the vanguard whose work announced the new era in black women's writings in America in the 1970s, it is not unexpected that much of the attention on her centers on her place in the tradition of Afro-American and American Letters. The majority of the essays in this collection address this issue.

Of the eight essays on the novels in this volume, two (Brenner on *Song of Solomon* and Traylor on *Tar Baby*) were previously published elsewhere in their entirety, and one (Fabre on *Song of Solomon*) is a shortened version of an address at a 1985 American Studies Seminar at Salzburg. The remainder were written especially for this collection. The new essays, differing in perspectives and approaches, were chosen to indicate the range of ideas embodied in the new criticism that is emerging on Morrison, and for the light they shed on new readings of the novels. The two previously published essays complement and oppose each other in their discourse on Morrison and traditions and correspond to the spirit of this volume. The entire group represents the work of black and white, male and female, younger and older, national and international scholars currently engaged in Afro-American and/or women's literature.

"Conversations from Abroad," two interviews that Morrison granted to American women currently living outside of the United States, open the main body of this collection and "The German Reception of Toni Morrison," seen through the eyes of a black American woman at home, ends it. Historically, black Americans have had favorable interactions with Europeans, and expatriate blacks, writers, and others, have been laudatory of Europeans since the late 1800s. Framing the book in this way emphasizes the interplay between black and white, old and new world connections, and the symbolic space that black American women occupy within them. It acknowledges that the many tributaries of the black woman's tradition in writing move back and forth, meandering through concentric circles of Anglo-European, ethnically diverse American, African, male, and female visions of reality. Yet, if Morrison is correct, it is as distinctive as the unmistakable blackness of and differences between John Coltrane and Louis Armstrong.

Sandi Russell is a black American woman living and writing (mainly about black women writers in the United States) in England; Rosemarie K. Lester is a white American woman living, writing, and teaching in Germany. The women have different relationships to Europe as well as to the United States (Lester's roots are German; Russell has no kinship ties to Britain), and they have different kinds of conversations with Morrison.

Russell is an outsider in Britain at a time when race relations in that country are poor. In their common writers and sister-strangers-in-a-strange-land status she seeks to establish bonds of race, gender, and nationality with Morrison. Her essay, reprinted from the London *Women's Review*, focuses on black ties and roots through language, a prominent theme in Morrison's writings. Here Morrison's attitude reinforces her assertion that she writes for black women so that they may "repossess, re-name, re-own" their cultural bonds.

Lester is an academic who identifies herself as a feminist. Her interview with Morrison in Frankfurt, during the latter's publicity tour for *Tar Baby*, aired on a women's radio program with Lester as interpreter. Lester's political philosophy leads her to focus on Morrison's activities, and she casts her as the successful multidimensional woman in the modern world. Morrison answers questions frankly. Claiming the world for her canvas, she tells Lester that she writes without a focus on gender and out of the "sensibility" of what she considers provocative and touches on her woman's sensibility.

The essays on individual novels focus on Morrison and the literary tradition. Michael Awkward, Deborah McDowell, and Robert Grant, in close textual readings, explore Morrison's narrative strategies for revising the conventions of the race-conscious, male-centered black literary tradition. On the other hand, Trudier Harris, Genevieve Fabre, Kathleen O'Shaughnessy, and Eleanor Traylor, in thematic studies, argue for Morrison's strong roots in black culture; Gerry Brenner and Craig Werner examine separate novels against theories of modernism.

Awkward, in a discussion of *The Bluest Eye*, and McDowell and Grant, on *Sula*, agree that Morrison's novels deliberately reject literary realism and the tradition in which race is the dominant discourse and men are always at its center. They see her use of women as central characters in these novels as a refiguring of the nature of the Afro-American literary canon and a bid for new directions in that creative venture.

In "Roadblocks and Relatives: Critical Revision in Toni Morrison's *The Bluest Eye*," Michael Awkward does an intertextual reading of scenes from *The Bluest Eye* and from novels by Richard Wright and Ralph Ellison. He claims the works of the men represented literary "roadblocks" to female "artistic self-hood." As he sees it, in revising Wright's and Ellison's work and manipulating the prefatory primer (the white stance), Morrison gives "authentication and voice to specific types of black and female experiences." The result of these strategies, he feels, is that *The Bluest Eye* created canonical space for several of the black female novels that followed it and revised the "overwhelmingly male disposition of the Afro-American literary canon."

Deborah McDowell has a different critical approach in "The Self and the Other: Reading Toni Morrison's *Sula* and the Black Female Text." Drawing on both reader-response theories and recent discussions of character in narrative, she points out that *Sula* reorders the priorities of a race- and male-centered Afro-American narrative and literary criticism. She adds that in complicating familiar conceptions of unified character and self, Morrison disappoints the Afro-American reader's desire for a "positive" *self* as opposed to a "negative" *other*. She asserts that such oppositions give way in *Sula* to blurred and confused boundaries in this fragmentary, episodic, elliptical novel. She theorizes that by its nature, *Sula* "lights a way out of the prison of binary thinking" that has long trapped black American literature and criticism. She concludes that Morrison offers a revisionist model for the act of reading that bypasses self-recognition and self-affirmation in favor of self-exploration.

Robert Grant's essay concurs with both Awkward (on *The Bluest Eye*) and McDowell (on *Sula*), stating that Morrison shatters traditional literary boundaries and defines new ones. In his "Absence into Presence: The Thematics of Memory and 'Missing' Subjects in Toni Morrison's *Sula*," he admits the book's kinship to the modernist, Afro-American, and feminist traditions, but argues persuasively that Morrison moves beyond those recognizable frames. Among other things, he points to the title character's lack of a conventionally unified sensibility and personality as aspects that make the novel, thematically and politically, sui generis, therefore, an unpredictable text. Focusing on *Sula*'s missing subjects and objects (Eva's leg and her comb) and missing people (Chicken Little, Jude, Ajax), he claims that Morrison's skillful techniques turn these interstices and indeterminate spaces into "sources of figurative fulfillment through memory and/or imaginative projection." He concludes that the absences enlarge the female hero and deconstruct the reader's "expectation[s] of politicized 'determinacy.'"

On the other side of literary traditions, Harris, Fabre, O'Shaughnessy, and Traylor explore the thematic underpinnings of the novels. The essays reveal a variety of perspectives on the subject. Working with *The Bluest Eye*, Harris explores positive aspects of cultural heritage; Fabre and O'Shaughnessy locate literary heritage in *Song of Solomon* in oral elements of black folk culture; and Traylor connects *Tar Baby* (as written word) to the oral tradition and the visual arts. In addition, she also identifies the historical role of black women in black culture.

In "Reconnecting Fragments: Afro-American Folk Tradition in *The Bluest Eye*," Harris sees *The Bluest Eye* as "Afro-American folk culture in progress." The black population of Lorain, Ohio, participates in traditions that foster black survival, comfort in times of need, and enduring creativity. Against this grain, Pauline and Cholly Breedlove erroneously accept the myth of the North as a place where blacks become socially and economically free. As a result, they lose their abilities to use the old folk forms that sustained generations of rural blacks, and thus they broke chains of continuity in black culture.

In "Genealogical Archaeology or the Quest For Legacy in Toni

Morrison's *Song of Solomon*," Genevieve Fabre begins with the idea that *Song of Solomon* is both a "lyric epic adventure" and an "incursion" into "mystery, poetry and prophesy." She notes that with great skill Morrison uses ironic overtones and paradox to "celebrate narrative and parable and dramatize an archetypal journey across ancestral territory." But Milkman, she points out, by temperament is an unlikely hero for the task that Morrison gives him: to "de/re/construct" chronology and genealogy. Before he can do that there are riddles to solve and pitfalls and trials to overcome, all of which complicate the nature of his journey. In identifying specific elements in Morrison's connection to black folk culture Fabre points to the writer's use of oral tradition; her acknowledgment of the importance of naming; her appropriation of the role of the joke in black culture; and her respect for cultural mythology, among other elements. The novel, as Fabre sees it, documents the legacy of survival and the power of collective memory kept alive through names, stories, words, songs, and the rituals of life and death.

Kathleen O'Shaughnessy's essay, "'Life life life life': The Community as Chorus in *Song of Solomon*," focuses on the role of the community in the novel, a popular theme in Morrison criticism. Here "the chorus," or audience (within the novel, but also embodied in readers outside of it) participates in the action through ritual dance, song, and commentary. O'Shaughnessy traces the ritual qualities of music, with its roots in African traditions, and song and dance motifs, through the novel.

Eleanor Traylor's essay "The Fabulous World of Toni Morrison: *Tar Baby*" anchors Morrison's novel in issues of a cultural past that are a source of sustaining power in the present. By pulling *Tar Baby*, "Grandma say, Grandpa say," and Romare Bearden's paintings into the same circle, Traylor sees the novel as part of the unity of the oral, visual, and written in the Afro-American tradition. She calls our attention to the image of a man standing on the deck of a ship in the novel's opening scene. This image calls Olaudah Equiano, the African, to mind. His narrative, written by himself almost 200 years ago, makes use of a similar image. On the deck of a slave ship, having survived the horrors of the Middle Passage, Equiano vowed to learn to navigate the circumstances of his life that would otherwise destroy him. *Tar Baby*, says Traylor, is a "story about nourishment . . . the story of a man in search of nourishment [in order to navigate the circumstances of his life] and a woman whose nourishing power, cut off from its source, has been defused." This defusion of black people's ability to nourish themselves and each other, which Traylor calls the central tension in the story, can be avoided, she tells us. There are guides to prevent it, as Morrison's "fabulous" fiction demonstrates; guides to direct those who must live in the modern world. Such, says Traylor, include the women to whom the novel is dedicated: the author's female relatives.

Gerry Brenner, in "*Song of Solomon*: Rejecting Rank's Monomyth and Feminism," and Craig Werner's "The Briar Patch as Modernist Myth:

Morrison, Barthes and the Tar Baby As-Is" demonstrate that Morrison, although she shares characteristics with them, is "not *like*" the Anglo-European male literary figures to whom her name is often linked, or as Brenner also shows, she does not subscribe to the ideals of the contemporary white, feminist heroine. The latter should come as no surprise to those who have read Morrison's nonfiction prose. She has often voiced strong ambivalent feelings toward the white Women's Liberation Movement.[33]

Brenner first examines Morrison's Milkman against Otto Rank's powerful myth of the hero (distinguished parentage; prophesy of danger before birth; the hero's surrender to water; his rescue by animals; his nurturance by humble folk or animals; discovering his parents; revenge on and acknowledgment by his father; and final achievement of honors). As she sees it, Morrison appears to appropriate Rank's myth by creating a hero who superficially fits his criteria. Then, through Milkman's actions, she ridicules him and thus shows her disdain for heroes and hero worship. On the other hand, the celebratory prose in the novel goes to Pilate, who also disappoints reader expectations of an ideal feminist heroine. Feminist critics note that Pilate "originates" nothing, lacks conscious knowledge, and has an unclear sense of mission. Brenner calls these accusations into question by noting that the character is independent, wide-spirited, and a culture bearer. She sees Pilate's value in her self-acceptance, self-content, and ethic of love. Morrison, she says, goes her own way and has rejected the male model and the feminist ideal of heroism.

In his work, Craig Werner locates Morrison's *Tar Baby* amidst the tensions between the Euro-American and Afro-American understandings of shared myths. First, he claims that Morrison and Barthes share common ground in breaking with T. S. Eliot's notion of myth as the bearer of universal meaning, and subscribing to myth as sign and signifier. But Morrison also breaks with Barthes to impose an Afro-American under-standing of myth and the dehistorization of the meaning of experience on her novel. Werner focuses on the tensions between Euro-American and Afro-American understandings of myth and sees Morrison adapting the folk sensibility to the is-ness (things are) of Afro-American experience, and exploring is-ness as a texture of competing myths and understandings of myths. The Tar Baby story, with its possibilities for multiple meanings, is perfect for Morrison's purposes in such an exercise. According to Werner, Morrison makes a "panoramic presentation of the complex is-ness of [the] Afro-American experience" through the actions of black and white individuals who reflect the tar baby myth.

The three essays under "General Topics" are new in Toni Morrison criticism. Carolyn Denard examines Morrison's fiction for points of convergence between feminism and ethnicity; Margaret Wilkerson, a well-known drama critic, explores the significance of the stage (oral) voice in the novels; and Anne Adams looks at how Morrison's works are seen and discussed in Germany. These essays provide another view of the breadth of interest in Morrison scholarship and give this work an added dimension.

In "The Convergence of Feminism and Ethnicity in the Fiction of Toni Morrison," Denard explores Morrison's novels at the intersection of culture and feminist consciousness. While there has never been any doubt that Morrison grounds her work in black culture, issues of feminism have been more ambiguous for critics. This comes partly from the writer's often-stated rejection of many of the goals of white feminism, a stance which, in fact, is common among black women. At the same time, with the exception of *Song of Solomon*, Morrison's novels are woman-centered, and her female characters are mostly strong and independent human beings. What Denard argues is that Morrison rejects the feminism that removes black women from their cultural moorings and through women like Eva Peace and Pilate makes a case for a feminism that remains wedded to the interests of men and women in the black community.

Although Toni Morrison has written a play, which was first performed in January 1986, her writer's reputation rests solidly on her fiction.[34] Margaret Wilkerson, however, insists that, judging from the dramatic voices in her novels, Morrison could easily have appropriated drama as her mode of artistic expression. Her "Dramatic Voice in Toni Morrison's Novels," an effort to prove this thesis, is an essay that discusses a subject that probably has never been written about. Other pieces in this collection have made much of Morrison's skill in translating the black oral tradition into the written word and the uses that she makes of songs and sounds in the telling of her stories. Wilkerson isolates these qualities in Morrison's narratives and illustrates their potential for stage effectiveness. Chief among them is the writer's storytelling ability; the complexity and development in her characterizations; the conflict in her plot lines; her "crisp . . . revealing and concise" dialogue; the richness and scope of her vision; and the handling of climactic scenes as prime dramatic elements in her works. Wilkerson's essay brings something completely new and infinitely interesting to Morrison criticism. In essence, her conclusions link Toni Morrison to the ancestral griots, the African storytellers who were indeed dramatists handing down the history and literature of the culture from one generation to another when writing was unknown.

During this century there have been a number of well-known black American writers who have made their homes in Europe. The oppressiveness of race in America has been named most often as the reason for their expatriation. At the same time, the works of many black men and women writers, at home and abroad, have been translated into European languages. The present European interest in black American women writers makes this an opportune time for American scholars to take an interest in the translations and in the nature of the critical reception these writers are receiving on that continent. Anne Adams's essay, "Straining to Make Out the Words of the 'Lied': The German Reception of Toni

Morrison," makes a good beginning. To the best of my knowledge this is the only scholarly work that has been done in this area of Morrison criticism, and Adams's essay is fascinating in what it reveals about attempts to cross barriers of language and culture.

Toni Morrison is read in several foreign languages including German, Spanish, French, Finnish, and Italian. Currently, all her novels are available in German translations and enjoy wide circulation in that country. Anne Adams read the novels in translations, some in more than one translation. She also read the criticism that appeared in German journals, newspapers, and magazines, with an eye on differentiating academic and popular criticism. Her essay is a critique of several translations of the novels and of the scholarly and popular responses to them in Germany. Because of Morrison's extensive use of the black oral tradition, her books present special problems to translators. Among the interesting and informative aspects of this essay, Adams discusses these language difficulties as they apply especially to German translators. She also describes some of the results of the failures to capture the black idiom. For reasons of a history of cultural crossings, black English, she tells us, can more easily be translated into French. In German, such efforts often fail. Her essay calls our attention to the practical and intellectual problems of language and culture differences.

This volume indicates the vitality of the new scholarship on Morrison. If, as several critics state here, Morrison's work is crucial in the refiguring of the Afro-American literary tradition now under way, there are exciting years ahead with a great deal more to be said about her novels. On the other hand, we are doubly fortunate for, from all indications, Morrison has much more to say to us through her writing. The future holds work for everyone, including the critics who now vigorously discuss the "middle-aged, gray-haired, colored lady" who strives to have her writing be *"like* something that [until now] has only been fully expressed in [black] music."

This volume exists because many people encouraged and supported my efforts, and many other people worked hard to make it a reality. To everyone, I am very grateful.

I especially thank Professor Franklin Wilson, Chairman of the Afro-American Studies Department at the University of Wisconsin, Madison, who first encouraged me to undertake the project. For their encouragement and support along the way, I thank my friends and colleagues at the University of Wisconsin, Madison, especially William Andrews, Betsy Draine, Susan Friedman, Linda Gordon, Freida High Tesfagioris, Judy Leavitt, Gerda Lerner, Florencia Mallon, Elaine Marks, William Vendeburg, and Craig Werner. I thank Pamela Bromberg of Simmons College for her critical reading of the first draft of the introduction, Deborah McDowell of the University of Virginia, Charlottesville for wanting to offer only her "best" to the collection, and Julie Chase, of the University of Wisconsin, whose help with library research was invaluable. I am especially grateful to the scholars who wrote essays for the collection, to whom all credit for whatever strengths it has is due.

I thank Professor Werner Sollors, Chairman of the Afro-American Studies Department, Harvard University, for friendship, encouragement of my work, pleasant work space when the manuscript was in preparation, and his generosity in making the research facilities of the department available to me during this time. I am grateful to Professors Nathan Huggins and Carololivia Herron of Harvard University for gifts of friendship and colleagueship, and to Marcelyn Dallis and Caron Betts, of the Afro-American Studies Department at Harvard, for the many kindnesses they offered to me during my stay with them.

Without the help, beyond-the-call-of-duty cooperation, and hard work of Margaret Brandenburg and Eleanor Salmon, of the University of Wisconsin, Madison, all the rest would have been in vain. Their contributions to the preparation of the manuscript cannot be measured.

And finally, I thank my good friends Nell Irvin Painter, for caring so much; Mary Helen Washington, who, in addition to everything else, served as my on-call librarian as the manuscript went through its final stages; and Marilyn Richardson, for always being there. For the shortcomings of this book, I accept full blame.

NELLIE Y. MCKAY

University of Wisconsin—Madison

Notes

1. Nellie McKay, "An Interview With Toni Morrison," *Contemporary Literature* 24, no. 4 (Winter 1983): 426.

2. McKay, "Interview," 429.

3. Toni Morrison, "Rootedness: The Ancestor as Foundation," in Mari Evans, ed., *Black Women Writers (1950-1980)* (New York: Anchor Books, 1984), 340.

4. Morrison, "Rootedness," 342.

5. Hughes's poem, an early work of the Harlem Renaissance, spoke to the quality of blackness that concerns Morrison.

6. Gloria Naylor and Toni Morrison, "A Conversation," *Southern Review* 21 (July 1985): 567.

7. Toni Morrison, *The Bluest Eye* (New York: Washington Square Press, 1972), 9.

8. Naylor and Morrison, "Conversation," 568. Naylor claims that reading Toni Morrison's work had a great deal to do with her decision to become a writer.

9. Ibid., 589-90.

10. Morrison, "Rootedness," 343.

11. Naylor and Morrison, "Conversation," 590.

12. Morrison's new novel, *Beloved*, will probably be released while this book is in press.

13. Morrison, "Rootedness," 340.

14. Carole McAlpine Watson, *Prologue—The Novels of Black American Women,*

1891–1965 (Westport: Greenwood Press, 1985). This bibliography omits Harriet Wilson's *Our Nig*, which was subsequently "discovered."

15. Naylor and Morrison, "Conversation," 590.

16. Carolyn Sylvander, *Jessie Fauset, American Writer* (New York: Witson Press, 1980), 95–98.

17. Susan Blake, "Toni Morrison," *Dictionary of Literary Biography—Afro-American Writers After 1955* (Detroit: Gale Research Co., 1984), 188.

18. Ibid., 188.

19. Ibid., 190.

20. Margo Jefferson, "Toni Morrison: Passionate and Precise," *Ms.* 3 (December 1974): 39. Review of *Sula*.

21. Quoted from Blake, "Toni Morrison," 194.

22. Jean Strouse, "Toni Morrison's Black Magic," *Newsweek* 97 (30 March 1981): 52.

23. Blake, "Toni Morrison," 196.

24. Ruby Dee, "Black Family in Search for Identity," *Freedomways* 11 (Third Quarter 1971): 319.

25. Liz Grant, "Review of *The Bluest Eye*," *Black World* 20 (May 1971): 52.

26. Jerry H. Bryant, "Something Ominous Here," *Nation* 219 (6 July 1974): 23. Review of *Sula*.

27. Sara Blackburn, Review of *Sula*, *New York Times Book Review*, 30 December 1973, 3.

28. Ibid., 3.

29. Earl Frederick, "The Song of Milkman Dead," *Nation* 225 (19 November 1977): 536.

30. McKay, "Interview," 417.

31. Linda Hill, "An Island, A Vision, The Beauty, and Son," *Black Enterprise* 11 (July 1981): 70. Review of *Tar Baby*.

32. Bessie W. Watson and Audrey L. Vinson, *The World of Toni Morrison* (DuBuque: Kendall/Hunt, 1985). Essays by the authors, and the only other collection on Morrison, is intended as a teaching tool for Morrison's novels.

33. Morrison, "Rootedness," 344.

34. Morrison's play, *Dreaming Emmett*, commissioned by the New York State Writers Institute, was first performed in 1986. I am unaware of critical response to it.

REVIEWS

Black Family Search for Identity

Ruby Dee°

I've just finished reading Toni Morrison's book, *The Bluest Eye* and my heart hurts. It's all I can do not to lie down and cry myself into some kind of relief from the life-pain of Pecola, the central character. She is a girl born black, poor and, by majority standard, ugly. It is also an account of the people that surround her, especially Pauline, her mother and Cholly, her father. They are the kind of people that all black people know of—or are— to varying degrees. The author digs up for viewing deep secret thoughts, terrible yearnings and little-understood frustrations common to many of us. She says these are the gnawings we keep pushed back into the subconscious, unadmitted; but they must be worked on, ferreted up and out so we can breathe deeply, say loud and truly believe "Black is beautiful."

Pecola, soon after entering young womanhood, is raped by her father, and goes quietly mad into the fantasy world of her newly acquired blue eyes. Pauline, her mother, finds haven, hope, life and meaning as servant to the white, blond, blue-eyed, clean, rich, family to which she dedicates her love and her respect for an orderly life that poverty does not afford.

From her kitchen throne, she comes to view the reality of her own family with disgust and almost hatred. Cholly knew his father for one day. He learned about caring through his grandmother who died when he was a boy. Loving, mischievous, romantic, searching and with the resiliency common to youth, we watch him decay into middle age. He tries in one drunken moment to recapture the poetry—dimly remembered—when his soul was first moved. He had heard the poetry for the first time with Pauline and tried to capture it again from time to time. This time he tries with Pecola, his own daughter. It is around and through Pecola, the scorned and rejected girl who longs to be beautiful and to be loved, that most of the main characters plod through a desperate, pitiful search for meaning and personal definition.

Toni Morrison has not written a story really, but a series of painfully accurate impressions. How all of the people she talks about arrive where

°Review of *The Bluest Eye*. Reprinted from *Freedomways* 11 (3d quarter 1971): 319-20.

19

we meet them is what she is about with such great precision. She gives us a sense of some of the social elements of some of the people, black and white that contribute to the erosion of innocence and beauty. To read the book however, is to ache for remedy.

In *The Bluest Eye* she has split open the person and made us watch the heart beat. We feel faint, helpless and afraid—not knowing what to do to cover it up and keep it beating. We think of remedies past and remedies in progress to apply somehow while the thrashing heart still beats. We must think faster and work harder and hope that maybe a new breed of people, tight with God, in some dark privacy, has a plan ready to set it all—alright.

[Review of *The Bluest Eye*]   Haskel Frankel*

Shoemakers' children go barefoot, we are told. And physicians must be reminded to heal themselves. What happens to editors who write novels? The question is not academic, as Toni Morrison is an editor with a New York publishing firm, and this is her first novel. She reveals herself when she shucks the fuzziness born of flights of poetic imagery, as a writer of considerable power and tenderness, someone who can cast back to the living, bleeding heart of childhood and capture it on paper. But Miss Morrison has gotten lost in her construction.

The title pinpoints the focus of her book. Pecola Breedlove, in her first year of womanhood, is black, ugly and poor, living in a store front, sharing a bedroom with her brother, her crippled mother and her drunken father. Pregnant by her father, she goes to Soaphead Church, a man who believes himself possessed of holy powers. What she wants are blue eyes.

In this scene, in which a young black on the verge of madness seeks beauty and happiness in a wish for white girl's eyes, the author makes her most telling statement on the tragic effect of race prejudice on children. But the scene occurs late in the novel—far too late to achieve the impact it might have had in a different construction. For most of the way, Pecola yields center stage to Frieda and Claudia—who, aside from knowing her, and perhaps, offering contrast, by themselves being black and poor [though from a happier home], serve little purpose beyond distraction. Claudia tells the story part way into each of the four seasonal divisions of the book. From her, the narratives branch out to assorted portraits and events throughout the black community of Lorain, Ohio, with Pecola, whose story this eventually is, too often playing a secondary role until the novel zeroes in on her for the ending. Her mental breakdown, when it comes, has only the impact of reportage.

*Reprinted from *New York Times Book Review* 1 (November 1970): 46–47. © 1970 by The New York Times Company. Reprinted by permission.

Miss Morrison never bores as she wanders around town. There are vivid scenes: Pecola's first "ministratin'"; a "pretty milk-brown lady" driving Pecola from her home for the killing of a cat, by the woman's own son: the young Cholly Breedlove [later to be Pecola's father] caught during the sex act by white men and being forced to continue for their amusement. Given a scene that demands a writer's best, Miss Morrison responds with control and talent. Yet there are moments when the mind stops and questions. The novel begins: "Nuns go by as quiet as lust . . ." [How quiet is lust? Is it always?] Or: ". . . he will not unrazor his lips until spring." Does that mean he will not shave around his mouth all winter? And just what is "an ivory sleep"?

With the flaws and virtues tallied, I found myself still in favor of *The Bluest Eye*. There are many novelists willing to report the ugliness of the world as ugly. The writer who can reveal the beauty and the hope beneath the surface is a writer to seek out and encourage.

Beautiful, Needed, Mysterious   Barbara Smith°

While I was reading *Sula* the second time, my grandmother, who was 87, died. In one way her death was expected, since she was old and ill, but in many other ways it was not. I have been made familiar with the reality of loss several times since my mother died when I was nine, but I have never grown used to it.

My grandmother's funeral was brief and restrained, except when a woman I did not know sang in a worn and quavering voice, "What a Friend We Have in Jesus." The song made me think of my grandmother herself, singing the same words and many others throughout my childhood. It brought back *Church* and how important it had once been to me simply because it was so vitally important to the women who brought me up. I wondered about my grandmother's faith and whether the heaven she had believed in so deeply was there for her. I hoped that it was and imagined all the women in my family, now gone, greeting her with joy in a secure realm where Black spirits dwell.

Reading *Sula* at a time when I was doing so much remembering was comforting and right, because Toni Morrison remembers and recreates our lives so extremely well. Among many other things, she knows about the matters of death and faith that had been puzzling me. She writes of the funeral of a child:

As Reverend Deal moved into his sermon, the hands of the women unfolded like pairs of raven's wings and flew high above their hats in the air. They did not hear all of what he said; they heard the one word, or

°Review of *Sula*. Reprinted from *Freedomways*, no. 14 (1st quarter 1974): 69-72.

phrase, or inflection that was for them the connection between the event and themselves. For some it was the term "Sweet Jesus." And they saw the Lamb's eye and the truly innocent victim: themselves. They acknowledged the innocent child hiding in the corner of their hearts, holding a sugar-and-butter sandwich. That one. The one who lodged deep in their fat, thin, old, young skin, and was the one the world had hurt. Or they thought of their son newly killed and remembered his legs in short pants and wondered where the bullet went in. Or they remembered how dirty the room looked when their father left home and wondered if that is the way the slim, young Jew felt, he who for them was both son and lover and in whose downy face they could see the sugar-and-butter sandwiches and feel the oldest and most devastating pain there is: not the pain of childhood, but the remembrance of it.

Morrison is a virtuoso writer. The music and paintings she makes with words stun the reader's senses at the same time that they convince her of their totally natural rightness. She constantly achieves what critic Stephen Henderson calls the "mascon" image: *a massive concentration of Black experiential energy* which powerfully affects the meaning of Black speech, Black song, and Black poetry. . . .[1] These images are emblematic of the unique social-cultural heritage of Afro-American life and have deeply resonant associations for those who have experienced them first hand. Morrison's exquisite language and subject matter embody Black experience in a way rarely achieved by Black novelists, except for masters like Hurston and Toomer.

As significant as her rootedness in Black life, is the fact that her perspective is undeniably feminine. As in her first novel, *The Bluest Eye*, central to the work is the relationship between young Black girls, in this case Sula and Nel who are both 12 in 1922. Although Nel comes from a home that is rigidly respectable and Sula from one that is permissively free, they mesh immediately because they are both lonely and both dreamers. Morrison explains:

> So when they met, first in those chocolate halls and next through the ropes of the swing, they felt the ease and comfort of old friends. Because each had discovered years before that they were neither white nor male, and that all freedom and triumph was forbidden to them, they had set about creating something else to be. Their meeting was fortunate, for it let them use each other to grow on.

The girls share everything: games, hopes, fears and terrors until Nel marries Jude at age 17. Morrison explains that ". . . greater than her friendship [for Sula] was this new feeling of being needed by someone who saw her singly." If Nel needs to care for someone, her future husband needs very much to be cared for. His expectations succinctly define the traditional role of wife. Morrison writes:

> The more he thought about marriage, the more attractive it became. Whatever his fortune, whatever the cut of his garment, there would

always be the hem—the tuck and fold that hid his raveling edges; a someone sweet, industrious and loyal to shore him up. And in return he would shelter her, love her, grow old with her . . . The two of them together would make one Jude.

The image of a woman as "hem," existing to complete a man to the exclusion of her own needs is chilling, but accurate in terms of many women's lives.

Nel chooses conventional path of home and babies, while Sula leaves their small town for education and adventure. Ten years later she returns to raise havoc and inspire hatred in the Black people of the Bottom. Although Morrison says that she is "classically evil," I think that it is her unsettling noncomformity in a provincial place and time which makes her seem so wrong. Morrison explains that "she lived out her days exploring her own thoughts and emotions, giving them full rein, feeling no obligation to please anybody unless their pleasure pleased her." The reasons Morrison offers for Sula's numerous sexual encounters seem even closer to the source of her supposed wickedness.

In a way, her strangeness, her naiveté, her craving for the other half of her equation was the consequence of an idle imagination. Had she paints, or clay, or knew the discipline of the dance, or strings; had she anything to engage her tremendous curiosity and her gift for metaphor, she might have exchanged the restlessness and preoccupation with whim for an activity that provided her with all she yearned for. And like any artist with no art form, she became dangerous.

Sula is frightening because racial and sexual circumstance has determined that she will have no way of expressing her brilliant inner fire, yet she absolutely refuses to settle for the "colored woman's" lot of marriage, child-raising, labor and pain. I can verify the validity of Morrison's analysis. Having grown up in a family of talented women who worked as teachers in the segregated schools of the South and as domestics in the white kitchens of the North, I saw first hand the demoralizing effects of stymied intelligence and creativity. The people of the Bottom hate Sula with good reason because she is a living criticism of their dreadful lives of resignation.

To me the only case of true wickedness is Sula's casually sleeping with Nel's husband, who then takes the opportunity to desert his wife and their three children. The betrayal of the act itself is surpassed by Sula's inability to comprehend why she might have left him alone in the name of friendship. She retorts to Nel's accusations: "'I didn't kill him, I just fucked him. If we were such good friends, how come you couldn't get over it?'" Her bizarre insensitivity is consistent with her character, but I find it nearly unbearable. Morrison very skillfully gives the sympathetic reader a "last straw" so that she too will share the town's hatred and fear.

When Sula dies at age 30, the community falls on evil times. Morrison implies that her abrasive presence served a definite cathartic purpose for a people with so few hopeful possibilities.

The novel ends with Nel's discovery some 25 years later that the gray ball that had hovered just outside her field of vision ever since Jude left was not despair for him, but instead regret for the loss of Sula. Morrison writes:

> "All that time, all that time, I thought I was missing Jude." And the loss pressed down on her chest and came up into her throat. "We was girls together," she said as though explaining something. "O Lord, Sula," she cried, "girl, girl, girlgirlgirl."

The link between Black women who share each other's lives is strong. Morrison knows *and* feels this. She has made a book for us that is beautiful, mysterious and needed. I have only touched the surface. I loved it. Read it for yourself.

Note

1. Stephen Henderson, *Understanding the New Black Poetry*. New York, Morrow, 1973, page 44.

[Review of *Sula*]   Roseann P. Bell°

If there is validity in the maxim that the truth shall make us free, then Toni Morrison's *Sula* might well be regarded as a manifestation of truth, and hence, a corresponding avenue which leads toward some kind of freedom. We know the desperation of searching for truth and freedom in these perilous and confusing times, but the elegant craft and intense emotional power of *Sula* remind us that our search is not new; it is part of the continuum of self-discovery we must know before we come to the greatest of all freedoms: the understanding of human frailty and the understanding of other equally universal laws.

It is impossible to select one character who symbolizes a truth/freedom quest more than the others; they all represent the quest. But aside from the central character Sula, Eva deserves the most critical attention.

I am sure that some readers see Eva as a stereotyped "Black matriarch." She is not. The only thing Eva has in common with the Dilseys, the Berenices and the hundreds of other heavy-set, Black "domineering" mamas of traditional American literature, is that she is Black and she is the head of her household. True, Eva is a woman without a man, but she is not without men; they are there to complement that feminine, spiritual,

°Reprinted from *Obsidian* 2 (Winter 1976): 93–95.

physical and emotional part of herself which many American writers, Black and white, have not created because they have not seen, felt, or understood the three dimensional humanity of *human* Black women, as opposed to stereotypes.

The point is that Eva is *only* human, and that she dominates only one thing, her control over her own perception of reality, a reality which functions under the aegis of an inflexible moral code. She knew, for example, that it was wrong for children to go uncared for. She took in those indigent waifs "she had seen from the balcony of her bedroom or whose circumstances she had heard about from the gossipy old men who came to play checkers or read the *Courier*, or write her number" (p. 37).

The honesty in Eva which allowed her to "adopt" (i.e., take in) wayward, neglected children also fed her healthy hatreds. When her daughter, Hannah, accused her of hating colored people, "Eva said she only hated one, Hannah's father, Boyboy [who had deserted his children], and it was hating him that kept her alive and happy" (p. 37).

The most powerful statement of Eva's fully developed humanity is in the description of the death of Plum, her son. Early in the structure of the novel, we glide over the curious incidents which reinforce the accepted generalizations that make us comfortable and assure us that our thinking is not abnormal: we suffer through Eva's tribulations as she tries successfully to save her children from cold, poverty, and the psychological trauma of being deserted by Boyboy, their father. Some critics suck their teeth in that early part of the tale and attest to the limitless strength of Black women; this sets the mold for their subsequent speculations. But like the surprising truth of everyday accidents, these critics are lost when they encounter this same strong Eva in her addicted son's room, participating in a truth/freedom ritual while Plum is euphoric and close to the sublime:

> Plum on the rim of a warm light sleep was still chuckling. Mama. She sure was something. He felt twilight. Now there seemed to be some kind of wet light traveling over his legs and stomach with a deeply attractive smell. It wound itself—this wet light—all about him, splashing and running into his skin. He opened his eyes and saw what he imagined was the great wing of an eagle pouring a wet lightness over him. Some kind of baptism, some kind of blessing, he thought. . . . Eva stepped back from the bed and let the crutches rest under her arms. She rolled a bit of newspaper into a tight stick about six inches long, lit it and threw it onto the bed where the kerosene-soaked Plum lay in snug delight. Quickly as the *whoosh* of flames engulfed him, she shut the door and made her slow and painful journey back to the top of the house. (p. 47)

People who've read *Sula* invariably begin their exploration into the mysteries of the entire work with Eva's killing of Plum. Few see Eva's deed as an act of euthanasia, primarily because we do not wish to admit that "strong Black matriarchs" kill off their own children (except in some emotional ways). When we view the truth, however, we must focus on the symbolic meanings of life and death. To Eva, death was the ultimate reality. Having given Plum life through tremendous struggles, she could not endure his meandering in the artificial pastiche of death; she took him out of his dope-ridden misery and gave him the real thing. Present day mothers in Harlem or Atlanta or Watts or wherever have wished for a similar courage as they've watched the products of their love and suffering shrink into vegetables that would ultimately die the terrible death, foaming at the mouth and ignorant of the promise of life their mothers and fathers gave to them.

It is unlikely that Eva will ever suffer the shame or popularity of inspiring stereotypes; her truths and her freedoms cannot be confined to such restrictive characterizations. It is also doubtful that many other writers will fashion the chrysalis of universal truths with which an Eva could effectively interplay, as Toni Morrison has done. In addition to soul-wrenching testaments on the human animal, author Morrison boldly places the wonder of God, history, and the cosmos under the artistic glass. Unabashed, she steps to the lectern through the descriptions of her characters and their musings, and makes her own judgment about man and his toys: the need for belief in God and a palatable explanation of good and evil. The people of Medallion, denizens of a valley where "they tore the nightshade and blackberry patches from their roots to make room for the Medallion City Golf Course" (p. 3), are like thousands of Black people all over the United States, uprooted, defrocked, and "urban renewed." They have their own attitudes about natural, moral checks and balances:

> What was taken by outsiders to be slackness, slovenliness or even generosity was in fact a full recognition of the legitimacy of forces other than good ones. They did not believe doctors could heal—for them, none ever had done so. They did not believe that death was accidental—life might be, but death was deliberate. They did not believe that Nature was even askew—only inconvenient. Plague and drought were as "natural" as springtime. If milk could curdle, God knows robins could fall. The purpose of evil was to survive it and they determined (without ever knowing why they had made up their minds to do it) to survive floods, white people, tuberculosis, famine and ignorance. They knew anger well but not despair, and they didn't stone sinners for the same reason they didn't commit suicide—it was beneath them. (p. 90)

Eva comes from this milieu, and she is given more respect than others in the novel whom Christians might revere. Eva understands the presence of evil, and the entire tale is a description of her methods (successful ones) to recognize, deal with, survive, outwit and ultimately triumph over it.

It should not be surprising that *Sula* is regarded as an important statement in the contemporary discussions on the Black Aesthetic. Our aesthetic is what we are and what we perceive to be true, good, beautiful and useful. We can use Toni Morrison's art to help us answer questions about the length of time we have to continue functioning in a bankrupt and corrupt manner, aping the cynicism of decadent white societies while justifying violence, greed, and exploitation of ourselves and others, and all the while blaming the outcomes on our recent history of depression and despair. *Sula* (and especially the character Eva) suggests a positive way of freeing our fettered minds from the oppressive tentacles of a past which, when given neurotic attention, prevents us from progressing and projecting a new vision for ourselves and others interested in a more realistic human existence.

"If You Surrender to the Air. . . ." Melvin Dixon°

Once you begin hearing aloud the clipped voices of these characters and feel their lingering presence long after you've closed the book, once you start suspecting even the simplest gestures of the hand or the eyes of people around you and then want to keep the light on to avoid sleep and night, you are already entangled in history, myth, nightmare, and magic. You learn about greed, pain, sexual abandonment, and terror in the lives of people you wouldn't dare know nor even care about until now.

Such is the effect of *Song of Solomon*, Toni Morrison's third and most ambitious novel. The story weaves from the unspoken demands of hate and love in the lives of midwestern black men and women who, uprooted from the historical bond of the south and slavery, stutter to rename themselves in the uncertain struggles for land, family, posterity, and progress.

Macon Dead is one of these men. He advises his son, who is named after him but called Milkman, of "the most important thing you'll ever need to know: Own things. And let the things you own own other things. Then you'll own yourself and other people too."

The son of a former slave, now a prosperous landowner, Macon and his sister Pilate witness the brutal murder of their father by local whites. Forced into flight, the two live off the wilderness with the help of Circe, a domestic of the very family that committed the murder. In the woods the children are both comforted and haunted by the specter of their father. The ghost appears to be guiding them to safety, but in actuality, it is searching for its dead wife and its own eternal rest. The children are accosted and threatened by a white miner whom they kill; they flee from the scene, leaving behind the miner's gold. Their flight, the sack of gold, the father they half-buried along an eroding riverbank forever separate Pilate and Macon from each other.

Pilate, who was born without a navel minutes after her own mother expired in childbirth, becomes everything Macon is not. She seeks out

°Review of *Song of Solomon*. Reprinted from *Callaloo* 1, no. 4 (1978): 170–73.

distant relatives further south. Finding none, she turns her hand to helping others, even when they fear and ostracize her because of her "smooth stomach." Years later, with her daughter Rheba and granddaughter Hagar, Pilate arrives in the town where her brother has become the chief landlord for poorer blacks. Except for Macon, her only reminder of the past is a single brass box earring with her name written on brown paper and folded inside and a sack of bones believed to be those of the unburied miner. The ghost of the father had told her "You just can't fly on off and leave a body." And she discovers that "the dead you kill is yours. They stay with you anyway, in your mind. So it's a better thing to have the bones right there with you wherever you go. That way it frees up your mind."

Macon has chosen to emulate his father by acquiring as much real estate and hard cash as he can. More out of ambition than love, he marries Ruth, the daughter of the most respected black doctor in their Michigan town, and sires two daughters, First Corinthians and Magdalene called Lena. The novel begins sixteen years later on the morning of an incredible suicidal flight by a man rigged with wings. Ruth witnesses the horror of the flight and goes into labor. Milkman, Macon's only son, is born in the emergency ward of nearby Not Mercy Hospital where blacks were previously refused treatment.

The novel centers on Milkman who, growing up to despise his father and his wealth, prefers the company of Guitar, a member of the violent vigilant group Seven Days, and Pilate, whose poor and much disarrayed household brings him love. When Milkman meets Hagar they share a passion that eventually consumes Hagar and sends Milkman off to search for the miner's abandoned gold. Milkman's search, which dominates the second part of the novel, is only one brief stop in the larger journey toward reconciliation with his family as he uncovers what the mysterious song of Solomon portends for the unburied bones, his grandfather, Pilate, and himself.

The complexity of events in the novel forms an extremely rich mosaic of narrative and point of view. But it is only part of the full beauty of the work. What finally takes hold of the reader is the sustained metaphor of flight which unfolds in a taut pattern of images like the suspended strings of a parachute, holding the reader absolutely breathless.

Although the story focuses on Milkman and gains his point of view, it provides a generously omniscient perspective on the troubled lives of everyone connected to him by friendship or blood. Ruth, his mother, starved for physical affection, had nursed Milkman well beyond his infancy and earned him the nickname when both mother and son were discovered by the family's handyman. Ruth now knows herself only through emotional isolation: "I am not a strange woman. I am a small one . . . I lived in a great big house that pressed me into a small package." Milkman, however, never even learns who he is or why he's called Milkman, except to quit the stifling atmosphere of Ruth's pain and the

steady awful silence of his sisters First Corinthians and Magdalene called
Lena. The sisters' sterile, confined lives reverse whatever notions readers
may recall of Biblical love and redemption. This novel does not accord the
characters or the readers such easy hope. Then there is Pilate living in total
disarray from the wine she bootlegs. Her name suggests the judgment of
Christ and its attendant relinquishing of responsibility. But Morrison has
depicted a positive, full, aggressively alive character who recalls the name's
near homonym, pilot: one who guides flight, directs it, takes charge.

It was Pilate who conjured an aphrodisiac to make Ruth once more
attractive enough to Macon to have them conceive Milkman. And it was
Pilate again who nourished his birth in spite of Macon's efforts to have the
pregnancy aborted. Milkman, born on the moment of suicidal flight,
discovers that he comes from a family of flying Africans who sought
freedom from slavery by escaping North or "flying" back to Africa. When
he finally hears his name in the song of Solomon, he frees himself from the
emotional death of Macon Dead, the obsessive terrorism of Guitar, and the
clinging guilt of Hagar's love. Milkman and Pilate bury his grandfather's
bones. They silence the dead, and Milkman finds the strength to lift himself
in one last leap of defiance from the mountaintop.

But let the novelist herself tell it. Hear in her ripe tongue the voices of
men and women pushed to the very edge of their ability to summon the
power of the dead, the living, and the unborn. Listen as Milkman learns to
read again the names that signal him:

> He read the road signs with interest now, wondering what lay beneath the
> names. The Algonquins had named the territory he lived in Great Water,
> *michi gami*. How many dead lives and fading memories were buried in
> and beneath the names of the places in this country. Under the recorded
> names the other names, just as "Macon Dead," recorded for all time in
> some dusty file, hid from view the real names of people, places and things.
> Names that had meaning. No wonder Pilate put hers in her ear. When you
> know your name, you should hang on to it, for unless you do . . . He closed
> his eyes and thought of the black men in Shalimar, Roanoke, Petersburg,
> Newport News, Danville, in the Blood Bank, on Darling Street, in the pool
> halls, the barbershops. Their names. Names they got from yearnings,
> gestures, flaws, events, mistakes, weaknesses. Names that bore witness.

In *Song of Solomon*, Morrison has captured our sometimes painful
search to discover our names and articulate their meaning. And she has
named the myths that linger after the nightmare to tell us we have survived.
Her language recreates the self and alters the Classical and Biblical legends
we've inherited by revealing their connection to our contemporary pain.
Like Milkman we can no longer passively rely on what we have merely
inherited from the past; we must make it live for us and with us now, even if
it attempts to stagger us in defeat.

Song of Solomon is a brilliant, compelling achievement. It demands to
be discussed, if only to force the reader to wrench himself free from a prose

which spins a relentless web of conjure. More than *Sula* or *The Bluest Eye*, Toni Morrison's previously acclaimed novels, *Song* challenges every emotion, making love or hatred vague and inappropriate feeling until we endure their steady cutting edges. Like Pilate, Macon, Ruth, Hagar, Milkman, we are no longer safe. Nor should we, after reading this novel, want to be.

[Review of *Song of Solomon*]   Samuel Allen*

Toni Morrison is drawn to challenges and in her latest work has accepted a difficult one and met it. Her first two novels, *Bluest Eye* and *Sula*, established worlds filtered through the sensibilities of a number of memorable Black women. In *Song of Solomon* which, briefly put, defines the growth into manhood of a young Black man in a midwestern town, the focusing consciousness is male. In a story in which names carry a symbolic meaning, Milkman Dead is the perversely living son of Macon Dead, the richest man in the Black community, whose family acquired its intriguing surname following the Civil War through the clerical error of a drunken Yankee soldier. Milkman's transformation from an indulged and self-indulging child into a dangerously won maturity shapes the narrative line of event and of perception. Morrison achieves an unusually skillful transition from a precisely described Michigan town into a timeless mythological world of quest for meaning and identity. At the end of Milkman's journey is not the gold which triggered it, but the dismantling of his personality and the acquisition of a difficult knowledge of himself and those closest to him.

Although Morrison's characters live convincingly beyond the borders of the page, the dramatic tension of the story results largely from the fact that the fate of three pivotal figures is molded by three distinct sets of values. Macon Dead, the industrious, ambitious businessman, standard-bearer of bourgeois horrors, serves as foil for his sister, Pilate, deformed in the world's view and derelict, but whose gift is forbearance and love and a surrendering to life to possess it. "If I'd a known more people, I'd a loved more." Pilate is an arresting figure who emerges as the focus of moral concern, a guardian for those lacking her strength, whose major significance becomes progressively evident. She has carried with her, unwittingly, the clue to her inheritance, a sack of bones and rocks from her childhood, with a spool of thread for each element of the Afro-American's dual tradition. Through her death, rendered in place of her nephew's, the invitation to soar, a central motif, is extended. The thrust of her function as

*Reprinted from the *Boston University Journal* 26, no. 1 (1978): 67–69. Reprinted by permission of The Trustees of Boston University.

a kind of moral lodestone suggests, finally, that although the protagonist is male, the ultimate concern of this latest of the author's novels is, also, the Black woman. The compassionate response of Pilate to the tragedy of her granddaughter's hopeless pursuit of Milkman appears particularly to reinforce such an assessment.

Against these two, brother and sister, is posed the chilling racial evangelism of Milkman's friend, Guitar, who contributes another song to the story. His is another kind of love, a coin whose other side is a hatred which will make him capable, eventually, of killing his closest friend. Guitar is a committed member of the Seven Days, a group dedicated to a random retribution for each unprosecuted killing of an Emmett Till. Milkman clearly rejects their grim arithmetic, but the prominence assigned Guitar in Milkman's search implies the measure of the author's awareness of the sense of injustice out of which their strategy developed.

James Baldwin has remarked upon the complex condition which in the multiple forces influencing it, is the Afro-American experience. The stylistic means with which Morrison, in *Song of Solomon*, continues her exploration of that condition reflect this complexity. The extensive array includes inversion, paradox, the play of opposites, criss-crossing conversations and an appropriately masculine metaphorical language. There appears to be, also, a pattern similar to that of Black music which could probably aptly be described as an off-the-beat symbolic reference. The name approaches but misses, in varying degrees, the congruence suggested by the context in a manner analogous to the defeat of expectation, through the deferment or acceleration of stress, in syncopated music. Pilate, for example, takes on Christ-like attributes and, within the suggested meaning of the flying motif, may be viewed as a pilot; Magdalene observes while her sister strays from a life of propriety; the Weimaraner dogs, Horst and Helmut, in the decaying house of the grandfather's murderers, suggest but fall short of the name of the Munich beer-drinking song.

The novel most notably excels, however, in its imaginative use of myth and folklore. There is an achieved fusion of fantasy and fact, of ancient myth and Virginia coon hunt. Morrison first establishes a cast of plausible characters fixed in a specified year on the calendar in a well detailed midwestern town. Time, however, at a certain point is suspended altogether and, in a movement reminiscent of the world of Jack and the Beanstalk, the story slips beneath the bottom line of Macon Dead's property accounts into the mythological realm of the author's proper concern. In the launching of the search for gold, the novel which previously may have labored is, as later is Milkman himself, made convincingly whole.

In Ellison's adroit use of Black folklore in *Invisible Man*, the journey proceeds prototypically from rural South to urban North. Morrison reverses the age-old escape route and here she is contemporary, to send her hero by stages back into a heritage common to practically all Black families in America, the rural South of fable and legend. From the Black folk tradition, she joins, in Stephen Henderson's lexicon, a virtuoso rapping with an old Negro spiritual to convey an eloquent carpe diem:

> Stop picking around the edges of the world . . . We live here. On this planet, in this nation, in this country right here . . . We got a home in this rock, don't you see . . . Grab this land. Take it, hold it, my brothers, make it, my brothers, shake it . . . Pass it on.

It is characteristic of her fine balancing of inspirational appeal and the nuts and bolts of a tangible world that she tells us in the next sentence:

> But they shot the top of his head off, and ate his fine Georgia peaches.

Morrison has recourse not only to Black folklore but avails herself equally of other accessible cultural resources, including a range of classical Western myths. Reaching out to embrace rather than to exclude is her characteristic gesture; the diversity of her references makes clear that she finds no need for herself or anyone else to forgo any element of the American composite. "Medina, Yaraba, Hamlet too," the children chant in the song of the title piece. The dominant motif of flying may appropriately derive from either the Western myth of Daedalus or the Black folk legend of flying back to Africa, or from both.

Morrison's capacity to install herself in the consciousness of another is persuasively evident in her portrayal of the male of the species. Although there is probably, on occasion, an excess of macho, the central relationship between Milkman and "my man," Guitar, is psychologically true and extraordinarily well drawn. The idiom of much of Black male speech is rendered with unusual accuracy: the irony and the laconic wit, the unbridged shifts in rhythm and context, the veiled and unveiled violence, as well as the warmth and the braggadocio. The dialogue of confrontation is particularly convincing, reminiscent of that of Richard Wright. With a sensitive ear, Morrison has reproduced the cadences distilled from a long history of interaction on American soil of European and African speech patterns.

A sure sense of parody and a Nabokovian talent for the macabre only intimated in her previous work emerge in *Song of Solomon*. One does not readily forget the suggestive fate of Guitar's father, his body sliced in half for packing, an eye upon a staring eye as he begins his sojourn in eternity; or the horror comedy of the granddaughter's doomed pursuit of another "bluest eye."

The novel is the product of a skilled artisan who has grounded her work in the lore of two traditions, both gospel and barcarole, to achieve a surprisingly eloquent synthesis. It moves at its own pace, ultimately to invade the consciousness in force.

"Tar Baby, She Don' Say Nothin'" Robert G. O'Meally°

The promotion of *Tar Baby* was a stunning show. For a book that promised to be not just a good read for this season but Literature of Lasting Value, the Madison Avenue machinery spun into highest gear. Certain book stores displayed signed advance copies: trade edition and the illustrated Franklin, leather-bound; key publications featured front page coverage, full reviews (the *New York Times* reviewed it twice), and interviews. "I can't believe *Newsweek* will have a middle-aged colored woman on its cover," said Morrison. Yet there she was, posing between readings, guest spots on television, book parties. For a shining moment she was the toast of the literary world. And—never mind that nobody in the subway seemed to have put down the usual romances and mysteries for *Tar Baby*—the books were *selling*: by August *Tar Baby* was selling out of its sixth edition. When it appears in paperback, it will, one supposes, take the next step toward permanence in the Lasting Value market place of Faulkners and Ellisons: it will be taught in universities; it will attract scholarly attention.

All this hyping puts pressure on the scholar in the field of black literature. But what is the book's real value? I found it to contain a sheaf of images and scenes not quickly to be forgotten. Like a pretty and intricate geometric design and proof, *Tar Baby* is often very intriguing. Yet I also found *Tar Baby* deeply flawed: somehow it has all the makings of a good novel; what's missing is the spark of life that makes a good novel not a formula but vibrant art.

Essentially, *Tar Baby* is the story of Jadine Childs and Son Green. "Jade"[1] is a green-eyed Negro woman of fair-complexion who, at twenty-five, has squeezed much ritsy living into her years. High fashion model, painter, actress, graduate of the Sorbonne, Jadine was born in black Baltimore but escaped with her guardians, Uncle Sydney Childs and Aunt Ondine Childs, to the Caribbean island of Dominique. Back in Baltimore, Sydney and Ondine had worked as butler and maid for Valerian Street; when Valerian moved to the West Indies he took them and fifteen year old Jadine, with him. Not long afterwards, Valerian met and married Margaret Street; she looked so much like one of the candies from which he'd made his fortune. Their son, Michael, grew up in Dominique, at "L'arbre de la Croix," the big house that both the Streets and the Childses call home.

Set in the seventies, the novel begins when Jadine is home from Europe for Christmas. In the midst of a longstanding squabble with Valerian, Margaret runs to her room, opens her closet door and screams: a black man, Son Green, is there in the dark, hiding. Son is a Floridan who had jumped ship and stowed away at "L'arbre de la Croix" for several days.

°Review of *Tar Baby*. Reprinted from *Callaloo* 4, nos. 1–3 (Feb.–Oct. 1981): 193–98.

Sleeping in closets by day and roaming the house and grounds by night, hunting for food, Son has come to feel comfortable in the place. In part to irritate Margaret and the Childses, Valerian lets Son stay on. Not having "seen a Black like him in ten years," Jadine is rankled at first, and then interested. She and Son make love and take off for New York City. But after a visit to Son's villagelike hometown, Eloe, and after a particularly wracking clash back in New York, Jadine leaves Son, returns to Dominique, and then to Paris with her white lover, Ryk. Bepuzzled, and one step behind in Dominique, Son is left to figure out the meaning of his brief encounter with "Jade."

In this novel of classic confrontation between the "bourgeois" black woman and the "downhome" black man, some of the most passionate writing emerges from passages concerning the meaning of blackness. As in Ellison's novel, here "blackness is . . . and it ain't"; "it ain't," for one thing, easy to reduce to a few easy terms. Jadine just wants to be *herself*, and "was uncomfortable with the way Margaret stirred her into blackening up or universaling out, always alluding to or ferreting out what she believed were racial characteristics. She ended by resisting both, but it kept her alert about things she did not wish to be alert about."

> Back in New York to meet Son, Jadine is on her own turf. She remembers that "if ever there was a black woman's town, New York was it": No, no, not over there making land-use decisions, or deciding what was or was not information. But there, there, there and there. Snapping whips behind the tellers' windows, kicking ass at Con Edison offices, barking orders in the record companies, hospitals, public schools. They refused loans at Household Finance, withheld unemployment checks and drivers' licenses, issued parking tickets and summonses. Gave enemas, blood transfusions and please lady don't make me mad. They jacked up meetings in boardrooms, turned out luncheons, energized parties, redefined fashion, tipped scales, removed lids, cracked covers and turned an entire telephone company into such a diamondhead of hostility the company paid you for not talking to their operators. The manifesto was simple: "Talk shit. Take none." Jadine remembered and loved it all.

But then there's the tense and wonderful portrait of Eloe, Son's all-black homeplace that looked to Jadine not like a town at all, more like a single block in Queens. With Son gone off to talk with his father, Jadine hunched behind her camera and tried to get a fix on these Eloe dwellers, also part of Morrison's huge and varied cavalcade of Afro-Americans:

> The children were happy to pose, and so were some of the younger women. Only the old folks refused to smile and glared into her camera as though looking at hell with the lid off. The men were enjoying the crease in her behind so clearly defined in the sunlight, click, click. Jadine had remembered her camera just before she thought she would go nuts, trying to keep a conversation going with Ellen and the neighbor women who came in to see Son's Northern girl. They looked at her with downright

admiration, each one saying, "I was in Baltimore once," or, "My cousin she live in New York." They did not ask her what they really wanted to know: where did she know Son from and how much did her boots cost. Jadine smiled, drank glasses of water and tried to talk "down home" like Ondine. But their worshipful stares and nonconversation made Son's absence seem much too long.

Back in Isle des Chevaliers, and through with Son and his backwater dreams and his contempt for her striving after social advancement, Jadine gets ready to take off for Paris. But before she can get away, Ondine tries to tell Jadine that she still needs to learn that being a good black woman involves being a good daughter. "Jadine," she tells her niece, "a girl has got to be a daughter first. And if she never learns how to be a daughter, she can't never learn how to be a woman. I mean a real woman: a woman good enough for a child; good enough for a man—good enough even for the respect of other women. . . . You don't need your own natural mother to be a daughter. All you need is to feel a certain way, a certain careful way about people older than you." But of course Jadine, who "has forgotten her ancient properties," misunderstands, thinks her aged aunt wants "parenting," that Ondine's idea of womanness is too restricting.

Morrison's unfailing ear for talk, and her willingness to let her novel not just delight but teach, give these passages distinction. Yet the novel's greatest achievement, I believe, is its effective orchestration of the "Tar Baby" folkstory. "In this novel," wrote Morrison in the Preface to the Franklin edition, "I did not retell that story and, needless to say, I did not improve it, I fondled it scratched and pressed it with my fingertips as one does the head and spine of a favorite cat—to get at the secret of its structure without disturbing its mystery." Made popular among nonblacks by Joel Chandler Harris and Walt Disney, the "Tar Baby" story is an Afro-American folktale with many variants collected in West Africa and in American black communities. "Tar Baby" is not, in other words, "fakelore"—Richard Dorson's term for creations by media producers interested in selling soap and hardware. "Tar Baby," the folktale, is a vibrant expression of black life and culture.

As such it makes for an effective subtext in a novel concerned, as this one is, with "the blackness of blackness."

Son accuses Jadine of being a kind of Tar Baby, a tricky white man's creation set to waylay black men whose real home is down in the brier patch: "gate keeper," thinks Son of Jadine, "advance bitch, housebitch, welfare office torpedo, corporate cunt, tar baby, side-of-the-road whore trap." This works as one key into the mystery of this novel: Son is Brer Rabbit in the farmer's patch, Jadine the dressed up Tar Baby, the "she" of the tales who "don' say nothin'." At the novel's end he is loosed from her grasp and runs: "lickety-lickety-lickety-split." Jadine—the twenty-five year old model whom the agencies make up to look like a nineteen year old with "the eyes and mouth of a woman of three decades"—traps Son with her sophisticated beauty. "He knew that any moment she might . . . press her dreams of gold and cloissone and honey-colored silk into him—and then who would mind the pie table in the basement of the church?"

Of the "Tar Baby" folktale, Morrison writes:

> It was a rather complicated story with a funny happy ending about the triumph of cunning over law, of wit over authority, of weakness over power. Its innocence and reassurance notwithstanding, it worried me: Why did the extraordinary solution the farmer came up with to trap the rabbit involve tar? Why was the rabbit's sole area of vulnerability having good manners? Why did the tar baby's silent complicity seem to me at once natural and obscene? Of the two views of the Brier Patch, the farmer's and the rabbit's, which was right? Why did it all seem so contemporary and, more to the point, so foreboding?

This tale, at once reassuring and yet "so foreboding," forms the nucleus of a novel that's by no means simple. For if Jadine is Tar Baby-like, so is the beautiful African woman in Paris, the woman with "skin like tar," who spat "an arrow of saliva" in Jadine's direction: the woman in a yellow dress who carried three white eggs and who seemed to personify something crucial and valuable about women and the black tradition. This African woman with "tar-black fingers" mocks Jadine's career successes (in something like the way Invisible Man's grandfather spoils his successes) and haunts her dreams. She appears in Jadine's Eloe nightmare in which a group of black women, including Jadine's mother and Ondine, point their breasts accusingly at the wayward daughter, "Jade." They could "impugn your character," these "diaspora mothers," just as the African woman with a single glance "could discredit your elements." Here we are left to wonder if Jadine does not fail to become, in the richest sense, a "Tar Baby," a black woman; a true daughter of the woman with skin like tar, with elements strong enough to hold not only one man but a people's traditions.

As a bearer of traditions, Son is also Tar Baby-like: a trickster of many names, a piano player and a folktale spinner. Son dreams not of high times in international cities but of Eloe, where his sacred memories include cleaning a tub of fresh fish for a precious dime, and minding the hot homemade pies in the basement of the church. Planted secretly in Jadine's bedroom, Son tries to instill in her his dream of "yellow houses with white doors which women opened and shouted Come on in, you honey you!" Not having washed for days, he was afraid his odor would wake her before he had time to "breathe into her the smell of tar and its shiney consistency." Here Son, the immature wanderer whom Jadine calls a "big old country baby," is the silent figure of tar hoping to capture the world traveller and take her home to blackness.

Morrison is playing with the Tar Baby story, "riffing on it" Albert Murray might say, to suggest a complex human situation. Both Jadine and Son are black inheritors of the Tar Baby story, and both see themselves as pulling the other from a sticky place, but, as the novel's narrator tells us, "this rescue was not going very well":

> Each was pulling the other away from a maw of hell—its very ridge top. Each knew the world as it was meant or ought to be. One had a past, the other a future and each one bore the culture to save the race in his hands. Mama-spoiled black man, will you mature with me? Culture-bearing black woman, whose culture are you bearing?

The subjects Morrison raises here are major ones, and unconfined to one race of people. One central aesthetic question is, How does spoken narrative relate to written narrative? When a folktale as stubbornly complicated as the "Tar Baby" story is a subtext, the writer must convert higher algebra into even higher calculus. This Morrison does, with an unstoppable voice that is compellingly her own. The novel fails, however, to bring these folk-characterlike figures to life. Finally, we do not care about Jade or Son, and their tiresome musings, for they seem stillborn. Stuck to each other or unstuck, these tar babies stir our minds but not—and here is the crucial test for all art—our deepest emotions. The novel is selling well, and I believe it will teach well, but for sheer storytelling that seems utterly uncontrived and lively, one must go to Morrison's better novels: *Sula* and the masterful *Song of Solomon*.

Note

1. Note: a "jade" is not only a precious gemstone which is—according to Webster's—"commonly green but sometimes whitish and takes a high polish"; a "jade" is also a low or sluggish woman . . . a flirtatious girl"; and a broken-down, vicious, or worthless horse." "To jade" is "to make into a jade" or "to lose heart, to flag, to weary."

Remembering One's Ancient Properties

Valerie A. Smith°

The tar baby of southern black folklore is reputed to haunt dark woods and entrap unsuspecting children. Melville Herskovits writes that "it was said to be impossible to pass the tar-baby without striking it . . . and when once you had struck it, you were lost."

The tar baby of Toni Morrison's new novel is a young, dirty southern black male fugitive called Son. One Christmas season he invades the Caribbean paradise inhabited by Valerian and Margaret Street (a white

°Review of *Tar Baby*. Reprinted from *Sewanee Review* 89, no. 4 (Fall 1981): cxv-cxvi. ©1981 by the University of the South. Reprinted with the permission of the editor of the *Sewanee Review*.

retired candy manufacturer and his wife), Sydney and Ondine Childs (their black servants), and Jadine Childs (the Streets' protegee and Sydney's niece). Although the Streets and the Childses are repelled by him, they cannot avoid his "touch." Their contact with him forces them to acknowledge secrets about themselves that they had previously ignored. Once they embrace the truth that lies beneath their surface complacency they cannot let it go.

Valerian has always remained unsullied by life. He retired young to avoid becoming an "industrial nuisance." After divorcing his first wife he married Margaret, a teenaged beauty queen, because his "youth lay in her red whiteness." He built himself a magnificent home, L'Arbe de la Croix, on his Caribbean island where he could "sleep the deep brandy sleep he deserved." And now he spends his days in the adjacent greenhouse surrounded by his most-loved plants and music.

Twenty years Valerian's junior, Margaret is not yet willing to share his self-imposed exile. She spends six months of each year at home in Philadelphia and urges him to return to the States to live. Valerian retaliates against her badgering by reminding her of her "ignorance and origins." Margaret is still a beauty, but she lacks his sophistication.

As Sydney often boasts, he and Ondine are "Philadelphia Negroes." Like Margaret they would rather be back home, but they have reconciled themselves to the tranquillity of the island. They value their security and their employer's generosity, since Valerian has Sorbonne-educated their niece and provided for their future by giving them stock each Christmas: "Stock. No slippers. No apron. Stock!"

Orphaned at the age of ten, Jadine is the center of her aunt's and uncle's life. Recently featured on the cover of *Elle*, pursued by "three count three gorgeous . . . men," and almost finished with a doctorate in art history, Jadine spends this particular Christmas at L'Arbe de la Croix deciding whether to marry the most "exciting and smart and fun and sexy" of her suitors.

When the novel opens, the family awaits futilely the homecoming of Michael, the Streets' son. In his absence they entertain an unanticipated guest instead. A horrified Margaret discovers Son (appropriately named) in her closet, and Valerian invites him to stay for the holidays.

The jarring presence of this outsider provokes the Streets and the Childses to display the profound emotions they customarily hide. Valerian's graciousness toward Son makes the elder Childses realize that they have never been treated as his equals. Angered by one of Valerian's decisions, at Christmas dinner Ondine reveals a secret she has concealed for twenty years: that Margaret abused Michael as a child. This disclosure forces Valerian to realize that he has refused to see his son's suffering in order to maintain his own naivete. And Margaret acknowledges the extremes to which she was driven by the boredom of her days as a young wife and mother.

Son has an equally profound impact on Jadine, with whom he enjoys a passionate affair. A country boy from Eloe, Florida, Son takes Jadine home with him to show her the superficiality of her cosmopolitan values. But as he cannot tolerate her rootless New York life, she cannot understand his people. In Eloe she is haunted by images of the substantial women of her past. Even after she leaves him, she never escapes her fear that she is inferior to these "night women."

Like Morrison's last book, *Song of Solomon*, *Tar Baby* is about the need to reconcile oneself to one's history. Ondine tells Jadine late in the novel that she must learn to be a daughter, "a woman that cares about where she came from and takes care of them that took care of her." Indeed, the proliferation of parent/child imagery underscores the fact that in the world of the novel no one knows himself until he explores and accepts his past.

Tar Baby is the most ambitious of Morrison's works. Besides presenting a wider range of characters, she weaves a richer mythic fabric into this novel than she did in the others. The imagery she uses to animate the local history and landscape occasionally rings false: "Fish heard [the clouds] hooves as they raced off to carry the news of the scatterbrained river to the peaks of hills and the tops of champion daisy trees." But the deft characterizations, flawless ear for dialogue, and free play of imagination that one expects from Morrison are as evident here as they are in *The Bluest Eye*, *Sula* and *Song*. *Tar Baby* is a provocative, complex, and exciting novel by an exceedingly gifted contemporary author.

ESSAYS AND
INTERVIEWS

Conversations from Abroad

"It's OK to say OK"

Sandi Russell°

Toni Morrison is not the person in her publisher's photograph. Her hair is in its natural state, and she ties it with a scarf. Her face is mobile, attentive, beautiful. The voice is informed and assured. Her ebullient talk reminds me of my friend Christine, and of all the black talk I have heard from women who never write a word. The creative energy of her writing and her power as a story teller are there in the talk.

She says she wrote her first two books because "they were the books I wanted to read." To me, she was like the teacher I never had, who upholds Afro-American culture instead of censoring in class the black speech I learned at home. "Did you know it's OK to say OK?" she asks, explaining that the word *okeah* is African in origin and was brought to America by slaves.

To be one with this life, to know it and embrace it and draw strength from it: that's what Toni Morrison affirms wholeheartedly. After the many years of suffering and endurance, she argues, blacks can now grasp life and make it their own. But they must be aware of *who they are and where they come from*. "We've done all that climbing—we're on the plateau. I'm not interested in misery, suffering—how many dead on your side, how many on ours. We've gone through the Middle Passage. We've paid the price. We've earned the right to be here. And we can stay on this plateau as long as we like. . . ."

But to reach that plateau intact, one has to have a sense of community. Toni Morrion grew up in Lorain, Ohio. As an adolescent, she "couldn't wait to leave." And leave she did. First for Howard University in Washington, D.C., and then for graduate work at Cornell. After a spell of teaching at Howard, and a broken marriage, she left again, for New York, with two young children. Her mother was astonished: "You don't have anybody there." But Toni disagreed: "You take the village with you. There is no need for the community if you have a sense of it inside."

In her essay on "Rootedness," Toni Morrison contracts the local community, whether in Africa or America, in which the art forms of an oral

°An interview essay. Reprinted from the *Women's Review* (London) 5 (March 1986): 22–24, by permission of the author.

culture thrived, and the conditions of the modern urban world in which, she believes, story-telling still has an important function. For her, roots are less a matter of geography than a sense of shared history; less to do with place, than with inner space: the freedom to be oneself, and yet a member of the tribe. So she identifies her art as a novelist with the ancestral tradition that is still alive in black music and religion.

The key to these forms of expression is participation: "There were spaces and places in which a single person could enter and behave as an individual within the context of the community. A small remnant of that you can see sometimes in black churches where people shout. It is a very personal grief and a personal statement done among people you trust. Done within the context of the community, therefore safe." Just as the black preacher or the blues singer leaves room for the hearer's response, so, Toni Morrison argues, "I have to provide places and spaces so that the reader can participate." Someone once asked of her, "Where are the adverbs?" She turned to me and smiled, "I allowed the reader to come in and experience, to work with me in the telling of the story. Black literature is open-ended, participatory. It was a measure of my ability to make this kind of contact with the reader."

The protective value of the black community is evident in *Sula*, her second novel. Although the community didn't like *Sula* and what she did, they allowed her to "be." She couldn't have had these freedoms elsewhere. In her first novel, *The Bluest Eye*, Toni Morrison had shown what can happen to a person alienated from positive black traditions. Pauline has lost her inner self, and the beauty of her own people. She tries to fill an aching void with the "white picture shows" and makes efforts to look like Jean Harlow. Her daughter, Pecola, is further removed from community strengths and longs for "the bluest eyes" to gain entrance into a world that doesn't accept her.

In *Song of Solomon*, Toni Morrison's third novel, the hero pursues material gain, but instead finds himself on a quest for his history. This journey eventually gains him spiritual freedom. Although the story has a male protagonist, the most powerful presence in it is a female ancestor, Pilate. Ms. Morrison's ability to incorporate fantasy and make it reality is brilliantly exemplified in the character of Pilate, who was born without a navel. "The navel allowed me to introduce the fantastic early in the book. It meant that Pilate could be 'inside and outside' at the same time. She was 'innocent wisdom.'"

Her fourth novel, *Tar Baby*, is what Toni Morrison calls "a very contemporary love story." Its main characters are Jadine (educated and cosmopolitan), and Son (uneducated, a provincial Southerner). Ms. Morrison says that "their problems are not so much *gender* as *class*; yet, in this very modern setting there is a deep and probing engagement with the past, as well as with nature. In moving into the present I keep ploughing back deeper and deeper into the past, in order to bring up sources that were important to the couple."

Beloved is Ms. Morrison's forthcoming novel, to be published in America later this year. In it, she returns to the painful past and tells the story of a runaway slave who killed her children to save them from slavery. Her trial is a "cause celebre" used by abolitionists. Toni Morrison speaks of this with hushed intensity: "she claimed the lives of these children . . . serenely. The story has lots of questions in it for me. The novel is an attempt to deal with those questions. It was an era I didn't want to get into—going back into and through grief." Her courage in re-entering an area that most black Americans understandably wish to leave behind them, testifies to the psychic strength that has increased with each of her fictions.

Paule Marshall has paid tribute to the women of Barbados whose talk at her mother's kitchen table in New York influenced her art as a writer. Toni Morrison also acknowledges a debt to the women of her family—four generations of them, including herself: "I remember my grandmother and my great-grandmother. I had to answer to those women, had to know that whatever I did was easy in comparison with what they had to go through." The very black great-grandmother with her very white hair was the most powerful presence in Toni's childhood. It was these women, this line of foremothers, who instructed her, told her to "Straighten her dress, wipe her feet, sit up straight." But also, she says, "They taught me how to dream."

"Adults asked us about our dreams, they were interested in them." She was not taught to hide "the secret self, the unwashed self," and adds, "I always liked that part of myself, the part that other people didn't like. I have to trust the uncontrolled, wild parts of myself, it's really dangerous."

We discussed why she began writing. "I felt a sense of loss, a void. Things were moving too fast in the early 1960–70s . . . it was exciting but it left me bereft." She filled this vacuum so that the women she knew, as well as herself, could speak, take their place in the telling. "There were no books about me, I didn't exist in all the literature I had read . . . this person, this female, this black did not exist centre-self."

Toni Morrison wanted to capture the relationships that black women have historically shared with one another. In Afro-American culture, and in the black church, sisterhood has a larger meaning than that of contemporary usage. "The term sister," Toni explains, "has a deep old meaning—it was valid, never secondary. Black women had to be real and genuine to each other, there was no one else. In pre-agency days they took care of the sick, the elderly, the children. There was a profound and real need there, for physical as well as psychological survival." She has rejected the suggestion that *Sula* is a lesbian novel, but identifies its theme as what happens when a relationship between women is not taken seriously: "In *Sula*, I wanted to throw that relationship into relief. There is such a thing as 'the other' . . . the friend that is the other, and women must hang on to that.

In the last half of the book, Sula is gone. When Nel misses her, we miss her. What was valued was their friendship . . . it was spiritual, of first order priority; the 'other I.'"

I asked her who she saw as her writing public, Toni Morrison was uncompromising: "I write for black women. We are not addressing the men, as some white female writers do. We are not attacking each other, as both black and white men do. Black women writers look at things in an unforgiving/loving way. They are writing to repossess, re-name, re-own." She drew my attention to the black woman writer's "unblinking gaze": Gloria Naylor's, for instance, in her description of the rape scene in *The Women of Brewster Place*. Eudora Welty, Lillian Hellman, Marilyn Robinson, Nadine Gordimer are white writers who have this uncompromising female gaze, but no white writers have yet gone as deep as their black contemporaries in exploring the roots of racism. "Where is the white woman who has written what it feels like to hate the black woman that reared her? I'd like to hear that."

As a former editor for Random House, who saw many books through the presses before her own got into print, what advice has Toni Morrison for new writers? "It's difficult for me to say this as a very well-known writer, but my advice is do not write for money, or put your trust in expensive publicity. It is not needed by the people who *read* books, but rather by those who gossip about personalities. The real work does get known by word of mouth." She also points out that, in spite of the current hype, mainstream publishers rarely find room for more than one new black woman writer at a time. Her advice is to avoid the big firms and publish with small presses who really care about your work; she adds: "Black women writers need to get together, form networks and meet one another. Someone needs to get on the telephone! It's no good addressing a larger audience unless they can speak to each other."

Toni Morrison considers herself as a "conduit" for the wisdom of her people. "I cannot be flattered because it isn't *me*; the ego isn't involved in the listening, the telling . . . there is room for everyone. When I wrote *Sula*, a young black woman was very excited about it, yet she was angry with me, saying: 'You told our secrets. We had this for ourselves; you have given it to them.' You can't keep it. The music used to be ours but it isn't anymore. It belongs to everyone, and you can hear us in the music everywhere. So now there is the novel. Black people didn't need it before, because we had the music. Now we need it. But it is not just mine. I have no ego in that way. When *Newsweek* did a story and I had my picture on the front page, I was so glad to see that half the article was devoted to other black female writers."

Toni Morrison, no longer an editor, now holds the Albert Schweitzer Chair in the Humanities at the State University of New York. As a distinguished professor with her own staff, she intends to initiate an international lecture which will "relate academic work to political action."

She is also responsible for a fellowship programme which will give younger writers the opportunity to work with her.

I experienced loss when I left Toni Morrison. I might have grieved, but I was actually full of joy because she had given so much of herself. Yet, in a sense, she had given me *myself*. And because of such gifts, I must confess that it was more than just OK; much, much more.

An Interview with Toni Morrison, Hessian Radio Network, Frankfurt, West Germany   Rosemarie K. Lester[*]

rkl: Toni Morrison—university teacher, editor, single parent, author not only of important literary works but also of essays on critical contemporary issues—how and where do you establish your priorities?

tm: I think it is a mistake to think of one's life in compartments and as conflict. We are trained to think that we have either / or choices all the time and I think this is inimical to what women are required to do. There are so many things, even if one has no career—within the household there is so much that one has to do, that it's important to think of them all as going together, and I tend to think that I don't have to make a choice between motherhood or a career—I just regard them all as pretty much the most important thing.

rkl: Is there a particular difficulty for a woman alone to raise two male children?

tm: Yes—I was not prepared for what appears obvious now: the differences between men and women, or boy children and girl children. I had two brothers who were younger than I and I thought I was very adept, but I had some other notions about what one has to deliver to the children— especially as a single parent. I thought that I should be mother and father, but that did not work at all. I was not a good father—I was a good head-of-household, in terms of my earning ability, and then I discovered (maybe a little late for them), that you can only be what you are, and deliver what you have, and that you can't provide the other things. They'll have to learn them elsewhere. As boys, my sons were attracted to danger and risk in a way that I was not. They had different spatial requirements than girls, or I ever had. And part of that may be education and socialization, but nevertheless, there they were—these male children who tended to eat up the house. They related to architecture and space differently. Their demands on a mother

[*]This is a shortened version of an interview conducted in the spring of 1983, and is published here for the first time by permission of the interviewer.

were very primitive; they didn't really care what I was about, they wanted service and attention and, at different points in their lives, conversation. They wanted me to be there as a base line from which they operated. They wanted different kinds of intimacy—it was all very strange. I don't have girl children, and perhaps if I did, I'd say something equally astonishing about them. It was curious—I found the boys useful when I was doing *Song of Solomon*, because having watched them grow up, I was able, I think, to enter into a male view of the world which, to me, means a delight in dominion—a definite need to exercise dominion over place and people. My upbringing was very strict, we were very passive girls and we took orders well. We did not issue orders with a great deal of ease, the way my children can do. This is all stereotypical and general, obviously there are variations in men and women, but if you think of the classic definition of masculinity versus femininity, then there is the question of dominion. I watched them in their play and in that desire to control, and when I was writing *Song of Solomon*, which is driven by male characters (it's the only book that has that focus), and I had to change the language a lot, the metaphors, so having children was helpful.

rkl: Philip Royster, the critic, has called this novel a *Bildungsroman*, a novel tracing the development of a person, a male person. These male attitudes, these male ways—do you feel that these are really inherently male and would you not go along with that school of thought that maintains they are forms of learned behavior?

tm: My true feeling is that they are inherent, though I'm perfectly willing to be persuaded that they are not, and I've read a lot of literature that suggests all of this business is obviously learned. I see it most clearly when I discover that women can learn to be something other than to be passive or secondary role creatures, and I can see that it is certainly learned—how to have less power than men. But I think that males— maleness—tends to be inherent, and I know that makes me disagree with eighty per cent of the literature on the subject. But there is an idea, a concept, of masculinity which can be transferred, certainly, and I think that's part of it.

rkl: You know what my next question has to be, then—how do you stand on feminist issues? Or perhaps I should modify it. Is it even possible to be a black feminist, or is there a decisive difference between black and white feminism? Where do women's concerns coincide, regardless of ethnic group—if such coincidence be possible?

tm: I think black women are in a very special position regarding black feminism, an advantageous one. White women generally define black women's role as the most repressed because they are both black and female, and these two categories invite a kind of repression that is pernicious. But in an interesting way, black women are much more suited to aggressiveness in the mode that feminists are recommending, because they have always been both mother and laborer, mother and worker, and the history of black women in the States is an extremely painful and unattractive one, but there are parts of that history that were conducive to doing more, rather than less, in the days of slavery. We think of slave women as women in the house, but they were not, most of them worked in the fields along with the men. They were required to do physical labor in competition with them, so that their relations with each other turned out to be more comradeship than male dominance/female subordination. When they were in the field plowing or collecting cotton or doing whatever, the owner of the slaves didn't care whether they were women or men—the punishment may have varied: they could beat both, and rape one, so that women could receive dual punishment, but the requirements were the same, the physical work requirements. So I have noticed among a certain generation of black men and women—older black men and women—the relationship is more one of comradeship than the you-do-this-and-I-do-this; and it's not very separate. In addition, even after slavery, all of us knew in my generation, that we always had to work, whether we were married or not. We anticipated it, so we did not have the luxury that I see certain middle class white women have, of whether to work OR to have a house. Work was always going to be part of it. When we feel that work and the house are mutually exclusive, then we have serious emotional or psychological problems, and we feel oppressed. But if we regard it as just one more thing you do, it's an enhancement. Black women are both ship and safe harbor.

rkl: That is a beautiful metaphor, indeed. Now, talking about work and strength, a bit earlier you mentioned that you were raised as a fairly passive young girl. How did it come about that you were motivated quite early to reject all the then prevailing saccharine images for girls? Did your ghost-story telling father have something to do with it? Did teachers? A lot of good, strong motivation seems to have come from your home.

tm: Yes, I was raised to take orders and to obey adults, but at the same time, they were giving me something else that I didn't recognize for what it was until much later. Their expectations of us were very high. When I left home and found that other people's expectations were low, I tended to surmount and transcend all kinds of obstacles because I had parents who thought we were all geniuses, and any difficulty that we had was external to us. Social obstacles, economic obstacles, or racism were obstacles, but we ourselves were extraordinary and superior people. My parents also responded to life like that. When we were in economic difficulty—I remember, once we were paying four dollars a month for rent (which doesn't seem like very much now but must have been an enormous amount then) and at one point my father wasn't working and didn't have it, and the landlord put a sign on the door: Evicted! And I remember my mother going outside and taking the sign down and tearing it up into little pieces—as though it made a difference. There was always some sort of aggressive and positive action following these things. Nobody tucked their tail between their legs and accepted them, you see. So I was accustomed to seeing men and women in my family address misfortune as though it was possible to do something about it. They never ran away, so to speak.

rkl: Talking about "creative aggression"—did your father really throw that fellow, who followed you, down the stairs, that white man? True story?

tm: It is true and it was memorable. Sometime we wonder where our first impressions come from. I do remember a white man following my sister and me into our house, up the stairs. We lived in an apartment on the second floor. My father was there, and he picked him up and threw him down the stairs, and then picked up our tricycle and threw the tricycle down after him. My father was not a tall man and this man loomed large. All he knew was that this man was behind his girls, and he was, you know, defending the household and all of that. But for me, it was interesting, because I had not seen abusive, physically abusive white people as many people have in the United States, so the first racial encounter I had as a child was one in which my father was triumphant, physically triumphant, and it's important that what I first saw was that kind of assertion on the part of my father.

rkl: When you went to Howard University during the early years of the civil rights movement—the time of Rosa Parks—you joined the Howard Players and went on tours in the South. Were your plays attended by the same whites who would not let you use their restaurants or share their bus seats? Who watched the plays?

tm: Our audiences were almost completely black. You really didn't come into contact with white people. Some people quarrel a little bit about that in my books, but we didn't really come in contact with white people. When black people talk about how much they love the South, some people are aghast, because it had this terrible reputation. But it's possible to almost live out your entire life there and never see one racial incident in any way that mattered. In a community of black people one felt safe, you know, fairly happy. The real pain came—even though it was progress—during the movement towards integration. Black people were thrown into contact with well-meaning white people, but also faced the ire and anger of those who were hostile to integration. Between the sudden intimacy with white people on their side, so to speak, and the others, it threw people into great disarray. I had a different background, in Lorain, Ohio. That was a poor steel town and there were many people from all over, first generation Europeans and Mexicans, and everybody worked in the steel mill. I never lived in a black neighborhood. What distinguished our neighborhoods was poverty, the same economic level.

rkl: In 1962, you went to Howard to teach. That was the time when civil rights battles were becoming more intense, Dr. Martin Luther King's movement was gaining momentum—how do you see yourself as a political person during that time?

tm: I think I witnessed the early stages of that at Howard University. Stokely Carmichael was a student of mine. He was the kind of student who makes average grades, but he was clever in class, the kind of student who made others respond. He was a wonderful, welcoming presence. In 1964 when he was graduating, I said, "Stokely, where are you going now?" and he said, "I've been accepted at Union Theological Seminary." He was going to study theology, but first, he was going to Mississippi to work for one summer in the field. Of course, he never got back to the theological seminary. Those kids, the first who were sitting in—many of them were in my classes. I was very young then. My son was born in 1961, and I think I was a little diverted from it. I know I always seem to be going into places backward. I was not in favor of integration. But I couldn't officially say that, because I knew the terror and the abuses of segregation. But integration also meant that we would not have a fine black college or fine black education. I didn't know why the assumption was that black children were going to learn better if they were in the company of white children. Since that time I've seen other things happen where there were black separatists who said, "we don't want to have anything to do with white people." I was always on the other side of the mirror of the moment, busing and such. In my heart, I didn't like it. But I knew that the racists also wanted segregation for their purposes . . . What I thought ought to happen was that the money should be there for the materials for education, for the fine faculty, and so on. I feel the same way about the public school. The public schools in black neighborhoods are awful because there is no tax base there, and I did not need to have my son bused from one part of New York to another in order to redress those ills. Put the money into black neighborhoods, get it there, and we will produce our own excellent faculty, curricula, etc. It wasn't the mixing of the human beings that was going to solve that problem . . . I understood exactly what was important about it, but I always thought that the fruits of that labor were going to carry perhaps a little poison, as well.

rkl: So, today—a decade and a half later—how do you evaluate the situation? The late fifties and the sixties were the years (in spite of the Vietnam war) when there was hope for change: social and political change, and I think everyone agrees that some progress was made then. But if I see that correctly—many of those gains have either come to a standstill or are in the process of reversal. The backlash which began in the late seventies certainly is upon us now, the mid eighties. Would you comment, please?

tm: Yes, you're right, there have been some gains made and held, but some terrible things have happened as a result. One, the civil rights movement got embezzled by the media, which made it into fashion. Then, as happened in post slavery days, when suffrage followed abolitionism in the United States, feminism followed the civil rights movement, so that the energies began to be turned away from liberation for black and minority peoples into the women's movement, and it put black women in a peculiar position of having to make choices that were fraudulent: to work for the black movement OR feminism. We are back to these impossible choices. Why should I have to choose between the black movement and women's liberation? More recently, the pain of seeing what has happened in the seventies, is that now the backlash, as you describe it, is profound. This administration has attempted to disassemble all of the legislation of the last twenty years—affirmative action, busing—government efforts to redress these wrongs.

rkl: Getting back briefly to Lorain, Ohio, you were saying that what united the people there was really a common poverty among the blacks and the many immigrants. Did you have good communication, was there social interchange between these poor people coming from many different ethnic backgrounds?

tm: Oh yes, immigrants had to learn, or be taught racism in a place like that. They didn't necessarily arrive there with it. What made our town or our neighborhoods and our schools coherent and free of any kind of conflict was the fact that the class was coherent. We were all in one economic class and therefore mutually dependent upon one another. There was a great deal of sharing of food and services, and caring. If someone was ill, people might come and take care of him or her regardless of race. When I was a little girl, there was a Greek family next door to us on one side; on the other side there was an Italian family: there were some black people; but there was privacy in their social gatherings. We didn't share in that. But as far as human responses, there was none of this acid, none of this vitriol, and what is interesting to me is that's a Northern city in Ohio, you know, right on Lake Erie, in an industrial area. In the South, where there were poor black people and poor white people, it was important to the upper classes to make sure, that those two groups of people believed that their lives were that different. So the Klan and poor white were doing the work of the landed gentry. It is interesting that before Martin Luther King died, on his poor people's march, he had been going into small Southern towns, talking to mixed audiences, poor white dirt farmers and poor black people, and he was persuading them that their interests were the same, that the enemy was the same, that the problems were not black liberation or white oppression—it was a class struggle that they were in, and that it was only to benefit the ruling class that they had always responded racially. Racism benefits the economic order, obviously. I saw a television show, I've only seen it once and nobody else in the world seems to have seen it but me. Just before he died, King was in a church, a white church, and there were poor white people, the ones we call "crackers," hillbillies, crying and listening to him. I remember a man for whom this was like an epiphany. It was the first time he realized how he, a white poor person, had been used, and that the enemy was not the black farmer next to him, who may have had, two feet more land, but the enemy was either in the banking structure or the law, at least elsewhere. Now that's a real revelation. If that idea was infectious and had spread across the country, something really important would have happened. So that King's death was terrible on every level. He had arrived at a point of influence, where something really dangerous was about to happen. There has never been a real class war (and I use the word "war" advisedly, I don't mean necessarily killing) but class cohesion, because they've had the liberty in a capitalist society of separating ethnic groups off into little pockets, so this could never be serious cooperation between classes. But I do know how it was in Lorain, Ohio, to live in a neighborhood that had class coherence—cooperation between classes.

rkl: Was Dr. Martin Luther King murdered because of that?

tm: I always thought that because he had reached the point where he could have influence concerning the Vietnam war, concerning the class problems, he was really dangerous, really dangerous, so that his death came at a moment when it was most useful to the reigning order.

rkl: The problems we are faced with today certainly do transcend race and class barriers—are you actively involved in politics at present—the Peace movement, the Freeze movement?

tm: I'm involved deeply in certain ways. I don't join anything because I'm the world's worst member of any organization. If they rely on me I might not show up . . . But I am active in terms of where I speak, and the things I write about. But there is something that I think is also needed in those movements, which is a person who is in and out, and who is in a position in some pressure points such as some of the boards that I sit on like government funding agencies. Because—what shall I call it—sabotage is possible there. You know, in a movement that is as complicated as this one, where primary things are important—peace and an antimilitary stance, some changes in the economic structure and so on—you need all kinds of people. There is a place for active demonstration, there's a place for journalism, a place for artists, for teachers, there's a place for all sorts. The movements can encompass all sorts of skills and talents.

rkl: One last question for you Toni Morrison: author (which connects, of course, with everything you have said—you are, after all, what you write). In an interview in *Essence* magazine you once said: "Of course, there are women who write for women, and then there are women who just write out of the matrix of what they know. . . . [Women] like Eudora Welty and Flannery O'Connor, have just written as people. Sometimes it's about men, sometimes not." Where do you stand?

tm: I'm in that latter category. I write without gender focus . . . It happens that what provokes my imagination as a writer has to do with the culture of black people. I regard the whole world as my canvas and I write out of that sensibility of what I find provocative *and* the sensibility of being a woman. But I don't write women's literature as such. I think it would confine me. I am valuable as a writer because I am a woman, because women, it seems to me, have some special knowledge about certain things. [It comes from] the ways in which they view the world, and from women's imagination. Once it is unruly and let loose, it can bring things to the surface that men—trained to be men in a certain way—have difficulty getting access to, although I can think immediately of several exceptions to that. I don't dislike the writing of women who write for women and about women exclusively, because some of it is quite powerful and quite beautiful. I just don't do it myself because it is a narrowing. It's like putting blinders on. When I write I want to feel as though all things are available to me.

THE NOVELS

The Bluest Eye

Roadblocks and Relatives: Critical Revision in Toni Morrison's *The Bluest Eye*

In "Rootedness: The Ancestor as Foundation," Toni Morrison insists that ancestors play an essential role in individual works in the Afro-American canon. She states:

> It seems to me interesting to evaluate Black literature on what the writer does with the presence of the ancestor. Which is to say a grandfather as in Ralph Ellison, or a grandmother as in Toni Cade Bambara, or a healer as in Bambara or Henry Dumas. There is always an elder there. And these ancestors are not just parents, they are sort of timeless people whose relationships to the characters are benevolent, instructive and protective, and they provide a certain kind of wisdom.[1]

Despite the apparent optimistic assurance of this statement, Morrison is well aware that "the presence of the ancestor" is not always viewed by the Afro-American writer as "benevolent, instructive and protective." Indeed, she argues—just a few sentences following the above declaration that the works of Richard Wright and James Baldwin exhibit particularly identifiable problems with the ancestor. For Morrison, Wright's corpus suggests that he "had great difficulty with that ancestor," and Baldwin's that he was "confounded and disturbed by the presence or absence of an ancestor."[2]

Morrison's singling out of Wright and Baldwin as figures in whose works ancestors represent troubling presences (or absences) is not, it seems to me, a random act. For, as Morrison is well aware, the Wright-Baldwin personal and literary relationship represents the most fabled *intertextual* association in Afro-American letters. Baldwin's attacks on his acknowledged precursor Wright[3] offer intriguing Afro-American examples of what Harold Bloom has termed "the anxiety of influence." In "Alas, Poor Richard," for example, Baldwin says of his method of creating canonical space for his own perceptions of Afro-American life: "I had used [Wright's] work as a kind of spring-board into my own. His own was a roadblock in

---

[°]This essay was written specifically for this volume and is published here for the first time by permission of the author.

my road, the sphinx, really, whose riddles I had to answer before I could become myself."[4]

An intertextual reading of Morrison's first novel, *The Bluest Eye* (1970), suggests that the works of older Afro-American writers also represented "roadblocks" in her journey to artistic selfhood. Specifically, Morrison's novel contains clear evidence of her (sometimes subtle) refigurations of Baldwin's discussion of Wright in "Many Thousands Gone" and the Trueblood episode in Ellison's *Invisible Man*. As we shall see, such revisionary acts, as well as her complex manipulation of her novel's prefatory primer, provide Morrison with the means of giving authentication and voice to specific types of black and feminine experiences whose validity and significance these texts—by overt and covert means—deny.

I

In "The Structuring of Emotion in Black American Fiction," Raymond Hedin astutely discusses Morrison's manipulation of the contents of *The Bluest Eye*'s prefatory primer. Hedin says:

> Morrison arranges the novel so that each of its sections provides a bitter gloss on key phrases from the novel's preface, a condensed version of the Dick and Jane reader. These phrases . . . describe the [American] cultural ideal of the healthy, supportive, well-to-do family. The seven central elements of Jane's world—house, family cat, Mother, father, dog, and friend—become, in turn, plot elements, but only after they are inverted to fit the realities of Pecola's world.[5]

Morrison employs the primer not only as prefatory material to the text proper, but also to introduce the chapters of *The Bluest Eye* that are recounted by the novel's omniscient narrative voice. The seven epigraphic sections are, as Hedin implies, thematically tied to the chapters which they directly precede.

For example, the chapter which introduces the Breedlove family to the reader is prefaced by the primer's reference to Jane's "very happy" family:

HEREISTHEFAMILYMOTHERFATHER
DICKANDJANETHEYLIVEINTHEGREEN
NANDWHITEHOUSETHEYAREVERYH[6]

But the family presented in the subsequent pages of the novel is the very antithesis of the standardized, ideal (white) American family of the primer. The reader learns, in fact, of the Breedloves' utter failure to conform to the standards by which the beauty and happiness of the primer family (and, by extension, American families in general) are measured.

But it is possible to make further claims for Morrison's employment of the primer as epigraph. In her systematic figuration of an inversive relationship between pretext (the primer) and text (her delineation of

Afro-American life), the author dissects, *deconstructs*, if you will, the bourgeois myths of ideal family life. Through her deconstruction, she exposes each individual element of the myth as not only deceptively inaccurate in general, but also wholly inapplicable to black American life. The emotional estrangement of the primer family members (an estrangement suggested by that family's inability to respond to the daughter Jane's desire for play) implies that theirs is solely a surface contentment. For despite Hedin's suggestion that this family is represented as "healthy" and "supportive," it appears to be made up of rigid, emotionless figures incapable of deep feeling.

Morrison manipulates the primer in such a manner I believe, in order to trope certain conventions prominently found in eighteenth-, nineteenth-, and early twentieth-century Afro-American texts. The convention that Morrison revises here is that of the authenticating document, usually written by whites to confirm a genuine black authorship of the subsequent text (for example, William Lloyd Garrison's preface to Frederick Douglass's *Narrative*). The Afro-American critic Robert Stepto has suggested that the manipulation of such white pretextual authorization of the black voice has had a significant influence in the development of the Afro-American narrative. The Afro-American narrative moves, as Stepto suggests in *From Behind the Veil*, from white authentication of blackness to, with the examples of Ralph Ellison and Richard Wright, black self-authentication.[7] Morrison's manipulation of *The Bluest Eye*'s prefatory primer signals, it seems to me, another step in the development of the Afro-American narrative as conceived by Stepto. Morrison returns to an earlier practice—of the white voice introducing the black text—to demonstrate her refusal to allow white standards to arbitrate the success or failure of the black experience. Her manipulation of the primer is meant to suggest, finally, the inappropriateness of the white voice's attempt to authorize or authenticate the black text or to dictate the contours of Afro-American art.

The Bluest Eye's first-person narrator, Claudia, performs a similar act in rejecting white criteria of judgment when she is able to view her childhood, which she had formerly conceived in a vocabulary of pain and degradation, as being characterized by "a productive and fructifying pain" and filled with the protective, "sweet," "thick and dark" love of a mother "who does not want me to die."[8] Like Nikki Giovanni's persona in "Nikki Rosa," Claudia discovers that despite the difficulties of poverty in an opulent America, "all the while I was quite happy."[9]

Claudia's achievement of a positive reading of her childhood, however, is not unproblematic, to be sure. Perhaps the most poignant (and certainly the most charged in an intertextual sense) of the incidents that result in her ability to reread her own life is her attempt to understand the rationale for standards that insist on white physical superiority. Claudia's efforts to comprehend the myth of white physical superiority while attempting, at the same time, to hold on to her views of her own people's beauty and cultural worth, exposes hers as a situation "betwixt and between" that the anthropologist Victor Turner has labeled liminality or marginality. Marginals, according to Turner,

> are simultaneous members (by ascription, optation, self-definition, or achievement) of two or more groups whose social definitions and cultural norms are distinct from, and often even opposed to, one another.[10]

To begin to resolve such social ambiguity, Turner argues, it is necessary that the marginal seek both the origin and an understanding of the often self-aggrandizing myths of the "more prestigious group."[11] The questing marginal must seek to understand the origins of myths, "*how things came to be what they are.*"[12] Consequently, adults' gifts of white dolls to Claudia are not pleasure-inducing toys, but, rather, signs (in a semiotic sense) that she must learn to interpret correctly. Such interpretation requires mining the dolls' surfaces—pink skins, blue eyes, blond hair—a literal search for sources:

> I had only one desire: to dismember [the doll]. To see of what it was made, to discover the dearness, to find the beauty, the desirability that had escaped me, but apparently only me. Adults, older girls, shops, magazines, newspapers, window signs—all the world had agreed that a blue-eyed, yellow-haired, pink-skinned doll was what every girl child treasured. "Here," they said "this is beautiful, and if you are on this day 'worthy' you may have." . . . I could not love it. But I could examine it to see what it was that all the world said was lovable.[13]

Claudia's search for the source of white beauty, however, is not confined solely to dolls. She says that the impulse to dismember white dolls gives way to "The truly horrifying thing":

> . . . the transference of the same impulse to little white girls. The indifference with which I could have axed them was shaken only by my desire to do so. To discover what eluded me: the secret of the magic they weaved on others. What made people look at them and say, "Awwwww," but not for me? . . .
> If I pinched them, their eyes—unlike the crazed glint of the baby doll's eyes—would fold in pain, and their cry would not be the sound of an icebox door, but a fascinating cry of pain.[14]

Claudia's somewhat sadistic dismemberment of white dolls and her subsequent torture of white girls are meant to recall, it seems to me, Bigger Thomas's axed mutilation of the dead body of Mary Dalton (presented by Wright as a symbol of young white female beauty) in *Native Son*.[15] Morrison's refiguration of Wright's scene, as we shall see, is her means of adding her voice to the discourse surrounding Bigger's murder, the most renowned of which belongs to James Baldwin.

Claudia's impulses lend nominal weight to Baldwin's claim in "Many

Thousands Gone" that "no Negro living in America . . . has not . . . wanted
. . . to break the bodies of all white people and bring them low."[16] But while
Baldwin suggests that such violent urges are "urges of the cruelest
vengeance" and motivated by "unanswerable hatred,"[17] Claudia's acts are
motivated in the main by a need to locate the source of white beauty that is
not immediately apparent to her. Baldwin believes that, in general, the
Afro-American refusal to give in to such urges and "smash any white face
he may encounter in a day" results from a noble embrace of humanity. He
states:

> the adjustment [from rage to accommodation] must be made—rather, it
> must be attempted, the tension perpetually sustained—for without this he
> [the Afro-American] has surrendered his birthright as a man no less than
> his birthright as a black man. The entire universe is then peopled only with
> his enemies, who are not only white men armed with rope and rifle, but
> his own far-flung and contemptible kinsmen. Their blackness is his
> degradation and it is their stupid and passive endurance which makes
> his end inevitable.[18]

For Baldwin, such "adjustment" allows the Afro-American to claim (or
reclaim) his humanity, and to demystify and devillainize whites and to love
his own people.

Claudia's adjustment, on the other hand, has significantly different
causes and consequences:

> When I learned how repulsive this disinterested violence [directed toward
> white girls] was, that it was repulsive because it was disinterested, my
> shame floundered about for refuge. The best hiding place was love. Thus
> the conversion from pristine sadism to fabricated hatred to fraudulent
> love. It was a small step to Shirley Temple. I learned much later to worship
> her. . . , knowing, even as I learned, that the change was *adjustment*
> *without improvement*. (my emphasis)[19]

Claudia's "conversion" is motivated not by an embrace of humanity, but
rather by "shame." The questing marginal's quandaries about the origins of
this standard remain unanswered. She learns only to feel ashamed of the
curiosity that led to her "disinterested violence," and that her failure to
accept without question the standards of white America is considered
"repulsive."

Claudia terminates her search for the source of white myths of
superiority and replaces the violent urges she had previously directed at
whites with "fraudulent love." But the suppression of violent urges by Afro-
Americans has significantly different implications for Morrison than for
Baldwin. For Morrison, the Afro-American's humanity is not what is at
stake, and "fraudulent love" of whites, the ultimate result of this rejection of
violence, is not better or more authentically human. It is only different,
only "adjustment" (an intentional repetition of Baldwin's terminology, it
would appear) "without improvement." Hence, Morrison suggests, in her

subtle rejection of Baldwin's reading of Bigger Thomas's humanity, that the adjustment of which the older writer speaks can lead to the devaluation of the authentically black.

II

We have seen how the revisionist impulses of *The Bluest Eye* plainly demonstrate Morrison's view of the terms in which a truly healthy black art and life are possible. Her provocative revision of Ellison suggests most clearly her view that energetic rejection of male (mis)representations of women is necessary for a faithful and responsible depiction of women's lives. I believe that at the heart of *The Bluest Eye*'s delineation of an incestuous encounter between Pecola and her father is Morrison's intertextually charged revision of the Ellisonian depiction of incest in the Trueblood episode of *Invisible Man*.

The Breedlove family in Morrison's text possesses a parodic relation to Ellison's incestuous clan. This relation is initially suggested in the names of the respective families. Ellison's designation suggests that the sharecropper and his family are the true (genuine) "bloods" (an Afro-American vernacular term for culturally immersed blacks). The Breedloves' name, however, is bestowed with bitter irony: theirs is a self-hating family in which no love is bred. In both texts the economically destitute families are forced to sleep in dangerously close(d) quarters. In *Invisible Man*, cold winters—and a lack of money with which to purchase fuel—force the nubile Matty Lou into bed between her still-procreative parents. In the case of *The Bluest Eye*, Pecola sleeps in the same room as her parents, a proximity that necessitates her hearing the "Choking sounds and silence" of their lovemaking.[20]

Further, there are stark similarities between mother and daughter in both texts that contribute to the incestuous act in both cases. In a discussion of the Trueblood Episode in Ralph Ellison's *Invisible Man*, Houston Baker argues that the daughter Matty Lou is her mother "Kate's double—a woman who looks just like her mother and who is fully grown and sexually mature."[21] And Cholly Breedlove's incestuous lust is awakened by Pecola's scratching of her leg in a manner that mirrored "what Pauline was doing the first time he saw her in Kentucky."[22]

It is possible, with the above evidence in place, to begin to suggest the specifics of what seems to me to be Morrison's purposefully feminist revision of Ellison. Read intertextually, *The Bluest Eye* provides—as I shall demonstrate below—an example par excellence of what the feminist critic Annette Kolodny has called revisionary reading [that] open[s] new avenues for comprehending male texts."[23]

In *The Resisting Reader*, Judith Fetterley argues that the reading of the Western canon's overwhelmingly male (and decidedly phallocentric) texts has encouraged women's agreement with the inscribed antifemale slant of the works. Having been taught to accept the phallocentric as indisputably universal, the woman reader unconsciously internalizes the often misogynistic messages of male texts. Fetterley insists that a female must, in order to participate successfully as a woman in the reading experience, "become a resisting rather than an assenting reader and, by this refusal to assent, . . . begin the process of exorcizing the male mind that has been implanted" in women.[24] The removal of the male implant results, for Fetterley, in "the capacity for what Adrienne Rich describes as re-vision, 'the act of looking back, of seeing with fresh eyes, of entering an old text from a new critical direction.'"[25] Feminist revision, according to Fetterley, offers the terms of a radically altered critical enterprise and the liberation of the critic: "books will . . . lose their power to bind us unknowingly to their designs."[26]

Houston Baker's "To Move Without Moving" is an excellent example in support of Fetterley's view of the (sometimes dangerously) persuasive powers of texts. For in this essay, we can observe the power of texts quite literally to bind even the most intellectually nimble readers / critics to their designs. Baker has exhibited, in a stunning reading of the economics of female slavery and the figuration of a community of female slaves in Linda Brent's *Incidents in the Life of a Slave Girl*,[27] his awareness of the ways in which feminist theory can help illuminate literary texts. This sensitivity to feminist concerns is, unfortunately, missing from his reading of Ellison. Instead, Baker's essay mirrors the strategies by which Trueblood (and Trueblood's creator) validates male perceptions of incest while, at the same time, silencing the female voice or relegating it to the evaluative periphery.

Baker begins his reading by citing Ellison's discussion in the essay "Richard Wright's Blues" of "The function, the psychology, of artistic selectivity."[28] This function, according to the novelist, "is to eliminate from art form all those elements of experience which contain *no compelling significance* (my emphasis).[29] Ellison's words provide a means to discuss the shortcomings of his own and Baker's treatments of the subject of incest. For Ellison's statement, situated as it is in Baker's essay, leads to an inquiry as to why neither Ellison's text nor Baker's critique of it treat the female perspective on, and reaction to, incest as containing "no compelling significance."

In the case of the novel, Trueblood's incestuous act is judged almost exclusively by men, from the black school administrators who wish to remove the sharecropper from the community to Trueblood's white protectors who pressure the administrators to allow the sharecropper to remain in his house and who "wanted to hear about the gal [Matty Lou] lots of times."[30] They form, as it were, an exclusively male-evaluate circle which views Trueblood's act as either shamefully repugnant or meritoriously salacious.

Except for the mother Kate's memorably violent reaction, the female perspective on Trueblood's act is effectively silenced and relegated to the periphery in Trueblood's recounting of the story. Never in the share-cropper's rendering of the story are Matty Lou's feelings in the foreground or even actually shared with the reader. Further, Trueblood is well aware of the silent scorn that the women who help Kate attend to the unconscious Matty Lou bear for him. When he returns home after an exile precipitated, in his view, by the inability of others to distinguish between "blood-sin" and "dream-sin," he orders the scornful community of women that has formed in response to his "dirty lowdown wicked dog" act off his property: "There's a heap of women here with Kate and I runs 'em out."[31] Having effectively run out the openly critical female community and silenced, by means of his abominable act, his wife and daughter, Trueblood is able to interpret his act in an extremely self-serving way, untroubled by the radically incompatible perspectives of women. Thus he can, despite his belief that he is a good family man, fail to see the bitter irony in his own assessment of his family situation: "Except that my wife and daughter won't speak to me, I'm better off than I ever been before."[32]

From a feminist perspective, Baker's reading of the Trueblood episode proves as problematic as the sharecropper's own because he, too, relegates the woman's voice to the evaluative periphery and sketches his own circle of males to justify and validate Trueblood's act. Baker asserts that one of the dominant themes of *Invisible Man* is "black male sexuality"[33] and invokes male social thinkers to suggest the accuracy of this reading vis-à-vis the Trueblood episode. And while statements from Clifford Geertz and Freud help Baker to substantiate points about the uncontrollability of phallic energy and about Trueblood's dream signalling a historical regression,[34] they fail, because they invoke worlds in which women are indisputably at the mercy of the phallic and legislative powers of men, to allow the critic to consider the response of the victim to her father's act.

And though Baker makes a valiant effort to endow the hastily considered Matty Lou with positive qualities, viewing her—along with her mother—as one of the "bearers of new black life,"[35] she remains in the critic's interpretation of the episode—as she does in the sharecropper's narration—simply an absence. While Baker's essay adds immeasurably to our understanding of Ellison's art, it fails, unfortunately, to consider the subsequently silenced victim of Trueblood's unrestrained phallus. Only by failing to grapple seriously with the implications of Trueblood's repre-sentation of Matty Lou's state following the incestuous act—"Matty Lou won't look at me and won't speak a word to nobody"[36]—can Baker conceive of the consequences of the taboo-breaking act as generally beneficial.

Unlike Baker's reading of the Trueblood episode of *Invisible Man* in which incest is conceptualized as material and tribal gain, Morrison's revision depicts it as painfully devastating loss. Actually, Morrison's reading of Ellison's text must be remarkably similar to Baker's, for in refiguring Trueblood in the character of Cholly Breedlove, she surrounds her creation with images consistent with Baker's conception of the Ellisonian character as majestic Afro-American vernacular artist free from social restraints. Morrison says:

> Only a musician would sense, know, without even knowing that he knew, that Cholly was free. Dangerously free. Free to feel whatever he felt— fear, guilt, shame, love, grief, pity. Free to be tender or violent, to whistle or weep . . . . He was free to live his fantasies, and free even to die, the how and when of which held no interest for him. . . .[37]

It was in this godlike state that he met Pauline Williams.[38] Only an Afro-American artist with the blues sensibility that Baker argues for Trueblood can organize and transform into meaningfully unified expression the utter chaos of Cholly's life. But Morrison—the remarkably skilled craftsperson who does transform Cholly's life into art—provides the blues song that is *The Bluest Eye* with a decidedly feminist slant. For while Ellison furnishes his depiction of incest with a vocabulary of naturalism and historical regression that permit it to be read in relation to undeniably phallocentric socio-cultural interpretations of human history, Morrison's representation is rendered in startlingly blunt terms.

Trueblood's presence inside his sexually inexperienced daughter's vagina is described in ways that suggest a significant symbolic import. The sharecropper's dream of sexual contact with a white woman while in the home of an affluent white man necessarily brings to mind images of lynching and castration of black men because of the threat of black male sexuality. Consequently, Trueblood's actual presence inside his daughter assumes less of an importance in the text than his dream encounter with an unnamed white woman. Morrison, however, provides her depiction of incest with no such historically symbolic significance:

> [Cholly's] mouth trembled at the firm sweetness of the flesh. He closed his eyes, letting his fingers dig into her waist. The rigidness of her shocked body, the silence of her stunned throat, was better than Pauline's easy laughter had been. The confused mixture of his memories of Pauline and the doing of a wild and forbidden thing excited him, and a bolt of desire ran down his genitals, giving it length, and softening the lips of his anus. Surrounding all of this lust was a border of politeness. He wanted to fuck her—tenderly. But the tenderness would not hold. The tightness of her vagina was more than he could bear. His soul seemed to slip down to his guts and fly out into her, and the gigantic thrust he made into her then provoked the only sound she made—a hollow suck of air in the back of her throat.[39]

Cholly is far from the majestic figure that Baker argues for Trueblood during his efforts to "move without movin'" in his daughter's vagina. And though Morrison does give the incestuous male figure the capacity for sympathy—citing, for example, the "border of politeness" that accompanies his lust—Cholly's "wild," "confused" act lacks the inscribed symbolic weight of Trueblood's transgression. While the sharecropper's inability to withdraw from his daughter's vagina represents, according to Baker, Trueblood's "say[ing] a resounding 'no' to the castratingly tight spots of his existence as a poor farmer in the undemocratic south,"[40] the tight sexual space represents for Cholly the forbidden area that must be forcibly entered and exited. The text of *The Bluest Eye* informs us: "Removing himself from her was so painful to him he cut it short and snatched his genitals out of the dry harbor of her vagina."[41]

Morrison finally seems to be taking Ellison to task for the phallocentric nature of his representation of incest that marginalizes and renders as irrelevant the consequences of the act for the female victim. Morrison writes her way into the Afro-American literary tradition by bringing to the foreground the effects of incest for female victims in direct response to Ellison's refusal to consider them seriously. So while the victims of incest in both novels ultimately occupy similarly asocial, silent positions in their respective communities, Morrison explicitly details Pecola's tragic and painful journey, while Ellison, in confining Matty Lou to the periphery, suggests that her perspective contains for him "no compelling significance."

While the criticism of *The Bluest Eye* has correctly demonstrated Morrison's revisionary intentions vis-à-vis its prefatory primer, it has failed to chart its refigurations of such key texts as Baldwin's and Ellison's. The stunning success of Morrison's revisionist gestures is on a par with Baldwin's efforts to clear away the roadblock to his entry into the Afro-American literary tradition, Richard Wright. But unlike Baldwin, Morrison locates her disputes with ancestors primarily within fictional texts. As a result, she is able to create a first novel that represents an important revisionary moment in Afro-American letters, one in which like no novel before it with the exception of Zora Neale Hurston's *Their Eyes Were Watching God*,[42] nationalist and feminist concerns combine to produce what Morrison elsewhere has called a "genuine Black . . . Book."[43] Morrison's revisionary gestures, it seems to me, create canonical space for subsequent black *and* feminist texts such as Ntozake Shange's *For Colored Girls*, Gloria Naylor's *The Women of Brewster Place*, and Morrison's own *Sula*, as well as for the rediscovery of Hurston's classic novel. *The Bluest Eye*, then, has served to change permanently the overwhelmingly male disposition of the Afro-American literary canon.

Notes

1. Toni Morrison, "Rootedness: The Ancestor as Foundation," in *Black Women Writers* (*1950–1980*), ed. Mari Evans (New York: Doubleday, 1984), 343.

2. Ibid.

3. James Baldwin, "Everybody's Protest Novel," and "Many Thousands Gone," in

Notes of a Native Son (New York: Bantam, 1955), 9–17, 18–36; Baldwin, "Alas, Poor Richard," *Nobody Knows My Name* (New York: Dial, 1961), 181–215.

4. Baldwin, "Alas, Poor Richard," 197.

5. Raymond Hedin, "The Structuring of Emotion in Black American Fiction," *Novel* 16, no. 1 (Fall 1982): 50.

6. Toni Morrison, *The Bluest Eye* (New York: Washington Square Press, 1970), 34.

7. See Robert Stepto, *From behind the Veil* (Urbana: University of Illinois Press, 1979).

8. Morrison, *Bluest Eye*, 14.

9. Nikki Giovanni, "Nikki Rosa," *Black Feelings, Black Talk, Black Judgement* (New York: Morrow Quill, 1970), 59.

10. Victor Turner, *Dramas, Fields, and Metaphors* (Ithaca, N.Y.: Cornell University Press, 1974), 233.

11. Ibid.

12. Ibid.

13. Morrison, *Bluest Eye*, 20.

14. Ibid., 22.

15. See Richard Wright, *Native Son* (New York: Harper and Row, 1940), 90–92.

16. Baldwin, "Many Thousands Gone," 30.

17. Ibid.

18. Ibid.

19. Morrison, *Bluest Eye*, 22.

20. Ibid., 49.

21. Houston Baker, "To Move Without Moving: Creativity and Commerce," in *Blues, Ideology, and Afro-American Literature* (Chicago: University of Chicago Press, 1984), 185.

22. Morrison, *Bluest Eye*, 28.

23. Annette Kolodny, "A Map of Rereading," in *The New Feminist Criticism*, ed. Elaine Showalter (New York: Pantheon, 1985), 55.

24. Judith Fetterley, *The Resisting Reader* (Bloomington: Indiana University Press, 1978), xxii.

25. Ibid.

26. Ibid., xxii–xxiii.

27. See Baker, "To Move Without Moving," 50–56.

28. Houston Baker, "Richard Wright's Blues," in *Shadow and Act* (New York: Vintage, 1964), 94.

29. Ibid., 93.

30. Ralph Ellison, *Invisible Man* (New York: Vintage, 1952), 52.

31. Ibid., 66.

32. Ibid., 67.

33. Baker, "To Move Without Moving," 180.

34. For Baker's discussion of Geertz and Freud (and others), see *Blues, Ideology, and Afro-American Literature*, 17–84.

35. Baker, "To Move Without Moving," 185.

36. Ellison, *Invisible Man*, 66.

37. Morrison, *Bluest Eye*, 125–126.

38. Ibid.

39. Ibid., 128.

40. Ibid., 187.

41. Ibid., 128.

42. For a discussion of the nationalist and feminist dimensions of Hurston's masterwork, see Michael Awkward, "The Inaudible Voice of It All: Silence, Voice, and Action in *Their Eyes Were Watching God*," in *Feminist Criticism of Black American Literature*, Studies in Black American Literature, vol. 3 (Greenwood, Fla.: Penkevill, 1986).

43. Toni Morrison, "Behind the Making of *The Black Book*," *Black World*, February 1974, 89.

Reconnecting Fragments: Afro-American Folk Tradition in *The Bluest Eye*

Trudier Harris*

The Bluest Eye is not only the story of the destructive effects of inter- and intraracial prejudice upon impressionable black girls in the midwest; it is also the story of Afro-American folk culture in process. Through subtle and not-so-subtle ways, Toni Morrison suggests that the vibrancy of the folk culture persists through the fortunes and misfortunes of the characters, and it serves to baptize them into kinship with each other. From folk wisdom to the blues, from folk speech to myths and other beliefs, Lorain, Ohio, shares with historical black folk communities patterns of survival and coping, traditions that comfort in times of loss, and beliefs that point to an enduring creativity.

The setting mirrors perhaps one of the greatest beliefs in black communities during and after slavery—that the North is a freer place for black people economically and socially. It does not matter that Lorain, Ohio, is just a shade north of south, or that Pauline Breedlove has only come from Kentucky, a couple of hundred miles away; it is still relevant that the city is north of where she was, that it holds out to her the traditional expectations of existence above the Mason Dixon line. It was irrelevant that some blacks arrived in the North and found conditions hardly better than the ones they thought they were escaping in the South. These migrants felt they had to hold out the promise to their relatives and friends in the South even if the promise had failed them. So tales circulated about how wonderful things could be "up North." Then, too, the myth was reinforced in those blacks who tamed the concrete jungle, acquired good jobs, and sent their children to school well clothed. In time they formed a middle class, separated from the hordes of their still-migrating sisters and brothers.

For Pauline and Cholly Breedlove, the myth of the North is temporarily a reality. For awhile, in Ohio, they have a house and the money they need. But Pauline's restlessness and Cholly's drinking eventually lead them to the triangular storefront house that comes to epitomize their

*This essay was written specifically for this volume and is published here by permission of the author.

economic and mental state. When Pauline loses a tooth and gives up trying to imitate white movie heroines, she resigns herself to poverty and ugliness. When her children are born, she conditions them to see the North as the nightmare into which her dream has turned. In short, her trading of myth for reality becomes detrimental to her whole family; even when the mythical images were those of the distorting silver screen, Pauline could believe that the promise of the North could be fulfilled. Once she loses faith in the possibility for change, she gives up beliefs that have tied her to historical black communities as well as to prevailing folk traditions. Giving up reflects, in part, her ultimate transference of identification from blacks to whites, as illustrated in her worship of the "little pink-and-yellow" Fisher girl. Her severing of ties to the folk culture in turn short circuits any connections she could pass on to Pecola that would aid her in reconnecting to that culture.

In general, Morrison's characters adhere to many folk beliefs, superstitions, and signs common to historical communities. This is especially true of beliefs surrounding sickness and death. For example, the novel opens with Claudia's remembrances of her mother's treatment for colds when she was growing up: a massage with Vicks salve, a bit to swallow, neck and chest wrapped in a "hot flannel." All were designed to induce sweating, which was believed to be effective in reducing fevers. In black communities where doctors were expensive or scarce, home remedies and items that could be purchased without prescription were relied on. Wrappings frequently became preventive medicine; children warded off colds and other ailments by wearing roots held on by flannel applied under their dresses and shirts. The belief extends to some of the older women in Morrison's community. Cholly's Aunt Jimmy wears her asefetida bag "around her neck";[1] other older women in the community "wrapped their heads in rags, and their breasts in flannel" (110). For them, belief in natural cures is a way of life, and they are not willing to part with their practices.

The specifics of these details are less important than that they show how people in such communities *cared* for each other, a caring that is in stark contrast to most of the characters in *The Bluest Eye*. Where such caring touches the lives of the characters, as with Claudia and with Cholly when Aunt Jimmy was alive, there is a positive influence upon behavior. When such caring disappears, as with Cholly after Aunt Jimmy's death, or was never available, as with Pecola, disastrous results ensue. Thus, through these sometimes casual references, Morrison offers a part of the pattern of black interaction that sustains against the dissolution represented by Pauline's refusal to mother her children, Geraldine's distortion of the notion of family, and Cholly's destructive abuse of his daughter.

The emphasis upon caring applies to the cures offered Aunt Jimmy during her illness. While they do not save her, they illustrate a variety of beliefs and convey the altruistic concern absent from many relationships in the novel. Taken ill after a camp meeting during a rainstorm, Jimmy is told: "Don't eat no whites of eggs," "Drink new milk," "Chew on this root" (108). Refusing such advice, Jimmy does not get better until M'Dear, the local healer, is brought in. "A competent and decisive diagnostician," M'Dear is usually called in when all the "ordinary means" of curing illnesses have failed. She determines that Jimmy has caught a cold in her womb and advises her to "drink pot liquor and nothing else" (108). Jimmy does well until a neighbor decides that she is strong enough to eat a peach cobbler; the next morning Cholly finds her dead. Since the community believes M'Dear "infallible," Jimmy could only have died from eating the peach cobbler. With the logic of the beliefs that guide their cures and preventions, the women rationally conclude that deviation from the advice (drink pot liquor) that had shown itself effective led to Jimmy's death. In their minds the peach cobbler was not blameless, or Jimmy's condition irreversible. A natural cure had been put into effect, and the natural flow was interrupted by the introduction of an alien element. That alien element was responsible for the death. The women accept that with the same stoicism that they combat the waywardness of their husbands and children and the racism of whites.

Their belief in and the very description of M'Dear is also reminiscent of historical folk communities where local healers, or conjurers, or hoodoo doctors usually had distinctive physical characteristics or deformities that set them apart from others in the community. Newbell Niles Puckett, in his study of conjuration in the South,[2] emphasized that many of the conjurers had one blue eye and one black eye, were extremely dark skinned, might be crippled or walked with a cane, and that they frequently lived apart from the rest of the community. M'Dear "was a quiet woman who lived in a shack near the woods" (108). Her power and the confidence the commuity has in her are reflected in her physical characteristics. Cholly expects her to be "shriveled and hunched over" because he has heard that "she was very, very old": "But M'Dear loomed taller than the preacher who accompanied her. She must have been over six feet tall. Four big white knots of hair gave power and authority to her soft black face. Standing straight as a poker, she seemed to need her hickory stick not for support but for communication" (108). The preacher's accompaniment lends power to M'Dear's authority, for in this realm of belief, the secular and the sacred come together. M'Dear's place in the community is as secure, or more so, than the preacher's; her practical status as midwife lends credence to, if not actual tolerance for, her other areas of expertise. Her ties to the community, despite her seeming outsider status, provide another contrast to Pecola, who, severed from those traditions that could incorporate her, merely remains outside the bonds of caring.

The community that believes in M'Dear's powers and in the killing power of peach cobbler also has its share of other folk beliefs and entertainments. Blue Jack, the old man who befriends Cholly after he quits school, is an active tradition bearer of various kinds of tales: "Blue used to tell him old-timey stories about how it was when the Emancipation Proclamation came. How the black people hollered, cried, and sang. And ghost stories about how a white man cut off his wife's head and buried her in the swamp, and the headless body came out at night and went stumbling around the yard, knocking over stuff because it couldn't see, and crying all the time for a comb. They talked about the women Blue had had, and the fights he'd been in when he was younger, about how he talked his way out of getting lynched once, and how others hadn't" (106). The story about the headless woman ties in to many tales of decapitation that circulate in oral tradition, those that are legendary in form, that is, told for true, and those that are etiological in form, explaining, for example, how the jack-o-lantern came into existence.

Blue becomes a folk hero to Cholly, and, long into adulthood, after he has killed three white men and become his own legend, Cholly remembers the good times he has had with Blue. The veneration comes as much from the stories Blue has told as from his admiration of Blue's life—carefree and without responsibilities to anyone. It also comes from the fact that Blue has been one of the few people, besides Aunt Jimmy, who cared for Cholly, who responded to him as a human being, rather than as a phallic symbol, a "nigger," or a burden. No such model exists for Pecola; even the prostitutes who befriend her are equally alienated from the community.

Elements of folk speech, like the folktales and folk heroes are also relevant to the novel. Metaphors comparable to those Zora Neale Hurston uses in *Jonah's Gourd Vine* (1934) occur intermittently, making contrasts between the characters like Geraldine, who deny any ties to folk roots, and those who are closer to the selves inherent in their blackness, such as Claudia's mother. When Mrs. MacTear exclaims that she has "as much business with another mouth to feed as a cat has with side pockets" (23), she exhibits philosophical ties with black people who express their conditions in metaphoric language that is arresting in its vividness. Pauline Breedlove's observation that it is as "cold as a witch's tit" (35) in her house is also a familiar folk expression. When Miss Marie notes that Pecola, on a visit to her house, is without socks, she describes her "as barelegged as a yard dog" (44), a comparison that again evokes the folk creativity that draws similes and metaphors from animals and the natural world. Such expressions tie these characters to historic folk communities even if they should later, as Pauline does, choose to reject most of those bonds of kinship.

Other traditions relevant to the shaping of black character are nicknaming and name calling, which again reflect patterns of caring and incorporation into community. Pauline is pained that she does not have a nickname and blames it on the family's pity for her, for the "slight deformity" she suffers, left from a nail puncture in her foot when she was two years old. Nicknaming is an old and venerated tradition in the black community, and not having been given one, Pauline felt excluded. Without that special favor bestowed upon her, and without being teased or having anecdotes told about her, Pauline "never felt at home anywhere, or that she belonged anyplace" (88). In their studies of nicknames in black communities, scholars have focused on the tremendous value they have, the special recognition they bestow upon an individual for a feat accomplished, a trait emphasized, or a characteristic noticed. Without a nickname, Pauline feels unclaimed by her family in any special way. When the rich white family for which she works in Ohio assigns her a nickname—Polly—it serves in part to explain Pauline's attachment to them: "they gave her what she never had" (101) and thereby claim her attention and her loyalty more so than anyone in her family had done. The white family tells anecdotes about her, of how they could "never find anybody like Polly," of how "she will *not* leave the kitchen until everything is in order," and of how she is ultimately the "ideal servant" (101). A perversion of the functions nicknames serve in black communities, Pauline, as Polly, illustrates the potential identity-shaping purpose such naming provides. She desperately clings to her relationship with the Fishers, but fails to see in her daughter a similar need to be claimed in a special way. Pecola's formal name, reminiscent of movies and books, suggests distance rather than claiming.

To be called "out of one's name," as Bernice Reagan has asserted in some of her research on naming, can be just as negatively powerful as a nickname can be positive.[3] The person so defamed is denied a confirming identity, and thereby suffers a lack comparable to what Pauline feels for not being singled out. The school children who shout names at Pecola shame her and use her features as a way of denying her admission into their society. When the boys circle her in a ritual of insult and shout "Black e mo Black e mo Ya daddy sleeps nekked" (55), Pecola becomes the victim who invites further abuse because she suffers visibly. The game is tantamount to a rite of separation. In the process, Pecola is given another opportunity to view her status as an outsider. Her rescue by Maureen Peal, Claudia, and Frieda is only temporary, because Maureen indulges Pecola only in an effort to discover if the insult the boys have shouted about her father is really true. Unsatisfied, the light-skinned Maureen draws a circle of acceptance around herself that excludes the other three girls: "I *am* cute! And you ugly! Black and ugly black e mos. I *am* cute!" (61). Conscious of her unattractiveness and her color, Pecola seems to disappear where she stands, unable to join Claudia and Frieda in returning insults to Maureen, or to appreciate that they are fighting for her. She senses too strongly rejection at an irredeemable level. Children, teachers, neighbors, and other adults have confirmed what her mother concluded upon her birth: that Pecola will never be an insider in the black community and cannot possibly hope for acceptance beyond it. All combine to reinforce Pecola's belief that the only escape for her is to become beautiful through obtaining the bluest eyes of all, ones that will dazzle everyone into loving her.

Her belief in what blue eyes will accomplish for her is just as strong as some of the folk beliefs expressed in the novel. Belief is the single most important factor in conjuration as in Christianity, the two systems to which Pecola is most frequently exposed. Her prayers to God to make her disappear are predicated upon the belief that such a feat is possible. Her giving of the poisoned meat to the old dog is similarly predicated upon the belief that, if a reaction occurs, her wish for blue eyes will be granted. Hope for a magical transformation underlies both desires, and Pecola's belief in the possible transformation ties her to all believers in sympathetic magic. Her conviction that the blue eyes have been granted her may be viewed as insanity, but it simultaneously fits the logic that has led to that final reward. It is no stranger than the community women's belief that Jimmy has died from eating a peach cobbler. Belief is the single most important element in both outcomes.

Pecola's basic wish for blue eyes ties her to all believers in fairy tales and other magical realms. It is Cinderella wanting to be transformed from char girl to belle of the ball, or Sleeping Beauty waiting a hundred years for the prince to awaken her. It is the classic tale of the ugly duckling turned beautiful swan, of the beast transformed through love and caring into the beautiful prince, of Sir Gawain's pig lady turned into a dazzling woman. While Pecola seems doomed whatever she does—if she resorts to fantasy, she is considered crazy, and if she tries to live in the real world, there is no place for her—her desire for blue eyes ties her to many heroines of fairy tales, and to many young girls who have wished for features other than the ones they have. While many of the latter desires are no more than passing fancies, Pecola's is more intense because she is never given the opportunity, in any realm (home, school, playground), to see anything positive in herself as she is. The patterns of caring and incorporation hinted at in some of the occurrences in the novel never reach her strongly enough to reshape her opinion of herself.

Belief in magical realms or in the power to make present conditions seem magical is also seen in the desire of Claudia and Frieda to influence Pecola's fate by planting the marigolds correctly. They hope, as Pecola does with the offering to the dog, to bring about a kind of sympathetic magic, to create a space and circumstances in which Pecola will have a healthier future. When they fail, they blame themselves for not performing the rites correctly, for not having the right amount of belief. Destined to live in the realistic world, which promises a sane future for them, Claudia and Frieda are encouraged to put aside their childish beliefs. Diverging into a different world, Pecola makes the transition into fantasy, into a world from which Claudia's and Frieda's destinies have effectively and happily shut them out.

Beliefs that are adhered to over long periods of time and repeated occurrences can be defined as rituals. One of these operative in Morrison's novel is the ritual surrounding the funeral of Aunt Jimmy; certainly the funeral itself is a ritual, but so too is the traditional gathering of neighbors, relatives, and friends immediately after the death. They come as if in a dance, to perform the movements that custom and tradition have assigned to them. First, they must prepare for the burial. Then, they prepare food for those who come from near and far. They, and the relatives, must divide the belongings of the loved one and see that those left homeless are provided for. Since Cholly has never witnessed the ceremonies surrounding a funeral, he gets an education simultaneous with our witnessing of the unfolding of a tradition. The ladies of Jimmy's generation take over: they "cleaned the house, aired everything out, notified everybody, and stitched together what looked like a white wedding dress for Aunt Jimmy" (111). They also manage to get clothes for Cholly to attend the funeral, and they ensure that all of his physical needs are met.

After the traditional viewing of the body, and the "tearful shrieks and shouts" (113) of the mourners, the processional moves to the cemetery. Although the funeral is not depicted in detail, Morrison captures its emotional intensity in the metaphoric language of classic tradition:

> It was like a street tragedy with spontaneity tucked softly into the corners of a highly formal structure. The deceased was the tragic hero, the survivors the innocent victims; there was the omnipresence of the deity, strophe and antistrophe of the chorus of mourners led by the preacher. There was grief over the waste of life, the stunned wonder at the ways of God, and the restoration of order in nature at the graveyard. (113)

The funeral serves to return order to a community disrupted by death. Like all rituals, it provides a functional release, a pattern into which grief can be shaped, for the entire community.

After the "thunderous beauty of the funeral," the funeral banquet is "a peal of joy"; it is "the exultation, the harmony, the acceptance of physical frailty, joy in the termination of misery. Laughter, relief, a steep hunger for food" (113). It is the sign that things can continue without the departed one, and it serves to put the grieving for her in the perspective of the larger force of ongoing life. Concerns return to the practical—who will take Cholly and what relatives will get which of Aunt Jimmy's belongings.

With the ritual over, the "accounts settled," and the spectacle completed, the individual families return to their own homes, content in the knowledge that they have played well the roles that tradition and custom have assigned to them. Now, comparable to Janie's burying of Tea Cake in Zora Neale Hurston's *Their Eyes Were Watching God*,[4] there are only the tales to be told, the stories carrying the memories of what happened at Jimmy's funeral, about how well she was "laid out" and how much her family and friends appreciated her. In death, as in life, the pattern of caring that eludes Pecola is a recurring strand in the novel, one that has touched Cholly and Pauline, but from which they have become disconnected in their pursuit of clothes and alcohol.

Jimmy's death provides for one kind of traditional ritual of caring and continuation. Another tradition Morrison draws upon in the novel is that of the blues. In many ways *The Bluest Eye* is similar to Ralph Ellison's *Invisible Man*[5] in its very theme and structure: "What did I do to be so black and blue?" Conscious of it or not, that question must reverberate in Pecola's mind throughout her adventures in the novel. Again and again, she is confronted with people who emphasize to her that she must "stay back" because of her blackness. Again and again, she is "boomeranged" over the head with the knowledge that little black boys do not want to "haul no coal" or be identified with a "stovepipe blonde" and that most of her friends, family, and neighbors believe that "white is right." She lives the blues twenty-four hours a day, through each of the long minutes drawn out in each of those hours. Mrs. MacTear can sing about "hard times, bad times, and somebody-done-gone-and-left-me-times" (24) and about "trains and Arkansas" (78); and Poland can sing about "blues in [her] mealbarrel / Blues up on the shelf" (44), but Pecola can give both of them lessons in living the blues. The ugliness that she believes is hers is just as blues-inducing as those levees breaking to release floodwaters in the Mississippi Delta. At least there was release from floods, and perhaps the pantry can be replenished, but Pecola's ugliness is there to stay. The potential for release from her state of the blues will never be fulfilled because the world around her does not believe that relief is her just due; it will always convey to her that the blues is her permanent condition, not a temporary state from which she can reasonably anticipate escape.

Her adventures, like those of her father, would "become coherent only in the head of a musician" (125), or in the structural composition of a novel that resembles a blues creation. Yet the blues are a way for people to touch their pain and that of others, to sing of what, in any given instance, is but an individualized account of collective suffering. But Pecola is unable to articulate the pain she feels or channel it through the form of the blues. Like her belief in fantasies derived from outside the black community, her state of the blues is familiar, but she has no model for it to serve as a way of connecting her to the community rather than cutting her off from it.

Pauline and Cholly Breedlove have both come into contact with forms of Afro-American culture used to tie black people to each other in caring, sharing ways. Yet their move to the North parallels a dissolution in their abilities to use the forms to which they have been exposed for any sustaining purposes. Thus they break the chains of continuity in culture and can only produce children who are outside that which had the potential to nurture them. Pecola and Cholly must therefore exist in a world of fragmentation, in a world where Mrs. MacTear and Poland might show signs of the more sustaining Southern black culture, but which they cannot effectively transmit to the Breedlove children. They, like other characters in their isolated existences in the novel, are tied together by cultural forces stronger than all of them, but the strands of that cultural net keep breaking away from Pecola to slip her back into a sea of confusion about herself and about her place in the world of Lorain, Ohio.

Notes

1. Toni Morrison, *The Bluest Eye* (New York: Pocket Books, 1972), 105. Subsequent references to this source appear in the text in parenthesis.

2. Newbell Niles Puckett, *Folk Beliefs of the Southern Negro* (Chapel Hill: University of North Carolina Press, 1926).

3. Bernice Reagan, "We Are 'Girl,' 'Chile,' 'Lady,' That and 'oman,' 'Hussy,' 'Heifer,' 'A Woman'; or, Naming That Imprisons and Naming That Sets You Free," Unpublished paper presented at the Annual Meeting of the Modern Language Association, Washington, D.C., 27 December 1984.

4. Zora Neale Hurston, *Their Eyes Were Watching God* (Philadelphia: J. B. Lippincott, 1937. reprint, Urbana: University of Illinois Press, 1978).

5. Ralph Ellison, *Invisible Man* (New York: Random House, 1972).

Sula

"The Self and the Other": Reading Toni Morrison's *Sula* and the Black Female Text

Deborah E. McDowell*

> What shall we call our "self"? Where does it begin? Where does it end? It overflows into everything that belongs to us.
> —Henry James, *Portrait of a Lady*

> She had clung to Nel as the closest thing to both an other and a self, only to discover that she and Nel were not one and the same thing.
> —Toni Morrison, *Sula*[1]

In "Negro Art," an essay published in the *Crisis* in 1921, W. E. B. DuBois described the desire of blacks for idealized literary representation. "We want everything said about us to tell of the best and highest and noblest in us . . . we fear that the evil in us will be called racial, while in others, it is viewed as individual."[2] A few years later, in 1926, DuBois seemed himself to want to see the "best and highest and noblest" image of the black SELF in literature. Concerned because blacks were being "continually painted at their worst and judged by the public as they [were] painted," DuBois organized a write-in symposium called "The Negro in Art: How Shall He Be Portrayed?" that ran from March–December in the *Crisis* magazine. The subject of intense debate, the symposium elicited applause and critiques from its respondents. Though not written directly in response to the symposium, one famous critique of its concerns was Langston Hughes's famous manifesto, published in the same year, "The Negro Artist and the Racial Mountain," in which he blasted the "Nordicized Negro intelligentsia" for demanding that black artists "be respectable, write about nice people, [and] show how good [black people] are."[3]

Roughly fifty years later, those in the vanguard of the Black Aesthetic movement described and called for black writers to inscribe the "positive" racial self in literature. In his 1977 essay "Blueprint for Black Criticism," for example, Addison Gayle appealed specifically for literary characters modeled upon such men and women as Sojourner Truth, Harriet Tubman, Martin Delaney, H. Rap Brown, and Fannie Lou Hamer—a kind of

---

*This essay was written specifically for this volume and is published here for the first time by permission of the author.

Plutarch's *Lives* of the black race. In that they offer images of "heroism, beauty, and courage," Gayle continues, "these men and women are positive" characters, functional "alternatives to the stereotypes of Blacks," and thus warriors in the "struggle against American racism."[4]

In the ten years since Gayle issued his blueprint, Afro-American literary criticism has finally seen the beginnings of a paradigm shift, one that has extended the boundaries and altered the terms of its inquiry. Falling in step with recent developments in contemporary critical theory, some critics of Afro-American literature have complicated some of our most common assumptions about the SELF, and about race as a meaningful category in literary study and critical theory.[5] These recent developments have made it difficult, if not impossible, to posit, with any assurance, a "positive" black SELF, always already unified, coherent, stable, and known.

And yet, despite these important and sophisticated developments, Afro-American critics of Afro-American literature, in both the popular media and academic journals, continue to resist any work that does not satisfy the nebulous demand for the "positive" racial SELF. And perhaps at no time has such resistance been more determined and judgments been more harsh than now, when diehard critics, reducing contemporary black women writers to a homogenized bloc, have alleged that their portrayal of black male characters is uniformly "negative."

A full inquiry into this debate, which has escaped the pages of literary journals and essay collections, and spilled over into the privileged organs of the literary establishment—the *New York Times Book Review* and the *New York Review of Books*—is not possible here, although it is in urgent need of address. But allow me to use Mel Watkins's comments from his June 1986 essay, "Sexism, Racism, and Black Women Writers," published in the *New York Times Book Review* to represent the insistent refrain. Watkins argues that in the great majority of their novels, black women indicate that "sexism is more oppressive than racism." In these works, black males are portrayed in an "unflinchingly candid and often negative manner," almost without exception, "thieves, sadists, rapists, and ne'er-do-wells." In choosing "Black men as a target," Watkins continues, "these writers have set themselves outside a tradition, devoted to "establishing humane, positive images of Blacks" (36).[6]

It is useful here to pause and extrapolate the interlocking assumptions of Watkins's essay most relevant to my concerns. These assumptions are the struts of the dominant Afro-American critical paradigm in which 1) the world is neatly divided into black and white; 2) race is the sole determinant of being and identity, subsuming sexual difference; 3) identity is preexistent, coherent, and known; and 4) literature has the power to unify and liberate the race. This paradigm pivots on a set of oppositions— black/white, positive/negative, self/other—among an interchangeable field. The overarching preoccupation with "positive" racial representation has worked side by side with a static view of the nature of identification in the act of reading. Further, when accepted and upheld, it has resulted in substantial figurations of myth akin to Alice Walker's description: "I am Black, beautiful, and strong, and almost always right."[7] *This* is the SELF, with which our hypothetical Afro-American critic, desperately seeking flattery, is likely to identify. It is uniformly "positive" and "good" and defined in contradistinction to its OTHER, uniformly "negative" and "bad."

Easily recognizable here is the classic condition of "otherness," a subject that is itself fast becoming an industry in current critical theory and practice. And, as feminist theorists consistently and emphatically point out, the opposition of "self" to "other," and all those analogous to it, relate hierarchically and reproduce the more fundamental opposition between male and female. Man is SELF, and woman, other.[8] And in this configuration, as Shoshana Felman puts it eloquently, echoing the dutiful terms of the dominant Afro-American paradigm, woman is "the negative of the positive."[9] We face here an exponential expression of what Henry Gates has observed about Afro-American narrative more generally. He notes astutely that the irony of the Afro-American writers' "attempt to posit a 'black self' in the very Western languages in which blackness [multiply femaleness] itself is a figure of absence [is] a negation."[10]

While these observations are commonplace in feminist discourse, their usefulness to students of Afro-American literary history has not been fully interrogated. Preventing such interrogation is an almost exclusive focus on race in Afro-American literary discourse, which is often tantamount to a focus on maleness. Further preventing such investigation is what might be called an orthodoxy of victimage that unifies and homogenizes black men. In reducing their relationship to white male power and privilege as exclusively one of victimization, this orthodoxy ignores the extent to which black men share in the ideologies and practices of male privilege. The subordination (if not the absolute erasure) of black women in discourses on blackness is well known. The black SELF has been assumed male historically, of which Gloria Hull, Patricia Bell-Scott, and Barbara Smith are well aware. They do not engage in cheap and idle rhetoric in entitling their landmark anthology: *All the Women Are White, All the Blacks Are Men,* for we are all too familiar with the fact that, in significant periods of their history, black women saw black men as the privileged centers of the race. While that pattern is widely evident, it stands out in noticeable relief both in Afro-American critical inquiry and in the Afro-American literary canon.[11] There, the "face" of the race, the "speaking subject," is male.[12]

While these issues need to be exposed, it will no longer suffice to leave the discourse at the point of simple descriptive exposure to which we are all inured. The next stage in the development of feminist criticism on Afro-American women writers must lead us beyond the descriptions that keep us locked in opposition and antagonism. Toni Morrison's novel, *Sula* (1973), is rife with liberating possibilities in that it transgresses all deterministic structures of opposition.

The novel invokes oppositions of good/evil, virgin/whore, self/ other, but moves beyond them, avoiding the false choices they imply and dictate. As Hortense Spillers puts it eloquently, when we read *Sula*, "No Manichean analysis demanding a polarity of interest—black/white, male/ female, good/bad [and I might add, positive/negative, self/other]—will do."[13] The narrative insistently blurs and confuses these and other binary oppositions. It glories in paradox and ambiguity beginning with the prologue that describes the setting, the Bottom, situated spatially in the top. We enter a new world here, a world where we never get to the "bottom" of things, a world that demands a shift from an either/or orientation to one that is both/and, full of shifts and contradictions.

In these, as well as other particulars, *Sula* opens up new literary and critical options, not only for the study of texts by Afro-American women, but for Afro-American literary study more generally. The novel certainly helps to set a new agenda for black women's social and narrative possiblities. Coming significantly on the heels of the Black Power Movement that rendered black women prone or the "queens" of the male warrior—an updated version of a familiar script—the narrative invites the reader to imagine a different script for women that transcends the boundaries of social and linguistic convention. Further, it offers a useful model of self, of identity and identification in the reading process, a model that springs the traditional Afro-American critic from the rhetoric of opposition that has kept the discourse in arrest.

2

Day and night are mingled in our gazes . . . If we divide light from night, we give up the lightness of our mixture . . . We put ourselves into watertight compartments, break ourselves up into parts, cut ourselves in two . . . we are always one and the other, at the same time.
                                                                    —Luce Irigaray[14]

To posit that we are always one and the other at the same time is to challenge effectively a fundamental assumption of Western metaphysics that has operated historically, in Afro-American literature and criticism: "the unity of the ego-centered individual self"[15] defined in opposition to an other. In *Sula*, Toni Morrison complicates and questions that assumption, evoking the very oppositions on which it has tended to rest. She transgresses and blurs the boundaries these oppositions create, boundaries separating us from others and rendering us "others" to ourselves.

Morrison's transgression begins with questioning traditional notions of SELF as they have been translated into narrative. She implicitly critiques such concepts as "protagonist," "hero," and "major character" by emphatically decentering and deferring the presence of Sula, the title character. Bearing *her* name, the narrative suggests that she is the protagonist, the privileged center, but her presence is constantly deferred. We are first introduced to a caravan of characters: Shadrack, Nel, Helene, Eva, the Deweys, Tar Baby, Hannah, and Plum before we get any sustained treatment of Sula. Economical to begin with, the novel is roughly one-third over when Sula is introduced and it continues almost that long after her death.

Not only does the narrative deny the reader a "central" character, but it also denies the whole notion of character as static *essence*, replacing it with the idea of character as *process*.[16] Whereas the former is based on the assumption that the self is knowable, centered, and unified, the latter is based on the assumption that the self is multiple, fluid, relational, and in a perpetual state of becoming. Significantly, Sula, whose eyes are "as steady and clear as rain," is associated throughout with water, fluidity. Her birthmark, which shifts in meaning depending on the viewer's perspective, acts as metaphor for her figurative "selves," her multiple identity. To Nel, it is a "stemmed rose"; to her children, a "scary black thing," a "black mark"; to Jude, a "copperhead" and a "rattlesnake"; to Shadrack, a "tadpole." The image of the tadpole reinforces this notion of SELF as perpetually in process. Sula never achieves completeness of being. She dies in the fetal position welcoming this "sleep of water," in a passage that clearly suggests, she is dying yet aborning (149). Morrison's reconceptualization of character has clear and direct implications for Afro-American literature and critical study, for if the self is perceived as perpetually in process, rather than a static entity always already formed, it is thereby difficult to posit its ideal or "positive" representation.

Appropriate to this conception of character as process, the narrative employs the double, a technique related, as Baruch Hoffman has observed, to the "rupturing of coherence in character."[17] It positions its doubles, Nel and Sula, in adolescence, a state of becoming when they are "unshaped, formless things" (53) "us[ing] each other to grow on," finding "in each other's eyes the intimacy they were looking for" (52). As doubles, Sula and Nel complement and flow into each other, their closeness evoked throughout the narrative in physical metaphors. Sula's return to the Bottom, after a ten-year absence is, for Nel, "like getting the use of an eye back, having a cataract removed" (95). The two are likened to "two throats and one eye" (147).

But while Sula and Nel are represented as two parts of a self, those parts are distinct; they are complementary, not identical. Although Sula and Nel might share a common vision (suggested by "one eye"), their needs and desires are distinct (they have "two throats").[18] Sula comes to understand the fact of their difference, as the epigraph to this essay suggests: "She clung to Nel as the closest thing to an *other* and a *self* only to discover that she and Nel were not one and the same thing." The relationship of other to self in this passage, and throughout the narrative, must be seen as "different but connected rather than separate and opposed," to borrow from Carole Gilligan.[19]

Sula's understanding of her relationship to Nel results from self-understanding and self-intimacy, a process that Nel's marriage to Jude interrupts. Like so many women writers, Morrison equates marriage with the death of the female self and imagination. Nel would be the "someone sweet, industrious, and loyal, to shore him up . . . the two of them would make one Jude" (83). After marriage she freezes into her wifely role, becoming one of the women who had "folded themselves into starched coffins" (122). Her definition of self becomes based on the community's "absolute" moral categories about "good" and "bad" women, categories that result in her separation from and opposition to Sula.

The narrative anticipates that opposition in one of its early descriptions of Nel and Sula. Nel is the color of "wet sandpaper," Sula is the "heavy brown" (52), a distinction that can be read as patriarchy's conventional fair lady / dark woman, virgin / whore dichotomy, one reflected in Sula's and Nel's separate matrilineages.

Sula's female heritage is an unbroken line of "manloving" women who exist as sexually desiring subjects rather than as objects of male desire. Her mother, Hannah, "ripple[s] with sex" (42), exasperating the "good" women of the community who call her "nasty." But that does not prevent her taking her lovers into the pantry for "some touching every day" (44). In contrast, Nel's is a split heritage. On one side is her grandmother, the whore of the Sundown House, and on the other her great-grandmother, who worshipped the Virgin Mary and counseled Helene "to be constantly on guard for any sign of her mother's wild blood" (17). Nel takes her great-grandmother's counsel to heart, spending her life warding off being "turn[ed] to jelly" and "custard" (22). Jelly and pudding here are metaphors of sexuality characteristic in classic blues lyrics.

Nel's sexuality is not expressed in itself and for her own pleasure, but rather, for the pleasure of her husband and in obedience to a system of ethical judgment and moral virtue, her "only mooring" (139). Because Nel's sexuality is harnessed to and only enacted within the institutions that sanction sexuality for women—marriage and family—she does not own it.[20] It is impossible for her to imagine sex without Jude. After she finds him and Sula in the sex act she describes her thighs—the metaphor for her sexuality—as "empty and dead . . . and it was Sula who had taken the life from them." She concludes that "the both of them . . . left her with no thighs and no heart, just her brain raveling away" (110).

Without Jude, Nel thinks her thighs are useless. Her sexuality is harnessed to duty and virtue in a simple cause / effect relationship as is clear from the plaintive questions she puts to an imaginary God after Jude leaves:

> even if I sew up those old pillow cases and rinse down the porch and feed my children and beat the rugs and haul the coal up out of the bin even then

nobody. . . . I could be a mule or plow the furrows with my hands if need be or hold these rickety walls up with my back if I knew that somewhere in this world in the pocket of some night I could open my legs to some cowboy lean hips but you are trying to tell me no and O my sweet Jesus, what kind of cross is that? (111)

Sula, on the other hand, "went to bed with men as frequently as she could" (122) and assumed responsibility for her own pleasure. In her first sexual experience with Ajax, significantly a reenactment of Hannah's sexual rituals in the pantry, Sula "stood wide-legged against the wall and pulled from his track-lean hips all the pleasure her thighs could hold" (125). This is not to suggest that Sula's sexual expression is uncomplicated or unprob-lematic, but rather that unlike Nel's, it is not attached to anything outside herself, especially not to social definitions of female sexuality and con-ventions of duty. Although initially she "liked the sootiness of sex," liked "to think of it as wicked" (122), she comes to realize that it was not wicked. Further, apart from bringing her "a special kind of joy," it brought her "misery and the ability to feel deep sorrow" and "a stinging awareness of the endings of things" (122, 123), a feeling of "her own abiding strength and limitless power" (123). In other words, Sula's sexuality is neither located in the realm of "moral" abstractions nor expressed within the institution of marriage that legitimates it for women. Rather it is in the realm of sensory experience and in the service of the self-exploration that leads to self-intimacy. After sex, Sula enters that "post-coital privateness in which she met herself, welcomed herself, and joined herself in matchless harmony" (123). Unlike Nel, Sula has no ego and therefore feels "no compulsion . . . to be consistent with herself" (119). In describing her, Morrison notes that Sula "examines herself . . . is experimental with herself [and] perfectly willing to think the unthinkable thing."[21] To Sula "there was only her own mood and whim" enabling her to explore "that version of herself which she sought to reach out to and touch with an ungloved hand," "to discover it and let others become as intimate with their own selves as she was" (121).

Not only is sexual expression an act of self-exploration, but it is also associated throughout the narrative with creativity as seen in the long prose poem she creates while making love to Ajax. But significantly that creativity is without sufficient outlet within her community. According to Morrison, "If Sula had any sense she'd go somewhere and sing or get into show business," implying that her "strangeness," her "lawlessness" can only be sanctioned in a world like the theater.[22] Because of her community's rigid norms for women, Sula's impulses cannot be absorbed. Without an "art form," her "tremendous curiosity and gift for metaphor" become destructive (121). Without art forms, Sula is the artist become her own work of art.[23] As she responds defiantly to Eva's injunction that she make babies to settle herself, "I don't want to make somebody else. I want to make myself" (92).

Because she resists self-exploration, such creativity is closed to Nel.

She has no "sparkle or splutter," just a "dull glow" (83). Her imagination has
been driven "underground" from years of obeying the normative female
script. She "belonged to the town and all of its ways" (120). The narrative
strongly suggests that one cannot belong to the community and preserve
the imagination, for the orthodox vocations for women—marriage and
motherhood—restrict if not preclude imaginative expression.

Obedience to community also precludes intimacy with self for
women. Nel rejects this intimacy that involves confronting what both Sula
and Shadrack have confronted: the unknown parts of themselves. In
turning her back on the unknown, Nel fails to grow, to change, or to learn
anything about herself until the last page of the novel. She thinks that "hell is
change" (108). "One of the last true pedestrians" in the Bottom, Nel walks
on the road's shoulder (on its edge, not on the road), "allowing herself to
accept rides only when the weather required it" (166).

Nel fits Docherty's description of the type of character who is "fixed
and centered up on one locatable ego," blocking "the possibility of
authentic response, genuine sentiment." According to this ego-centered
schema, "the self can only act in accord with a determined and limited
'characteristic' response" (80). Whereas Sula is an ambiguous character
with a repertoire of responses along a continuum and thus cannot be
defined as either totally "good" or "bad," Nel's is a limited response:
"goodness," "rightness," as her name "Wright" suggests. As it is classically
defined for women "goodness" is sexual faithfulness, self-abnegation, and
the idealization of marriage and motherhood.

After years of nursing the belief that Sula has irreparably wronged her
and violated their friendship, Nel goes to visit Sula on her deathbed as any
"good woman" would do. Virtue, "her only mooring," has hidden "from
her the true motives for her charity" (139). Their conversation, after years
of estrangement, is peppered with references to good and evil, right and
wrong. Nel protests, "I was good to you, Sula, why don't that matter?" And
Sula responds in her characteristically defiant way "Being good to
somebody is just like being mean to somebody. Risky. You don't get
nothing for it." Exasperated because "talking to [Sula] about right and
wrong" (144–45) was impossible, Nel leaves but not before Sula has the last
word. And significantly, that last word takes the form of a question, an
uncertainty, not an unambiguous statement of fact or truth:

> "How you know?" Sula asked.
> "Know what?" Nel still wouldn't look at her.
> "About who was good. How you know it was you?"
> "What you mean?"
> "I mean maybe it wasn't you. Maybe it was me."

In the space of the narrative Nel has another twenty-five years to
deflect the contemplation of Sula's question through desperate acts of
goodness: visits to "the sick and shut in," the category on the back page of

black church bulletins that pull on the chords of duty. But on one such mission to visit Eva, Nel is confronted with not only the question but the more *unsettling* suggestion of guilt.

> "Tell me how you killed that little boy."
> "What? What little boy?"
> "The one you threw in the water . . ."
> "I didn't throw no little boy in the river. That was Sula."
> "You, Sula. What's the difference?"

After years of repression, Nel must own her complicity in Chicken Little's drowning, a complicity that is both sign and symbol of the disowned piece of herself. She recalls the incident in its fullness, remembering "the good feeling she had had when Chicken's hands slipped" (170) and "the tranquillity that follow[ed] [that] joyful stimulation" (170). That remembrance makes space for Nel's psychic reconnection with Sula as a friend as well as symbol of that disowned self. Significantly, that reconnection occurs in the cemetery, a metaphor for Nel's buried shadow. The "circles and circles of sorrow" she cried at the narrative's end prepare her for what Sula strained to experience throughout her life: the process of mourning and remembering that leads to intimacy with the self, which is all that makes intimacy with others possible.

And the reader must mourn as Nel mourns, must undergo the process of development that Nel undergoes.[24] And as with Nel, that process begins with releasing the static and coherent conception of SELF and embracing what Sula represents: the self as process and fluid possibility. That embrace makes possible an altered understanding of the nature of identification in the reading process.

III

Recent theories of the act of reading have enriched and complicated—for the good—our understanding of what takes place in the act of reading. They have described the reading process as dialogical, as an interaction between a reader (a SELF) and an OTHER, an interaction in which neither remains the same.[25] In light of this information, we can conceive the act of reading as a process of self-exploration that the narrative strategies of Sula compel. What strategies does the narrative employ to generate that process? It deliberately miscues the reader, disappointing the very expectations the narrative arouses, forcing the reader to shift gears, to change perspective. Though these strategies might well apply to all readers, they have specific implications for Afro-American critics.

Sula threatens the readers' assumptions and disappoints their expectations at every turn. It begins by disappointing the reader's expectations of a "realistic" and unified narrative documenting black / white confrontation.

Although the novel's prologue, which describes a community's destruction by white greed and deception, gestures toward "realistic" documentation, leads the reader to expect "realistic" documentation of a black community's confrontation with an oppressive white world, that familiar and expected plot is in the background. In the foreground are the characters whose lives transcend their social circumstances. They laugh, they dance, they sing, and are "mightily preoccupied with earthly things—and each other" (6). The narrative retreats from linearity privileged in the realist mode. Though dates entitle the novel's chapters, they relate only indirectly to its central concerns and do not permit the reader to use chronology in order to intepret its events in any cause / effect fashion. In other words, the story's forward movement in time is deliberately nonsequential and without explicit reference to "real" time. It roves lightly over historical events, dates, and details as seen in the first chapter. Titled "1919," the chapter begins with a reference to World War II, then refers, in quick and, paradoxically, regressive succession, to National Suicide Day, instituted in 1920, then backwards to Shadrack running across a battlefield in France in World War I.

In addition, the narrative forces us to question our readings, to hold our judgment in check, and to continually revise it. Susan Blake is on the mark when she says that "the reader never knows quite what to think" of characters and events in *Sula*: "whether to applaud Eva's self-sacrifice or deplore her tyranny, whether to admire Sula's freedom or condemn her heartlessness."[26] The narrative is neither an apology for Sula's destruction nor an unsympathetic critique of Nel's smug conformity. It does not reduce a complex set of dynamics to a simple opposition or choice between two "pure" alternatives.

Among the strategies Morrison uses to complicate choice and block judgment are the dots within dots (. . . .) in the narrative that mark time breaks and function as stop signs. They compel the reader to pause, think back, evaluate the narrative's events, and formulate new expectations in light of them, expectations that are never quite fulfilled.[27] The Afro-American critic, wanting a world cleansed of uncertainty and contradictions and based on the rhetorical polarities—positive and negative—might ask in frustration, "Can we ever determine the right judgment?" The narrative implies that that answer can only come from within, from exploring all parts of the SELF. As Nel asks Eva in the scene mentioned earlier, "You think I'm guilty?" Eva whispers, "Who would know that better than you?" (169).

Not only does the narrative disappoint the reader's expectations of correct answers and appropriate judgment, but it also prevents a stable and unified reading of the text, though I have fabricated one here by tracing a dominant thread in the narrative: the relationship between self and other. But in exploring this relationship, Morrison deliberately provides echoing passages that cancel each other out, that thwart the reader's desire for stability and consistency:

"She clung to Nel as the closest thing to both an other and a self, only to discover that she and Nel were not one and the same thing."

But the following passage, which comes much later in the narrative, effectively cancels this passage out: Sula learned that

"there was no other that you could count on . . . [and] there was no *self* to count on either."

The novel's fragmentary, episodic, elliptical quality helps to thwart textual unity, to prevent a totalized interpretation. An early reviewer described the text as a series of scenes and glimpses, each "written . . . from scratch." Since none of them has anything much to do with the ones that preceded them, "we can never piece the glimpses into a coherent picture."[28] Whatever coherence and meaning resides in the narrative, the reader must struggle to create.

The gaps in the text allow for the reader's participation in the creation of meaning in the text. Morrison has commented on the importance of the "affective and participatory relationship between the artist and the audience," and her desire "to have the reader work *with* the author in the construction of the book." She adds, "What is left out is as important as what is there."[29] The reader must fill in the narrative's many gaps, for instance: Why is there no funeral for either Plum or Hannah? What happens to Jude? Where *was* Eva during her eighteen-month absence from the Bottom? What really happened to her leg? How does Sula support herself after she returns from her ten-year absence?

The reader's participation in the meaning-making process helps to fill in the gaps in the text, as well as to bridge the gaps separating the reader *from* the text. This returns us full circle to the beginning of this essay: the boundary separating some Afro-American readers from the black text that opposes a single unified image of the black SELF.

As Norman Holland and others have noted, each reader has a vision of the world arising from her/his identity theme. In the act of reading, the reader tries to re-create the text according to that identity theme. Holland continues, as we read, we use the "literary work to symbolize and finally to replicate ourselves,"[30] to reflect ourselves, to affirm ourselves by denying or demeaning the other. But, writing in a different context, Holland usefully suggests that, "one of literature's adaptive functions . . . is that it allows us to loosen boundaries between self and not self."[31]

Transgressing that boundary and viewing identity and the self in relation, rather than coherent, separate, and opposed, permits an analogous view of identification in the reading process. Just as the self is fluid, dynamic, and formed in relation, so is identification a process involving a relationship between the SELF and the "otherness" of writers, texts, and literary characters.

If we would approach that "unified" black community splintered, many argue, by black women writers' imaginative daring, those boundaries and the rigid identity themes and fantasies holding them up must be crossed. After all, as *Sula* playfully suggests, our conceptions of who we are never include all that we are anyway. One answer, then, to the epigraph: "What shall we call our 'self'?" is we shall call ourselves by many names. Our metaphors of self cannot then rest in stasis, but will glory in difference and overflow into everything that belongs to us.

Notes

1. Toni Morrison, *Sula* (New York: New American Library, 1973), 119. Subsequent references are to this edition and will be indicated parenthetically in the text.

2. W. E. B. DuBois, "Negro Art," *Crisis* (June 1921): 55–56.

3. Langston Hughes, "The Negro Artist and the Racial Mountain," in *Five Black Writers*, ed. Donald B. Gibson (New York: New York University Press, 1970), 227–28.

4. Addison Gayle, "Blueprint for Black Criticism," *First World* (January/February 1977): 44.

5. See three essays by Henry Louis Gates: "Preface to Blackness: Text and Pretext," in *Afro-American Literature: The Reconstruction of Instruction*, ed. Dexter Fischer and Robert Stepto (New York: MLA, 1979), 44–69; "Criticism in the Jungle," in *Black Literature and Literary Theory*, ed. Henry Gates (New York: Methuen, 1984), 1–24; and "Writing 'Race' and the Difference it Makes," *Critical Inquiry* 12 (Autumn 1985): 1–20. For critiques of the issue on "'Race,' Writing and Difference," in which the last essay appears, see *Critical Inquiry* 13 (Autumn 1986).

6. Mel Watkins, "Sexism, Racism, and Black Women Writers," *New York Times Book Review* (June 1986): 36. For similar discussions see Darryl Pinckney, "Black Victims, Black Villains," *New York Review of Books* 34 (29 January 1987): 17–20 and Richard Barksdale, "Castration Symbolism in Recent Black American Fiction," *College Language Association Journal* 29 (June 1986): 400–13.

7. Alice Walker, "The Unglamorous But Worthwhile Duties of the Black Revolutionary Artist, or of the Black Writer Who Simply Works and Writes," in *In Search of Our Mother's Gardens* (New York: Harcourt Brace Jovanovich, 1983), 137.

8. Although a whole field of binary oppositions can be viewed as analogous to the male/female opposition, Cary Nelson rightly cautions against so rigid a reading. He argues persuasively that when such dualities are considered in cultural and historical context, the basic male/female opposition breaks down and the qualities associated with each side are often reversed. See "Envoys of Otherness: Difference and Continuity in Feminist Criticism," in *For Alma Mater: Theory and Practice in Feminist Scholarship*, ed. Paula Treichler et al. (Urbana: University of Illinois Press, 1985), 91–118.

9. Shoshana Felman, "Women and Madness: The Critical Phallacy," *Diacritics* 5 (Winter 1975): 3.

10. See Gates, "Criticism in the Jungle," 7.

11. The historical equation of blackness with maleness in discourses on blackness and in the development of the Afro-American literary canon is an issue calling urgently for examination. Although I cannot address it here in any detail it is the subject of my essay-in-progress forthcoming in *Black American Literature Forum*. For a discussion of how this

equation has worked out in discourses on slavery see Deborah Gray White, *Ar'n't I a Woman: Female Slaves in the Plantation South* (New York: Norton, 1985). White examines slave women whose experiences are neglected, more often than not, from scholarship on slavery. According to White, the pattern began with the publication of Stanley Elkins's *Slavery, A Problem in American Institutional and Intellectual Life* (Chicago: University of Chicago Press, 1959) in which he posited his controversial "Sambo" thesis of male infantilism and incompetence which historians have since focussed their energies on negating. That focus has effectively eclipsed black women from view.

12. See Robert Stepto, *From Behind the Veil: A Study of Afro-American Narrative* (Urbana: University of Illinois Press, 1979), who defines the Afro-American narrative tradition in almost exclusively male terms. See also Henry Gates's preface to the special issue of *Critical Inquiry*, "'Race,' Writing, and Difference," in which he describes the beginning of that tradition: the writings of John Gronniosaw, John Marrant, Olaudah Equiano, Ottabah Cugoano, and John Jea, all male. They, he argues, posited both " the individual 'I' of the Black author as well as the collective 'I' of the race. Text created author; and Black authors, it was hoped would create or re-create the image of the race in European discourse" (11).

13. Hortense Spillers, "A Hateful Passion, A Lost Love," *Feminist Studies* 9 (Summer 1983): 296.

14. Luce Irigaray, *This Sex Which Is Not One* (Ithaca: Cornell University Press, 1985), 217.

15. Thomas Docherty, *Reading (Absent) Character: Toward a Theory of Characterization in Fiction* (Oxford: Clarendon Press, 1983), 265.

16. I am adapting Docherty's distinction between "character as a 'becoming' rather than as an 'essence.'" See Docherty, *Reading (Absent) Character*, 268.

17. Baruch Hoffman, *Character in Literature* (Ithaca: Cornell University Press, 1985), 79.

18. I borrow this point from Judith Kegan Gardiner, "The (US)es of (I)dentity: A Response to Abel on '(E)Merging Identities,'" *Signs* 6 (Spring 1981): 439.

19. Carole Gilligan, *In a Different Voice* (Cambridge: Harvard University Press, 1982), 147.

20. In *The Bluest Eye* Morrison is similarly concerned with those women who view sex as a marital duty rather than a source of their own pleasure. Called the Mobile women, they try to rid themselves of the "dreadful funkiness of passion," give their "bod[ies] sparingly and partially," and hope that they will "remain dry between [their] legs" (68–69).

21. Toni Morrison, "Intimate Things in Place," *Massachusetts Review* (Autumn 1977): 477.

22. See Bettye J. Parker, "Complexity: Toni Morrison's Women—An Interview Essay in *Sturdy Black Bridges: Visions of Black Women in Literature*, ed. Roseann P. Bell, Bettye J. Parker and Beverly Guy-Sheftall (New York: Anchor/Doubleday, 1979), 256.

23. For a discussion of this theme in other Morrison novels see Renita Weems, "'Artists Without Art Form': A Look At One Black Woman's World of Unrevered Black Women," *Conditions: Five* 2 (Autumn 1979): 46–58.

24. *Sula* is an intensely elegiac novel about loss, grieving, and the release of pain. The epigraph signals the concern. "It is sheer good fortune to miss somebody long before they leave you." It implies that leave-taking and loss are inevitable. At the end of the book Shadrack gives over to his grief for Sula, and when he does, he ceases to fill his life with compulsive activity. At Chicken Little's funeral, the women grieve for their own painful childhoods, the "most devastating pain there is" (65). The narrator grieves for a community that has become increasingly atomistic with the passage of time. Barbara Christian also sees these qualities in the novel, reading the epilogue as "a eulogy to the Bottom." See "Community and Nature: The Novels of Toni Morrison," *Journal of Ethnic Studies* 7 (Winter 1980): 64–78.

25. Wolfgang Iser, for example, discusses the two "selves" that interact in the reading process: one, the reader's own self or "disposition"; the other, that offered by the text. See *The Act of Reading* (Baltimore: Johns Hopkins, 1978), 37. For a thorough overview and synthesis of theories of reading see Susan R. Suleiman, "Introduction: Varieties of Audience-Oriented Criticism," in *The Reader in the Text*, ed. Susan Suleiman and Inge Crosman (Princeton: Princeton University Press, 1980), 3–45.

26. Susan Blake, "Toni Morrison," in *Dictionary of Literary Biography* (Detroit: Gale Research Co., 1984), 191.

27. I am indebted here to Jerome Beaty's afterward to *Sula* in *The Norton Introduction to the Short Novel*, 2d ed. (1987), 699.

28. Christopher Lehman-Haupt, Review of *Sula*, *New York Times* 123 (7 January 1974): 29.

29. "Rootedness: The Ancestor as Foundation," in *Black Women Writers: A Critical Evaluation*, ed. Mari Evans (New York: Anchor/Doubleday, 1984), 341.

30. "UNITY IDENTITY TEXT SELF" *PMLA* 90 (1975): 816. See also Jean Kennard, "Ourself Behind Ourself: A Theory for Lesbian Readers," in *Gender and Reading*, ed. Elizabeth Flynn and Patrocinio Schweikart (Baltimore: Johns Hopkins, 1986), 63–80.

31. See *Dynamics of Literary Response* (New York: Oxford University Press, 1968), 101.

Absence into Presence: The Thematics of Memory and "Missing" Subjects in Toni Morrison's *Sula*

Robert Grant*

Toni Morrison's *Sula*, both as text and as character, presents a conundrum to readers.[1] One reason for this, of course, is the degree to which in this novel Morrison deliberately avoids the rhetorical/polemical features generally associated with socio-political Afro-American novels, or the "protest fiction" exemplified in Richard Wright's *Uncle Tom's Children* and *Native Son*. Morrison's acknowledgments of white American racism's circumscription of black life are neither trumpeted nor elaborated. For instance, in the opening description of how the "Bottom" (the black section of Medallion where *Sula* is set) came to be created through a manipulative "Nigger joke" (4-5), or in the depiction of the white bargeman's and sheriff's casual disregard for the corpse of a drowned black child (63–64), Morrison's glances at racism are presented with an almost delicate irony. Keith Byerman defends the complexity of authorial vision underlying the holistic depiction of the relatively insulated black community of the Bottom when he argues that white "[c]ompulsion can cause suffering and sorrow, as it does in the exploitation that creates and maintains the Bottom, but it cannot be totalitarian." Not only is the Bottom "lovely" in a pastoral sense ("the bottom of Heaven," the narrator remarks) but Byerman notes

*This essay was written specifically for this volume and is published here for the first time by permission of the author.

how Morrison's fairly self-enclosed community allows for "Black refusal to be dehumanized by the 'nigger joke.'"[2]

Morrison in *Sula* focuses less on conventionally defined "protest" than on a depiction of the black experience. Her stance is in agreement with Michael Cooke who states that "a real difference exists between what is called '*the* black experience,' which is dogmatic and political, and . . . 'black experience,' which is merely axiomatic and comprehensive."[3] Justifiably, Morrison has been praised for her "comprehensive" grasp of those black communal "axioms" and rituals, for her powerful evocation of discrete black neighborhoods with the attendant "spirit of place," for her sensitivity to the real details—material and historical—forming the mental-emotional dialectic of the black experience. The community of the Bottom in *Sula* "breathes" for us with a splendid richness of description and *re*visionary vitality.

This black chorus-community in *Sula* is only one side of a complex triangular relationship in the novel; another is Nel Wright, arguably, a "co-protagonist" in the novel; and the third is the title character, Sula. It is the puzzling yet crucial question of Sula's *placement*—not just within her community in the novel, but within Morrison's "scheme" of what we, as readers, should "see" through Sula—that leads us into Morrison's purposeful design for a thematics of memory and mystery. Hortense Spillers has called *Sula* a "rebel idea" for its creator, as well as for black American literature and the heritage of black female portraiture generally. On many levels, "rebellious" is an apt descriptive for *Sula*, particularly if the reader keeps in mind that the cultural-semantic force of such terms as "rebels" and "rebelliousness" exists within a specific cultural and political dialectic, the analytical discourse of which inevitably "privileges" *both* tradition and transgression. This novel is one in which the relative social values of conservancy *and* iconoclasm are exquisitely balanced, and readers are hard put to determine "where" the author's ultimate moral-thematic sympathies were directed. *Sula* emerges out of several literary and politico-cultural traditions—modernist, Afro-American, and feminist —but thematically and politically, it is sui generis, and thus an "unpredictable" text. Morrison's anomalous textual configurations of signifiers, coupled with the convergence of more than one cultural expectation on the part of the reader, set up a variety of interpretational difficulties.

"Rebel ideas" in *Sula* are manifold, beginning, of course, with Sula as a "rebel," a willing pariah (122). The black female outcast here, however, is not a stereotyped Victim, in the mold of the pitiable Bessie in Wright's *Native Son* or the brutalized Mem in Alice Walker's *The Third Life of Grange Copeland*. Yet the ambiguous, ambivalent implications of the novel manifest social tensions. That is, on one hand, the black community, and by extension, the "black experience," is "celebrated" and lovingly presented. At the same time, however, the community is opposed and, to all events and purposes, *exposed* (overshadowed) by an independent protagonist "whose fanaticism is a reproach, not merely an eccentricity," to quote Flannery O'Connor's memorable phrase regarding "grotesque" characters.[4] Seemingly of the Devil's party, Sula commands the fascination and perhaps even the respect (if not entire admiration) of the reader despite the fact that her social and familial behavior refutes most of the "positive" black interpersonal values cited by sociologists researching the Afro-American social condition.[5] On one hand, Morrison is a literary subtilist writing with a secure sense of African-American history who understands how, for both "traditional" Afro-American folklorists and ideological partisans of the 1960s black cultural revolution, the historic reality and continuing ideal of black *community* are a sacral ethno-political sign *and* heuristic of, and for, the Afro-American omniverse. On the other hand, despite the novel's immersion in the material and ritualistic realities of small-town black American life, James Coleman is correct in declaring that the Bottom "community [in *Sula*] . . . was itself petty, hateful and spiteful."[6] Thus, in Morrison's world, the psychological "security" and cultural homogeneity afforded by an enclosed black community may *not* be an absolute, definable positive value for each black individual consciousness. This idea is, in many senses, a radically "feminist" consideration. But it is also a "rebel idea," an *anti*traditional notion disputing the communalistic, socio-centric claims and "verities" of much of African-American literature.

Aside from this, the reader is uncertain of Sula's behavioral motivations and the reasons for her defiance. Both the textual "evidence" and Morrison's own comments in interviews do little to dispel our sense of Sula as a moral and psychological enigma. The black community of the Bottom releases some of its uneasiness by classifying, and thus standard-izing, her as "evil." The omniscient, somewhat evasive narrator, however, is generally more carefully descriptive when it comes to Sula and more perceptive in understanding the community: "Their evidence against Sula was contrived, but their conclusions about her were not. Sula was distinctly different" (118). Indeed, the narrator *does* contribute a variety of causal considerations (some speculative, some persuasive, others generalized) to the reader's puzzling out of Sula, but the reader receives these attributions—just as the reader *perceives* Sula's multifarious actions—as an observer, a spectator. Unlike Nel, whose inner thoughts are relayed more directly and coherently to the reader, and whose pivotal emotional breakdown (after Jude's adultery with Sula) is communicated in an extended and unmediated first person point of view (104–6, 111), Sula resists our search for the conventional "unified" sensibility or personality. Thus, the reader's charged enterprise—to determine, to understand, and to consolidate meaning(s)—is complicated, if not entirely thwarted, by the fact that the novel's title character has no "center," no "self," no "ego." Sula fleetingly approaches a normative "womanly" or "wifely" behavior in her brief liaison with Ajax, during which she discovers a commonplace "romantic" possessiveness—which, ironically, drives Ajax away (131–34). Her final scene with Nel and the depiction of her death, however, sustain our impressions of her as an enigmatic and unregenerate rebel.

Throughout and beyond the narrative, questions of *intention* and coherence (in the characters) and *intentionality* and thematic design (from the author) often reformulate themselves as disorienting riddles. Feminist appropriations and interpretive distillations of *Sula* as solely a novel about "black female friendship," or as a "black lesbian novel,"[7] are too monistic. Despite Morrison's statement that she had intended to write "about good and evil and about friendship,"[8] *Sula* encompasses more than can be indicated by these stipulated boundaries and intentions and attempting to designate or simplify it in one catch-phrase is a little like describing Faulkner's *As I Lay Dying* as a novel about a family trip.

The point here is not to denaturalize or "universalize" Morrison's achievement rendering it faceless, raceless, or "gender-neutral," but simply to proclaim its "timelessness" to reveal, beneath its ardent funkiness, "archetypal" dynamics of an "individual versus society" conflict, as if these qualities were more important than the racial and sexual issues raised. The novel's linguistic, cultural, and spiritual bedrock of American "blackness" cannot be removed or dismissed without distorting its particular beauty, without conventionalizing its uniqueness. As Karen Stein has pointed out,[9] however, Morrison's technique is purposefully epical; her leading characters—Eva and Sula (Milkman and Pilate in *Song of Solomon*) attain mythic proportions, carrying with them echoes and silhouettes of biblical, classical, or "modernist" heroes. It is not surprising, then, that Sula's rebellion in the self-created form of a "dangerously free" black woman living in the first half of the twentieth century has Promethean overtones; "What's burning in me is mine!" she tells her grandmother, "And I'll split this town in two and everything in it before I'll let you put it out!" (93). And in other instances her "heroic," Sisyphean estrangements sound the extremities of existential anguish: "She went to bed with men as frequently as she could. It was the only place where she could find what she was looking for: misery and the ability to feel deep sorrow" (122). But these rebellious identities seem to be avatars of some unfathomable "daimon," some impenetrable psyche. Thus, Morrison's narration makes it clear that Sula's "evil" is merely a convenient social label. The cognitive-psychological "essence" of Sula remains a mystery.

Sula's rebellion both derives from and coheres with the author's own rebellion from certain black novelistic traditions that decree, and enforce upon readers the expectation, that all black texts must be politically determinate, amenable to some ideological translation be it "black protest" or "radical feminist." Morrison's carefully pinpointed temporal and historical markers (i.e., chapters headed by specific years such as "1919," "1927," etc.) and her equally astute integration of historically relevant, topical data into the narrative ground *Sula* within the economic and political realities of history. For example, at the penultimate moment of the novel, Shadrack's "National Suicide Day" finally becomes the communally celebrated "rational" solution to absurdity he had originally devised, precisely because of a collective release of "black rage," a collective (and self-destructive) reaction to historical disorder. But even this moment is simply one of many instances of chaos and "craziness" in Morrison's dialectical universe. Thus, occasional exaggerated ironies (for example, Eva Peace's killing of her son as a "sign" of her salvationist love), fictional textures of carnivalistic absurdity and surrealism are not meant to signify "intelligible" socio-political insights into, or lessons on, the ironies of the black American experience (as they do, for example, in *Invisible Man*).

Morrison's novel is a prime "postmodernist" text; its interpretational difficulties are a function of Morrison's calculated indeterminacies. The questions we labor over have less to do with verbal-rhetorical "strangeness" incorporated, or hybridized, *into* the text (as in the case of some of the works of Ishmael Reed and other experimental writers) than with what had been deliberately left *out* of the text. Thus, in addition to its value for certain historic-folkloric-communal "facts" and dimensions of black life and its distinctive ebb and flow of female friendship, Morrison's text engages on the structural and thematic levels memory, dialectic, and discontinuity. *Sula* in form and content is "about" gaps, lacks, "missing" subjects, and ambiguous psychic space, all of which must be "filled" and interpreted by the reader; further, the narrative content and technique are complementary in their appreciation of how the devices of memory "create" presence out of absence. Indeed, the novel's opening sentence is itself an inauguration of the mode and mood of memory as it paradoxically evokes a presence out of an absence: "In that place, where they tore the nightshade and blackberry patches from their roots to make room for Medallion City Golf Course, there was once a neighborhood" (3). The realities of time, mutability, and disorder introduced here are very much "actors" in the novel; just as crucially, the dialectic of memory, misperception, and discontinuity in *Sula* urges upon the reader seeking "order" the phenomenological connections between *interpretation* and *creation*.[10] Morrison has commented on her technique: "My writing expects, demands participatory reading. . . . It's not just about telling the story; it's about involving the reader. The reader supplies the emotions. The reader supplies even some of the color, some of the sound. *My language has to have holes and spaces so the reader can come into it*"[11] (emphasis mine).

I have always been struck by Morrison's claim that she "knew" she was a "writer" after she had completed *Sula*, her second novel.[12] Of course, completing a second book changed her from a "beginning" or "first-time" novelist. Morrison, however, seems to be referring here to the sense of maturity and *authority* that *Sula*, in which style, structure, and "vision" attain an almost breathtaking unity validated for her. Not surprisingly, at least one scholar-critic has praised the novel as Morrison's "most accomplished" work.[13] Her "meticulously crafted prose,"[14] the formalistic structures, metaphorical and imagistic polyphonies, and memorable deployment of such rhetorical/figurative features as simile, understatement, and synesthesia, all contribute to the "wrought" quality of her novels.

The architecture of *Sula* particularly deserves comment. Morrison and others have described the format of *Sula* in terms of the "circle" and "spiral," figures complementing the dramatic-thematic mirrorings and contrasts within the Nel-Sula relationship. The quasipalindromic design of the novel is also notable; *Sula* divides precisely into two equal parts ("I" and "II" contain almost exactly the same number of pages), and characters introduced and developed in "I" are brought back in "II" in inverse sequence. The novel begins "in memory" and concludes with Nel's crucial remembrance of Sula. Part 1 ends with the marriage of Nel and Jude and the departure of Sula from Medallion in 1927; part 2 begins ten years later (1937) with Sula's return to Medallion and with the narrator's hint of Nel's marital stagnation. Most intriguingly, parts 1 and 2 and specifically Sula's departure and return, literally frame a blank narrative "space" in the text. The actual center of the novel is perhaps the most noticeable of the novel's many gaps and discontinuities—in this case, the "missing" decade in which Sula traveled extensively, went to college, and ostensibly challenged herself through experience.

It was this "fixed" lacuna and a consideration of how major a part absence and indeterminacy played in this very formally "determined" novel that suggested to me how *Sula* might have what critic Frank Kermode has called narrative "secrets."[15] On the one hand, Morrison has described Sula as a "masculine" character, modeled admittedly upon the mobile and irresponsible black male "type." She is "adventuresome," "not scared," and "will leave and try anything." Yet in the novel itself we do not "see" or experience first hand Sula's exercising the options and opportunities that Morrison finds so appealing, the *mythoi* of "questing" Joycean heroes, and in "black literature about men: . . . the leaving home. And then there's no place that one settles . . . Curiosity, what's around the corner . . . Go find out what it is, you know! And in the process of finding, they are also making themselves."[16] Instead, Sula's traveling and educational experiences away from the Bottom/Medallion are *relayed* to the reader and, importantly, to Nel. The empty space at the literal center of the novel thus may be seen as an emblem of the work's missing subject(s), discerned from two standpoints.

From one vantage, the putative focus of the text is a "sociopathic" enigma, a character who is not clearly, in the psychological and psychoanalytical sense of the term, a coherent or unified Subject. Beyond this *Sula*, as a novel is seemingly without a "subject," in that familiar sense in which the term is used. Morrison may "really" be writing about the organismic and microcosmic black community presented so prominently in the work; about interconnections, perspectives, *relations* (a more comprehensive and precise term than "relationships," which suggests too narrowly only one-on-one interpersonal associations). Morrison's formal and characterizational avoidance of linearity and strict "determinacy" (in both the textual and psychological senses) accounts for the beguiling gaps that "dance" with and within the narrative's manifest content.

In *Sula* there are "missing" subjects (again, on several levels) and objects (e.g., Eva's leg and, later, her comb); absent persons are "missed" (Chicken Little, Jude, Ajax, and Sula); and missing persons are evoked in the memory through objects (e.g., Nel associates Jude with his tie, Shadrack recalls Sula from her belt). As suggested above, however, all these lacks become the sources of figurative fulfillment through memory and / or imaginative projection. A paradigmatic example is Morrison's coyly, evasively declarative description of Eva Peace's eventful yet mysterious absence from Medallion: "Two days later she left all of her children with Mrs. Suggs, saying she would be back the next day. Eighteen months later she swept down from a wagon with two crutches, a new black pocketbook, and one leg" (34). Such a passage would be hardly notable if there were, at some point, further elaboration and clarification. But both the fate of Eva's leg and an exact explanation of her whereabouts remain a mystery. More to the point, the mystery linking Eva's absence with her missing leg becomes an "open" space for communal storytelling, for oral interpretation and re-creation within the Peace family and the community at large. Thus, indeterminacy becomes the site for fable-building: "Unless Eva herself introduced the subject, no one ever spoke of her disability; they pretended to ignore it, unless, in some mood of fancy, she began some fearful story about it—generally to entertain the children. How the leg got up by itself one day and walked on off. How she hobbled after it but it ran too fast . . . Somebody [in the larger Bottom community] said Eva stuck it under a train and made them pay off. Another said she sold it to a hospital for $10,000. . ." (30–31).

Death, frequently violent, also asserts itself in the novel as a force of discontinuity. When the young Sula, in Nel's presence, accidentally kills Chicken Little by throwing him into the river where he drowns, the ensuing loss of innocence is signified by both girls' profound cognizance of space-as-*emptiness*, a specific and almost mystical awareness of vacuity. Thus, immediately after his death, Chicken Little can only be—indirectly yet unavoidably—referred to as "something newly missing"; and in images that will recur at pertinent junctures late in the novel, Chicken Little's startling "disappearance" is next signified by "the peace of the river" and "the dark closed place in the water" (61–62). The description of the funeral service reveals the multiple dimensions of memory as Morrison re-creates it in *Sula*. Understandably, for Sula and Nel the memorial service can only emphasize an absence: they "did not touch hands or look at each other during the funeral. There was a space, a separateness between them" (64).

Conversely, for the rest of the congregation, the memorial becomes an occasion for collective imaginative energy and empathic projection. Death, and its memory, "inspire" presences: "They did not hear all of what [Reverend Deal] said; they heard the one word, or phrase, or inflection that was for them the connection between the event and themselves . . . they saw the Lamb's eye and the truly innocent victim: themselves. They acknowledged the innocent child in the corner of their hearts . . . Or they thought of their son newly killed . . . Or they remembered how dirty the room looked when their father left home. . ." (65).

Morrison's own statements regarding Sula seem inexact and impressionistic and represent perhaps not so much "fuzziness" of design as an auctorial desire to inscribe a quality of plurisignification upon her title character. Sula's chameleon effects and "nature" are symbolically figured in the text by the prominent yet ambiguous discolored mark over her eye ("I"?), which observers perceive / interpret variously as a snake, a stemmed rose, a tadpole, and even as the ashes of her mother, Hannah. In interviews, Morrison has described Sula as "very atypical" and "not the average run-of-the-mill black woman,"[17] tracing her uniqueness and her strangeness from the fact of her being "a woman of force."[18] Sula's egocentric forcefulness and disregard for social expectations are more radical—and threatening—than mere unconventionality, however, since both her mother, Hannah, and her grandmother, Eva, are accepted and "absorbed" into the community despite their own colorful anomalies. Moreover, Morrison consistently places the "evil" which follows Sula after her arrival back in Medallion, accompanied by a "plague of robins" (89), in the realm of societal judgment rather than metaphysical reality; in both the novel's narration and in interviews the author generalizes with greater precision about the dynamics of superstition and social labeling. Sula, on the other hand, was admittedly "hard" and "very difficult" for Morrison to develop as a character; the parameters of the task, as Morrison has stated them, were decidedly challenging: to create in a character a type of pioneering self-centeredness—after all, Sula is an explorer "perfectly willing to think the unthinkable"—without making that same character "freakish, repulsive or unattractive."[19]

Many students and readers, however, do find something "freakish" about Sula as she is portrayed in the novel. As Morrison has remarked, qualities of mystery and myth are "distilled"[20] in Sula and her language to such an extent that she appeals to the reader as "unnatural." For example, even at the age of twelve she authoritatively wields power against a threatening gang of white teenage boys by combining an unnatural yet symbolic act—using her pocket-knife to slash off the tip of her finger—with a quietly stated, ominously rhetorical question: "If I can do that to myself, what you suppose I'll do to you?" (54-55). Significantly, this moment, with its hints of Sula's maturity and strangeness, occurs in the narrative *before* the frequently discussed incident in which she overhears her mother tell a neighbor ". . . I love Sula. I just don't like her" (57). Too often Hannah's comment is interpreted as a "determining" factor in Sula's personality formation, as if this one remark betokened a socio-behavioral pattern and "key"—that is, maternal neglect or insensitivity. The narrator does not deny that Hannah's comment does affect Sula, but the effect is to clarify an independence—to teach "her that there was no other that you could count on" (118–19)—and a fearlessness already exhibited. Moreover, Hannah may be lazy and sexually promiscuous, but Morrison speaks, and writes,[21] of her with great affection; she is not a "sinister" character, and there is no suggestion in the text that she "abuses" Sula in any way. Thus, I think the conventional deterministic search for sociological "reasons" and environmental "causes" has been misguided. Rather than view Hannah's "honest"[22] comment as an etiological solution, the reader should instead see it as a symptomatic effect, and a confirmation, of Sula's intractable enigma. Hannah's attitude inspires not an answer but a question: why wouldn't a mother (especially one as "tolerant" and unconventional as Hannah) like her own daughter? Hannah, we may infer, has intimations of Sula's unresolved "difference." And this strangeness in Sula, this curious detachment, is borne out most memorably and disturbingly when she "watches" her mother burn to death, offering no aid, primarily because (as Eva senses) "she was interested" (78). Even on her deathbed Sula makes a retrospective admission of this fact, which contains no confession of vengeance, of spitefulness against Hannah: "I never meant anything. I stood there watching her burn and was thrilled. I wanted her to keep on jerking like that, to keep on dancing" (147).

The reader struggles to "conceive" of such a character whose candor and awareness are alternately admirable, alienating, humorous, and a little frightening. After Sula returns to Medallion her existential self-assertion leads inevitably to confrontation. She argues to her grandmother: "I don't want to make somebody else. I want to make myself" (92), and even during her final illness she proclaims to Nel, "But my lonely is *mine*" (143). Needless to say, "social conversation was impossible for her because she could not lie" (121). Often, honesty and bluntness are coupled with an ironic, deconstructing vision into social hypocrisy, as when she obliterates Jude's self-pitying posture of the "victimized" black male with a priceless lecture on how the black man is "the envy of the world" (103–4), or when she responds to Nel-the-"wronged-wife's" accusation, "You had to take [Jude] away," with a withering retort: "What you mean take him away? I didn't kill him, I just fucked him" (145).

In her rhetoric, sense of humor, earthiness, ironic intelligence, and willingness to take chances and make leaps, Sula seems superior to her constricting environment. Yet obviously, in some ways she needs the Bottom as much as the community needs and "feeds off" her and her antics. Thus, Sula is not as autonomous existentially as she appears, and we note how Morrison takes pains to underline the fact that for all of her refreshing bravado she is an "unfinished" woman, an entity who may not need a primary relationship but who does need *to be in a relationship to* something or someone. Herein lies part of the answer to the question "Why does Sula return to Medallion, to the Bottom?" Yes, she is drawn back because of Nel, but Nel is only "one of the reasons" (128). On a deeper level, Sula—who has "no self," "no center," and "no ego" (119)—inchoately understands and responds to the process by which iconoclastic individuals and preservative communities define and "identify" themselves *against* each other. Thus she fashions and sustains her unique identity as a "rebel" only, and necessarily, in connection with the fairly orthodox and enclosed community of the Bottom. But at the same time she has no essential direction, is dependent upon "her own mood and whim," and is ultimately defined as much by a central *lack* as by anything else. Thus, we are told in one of the most famous passages in the novel, Sula craves "the other half of her equation" and is specifically "dangerous" because she is an "artist with no art form" (121).

Morrison understands the inscrutable network of interpersonal differences and similarities structuring the basis of friendship. A careful reading reveals that Nel and Sula are not so extremely different from each other, and that rather than place them in the gothically dichotomous worlds of "good" and "evil," the reader should perceive them occupying only relatively distant places on a moral continuum. Without minimizing the importance of their "separateness" and the conflict that evolves in Part 2, we should note frequent instances of intimate and almost telepathic "sharing" between Sula and Nel. Puberty becomes a juncture at which they meet in and partake of the "delirium of noon dreams" (51). So intimate is their sorority that, in one of the novel's most mystical sequences, they silently perform a subconsciously ritualized "play" expressing, through the "innocent" displacement of "fooling around outside," an intensely shared awareness of the secrets of *eros* and *thanatos* (58–59).

Morrison further underlines their kinship, however, by suggesting that the very issue that ultimately separates them—Sula's adultery with Nel's husband, Jude—actually establishes a near-identity of sisterhood. Thus, both characters are depicted experiencing very similar reactions to loss and loneliness; specifically, both women must confront an intimate absence and emptiness that memory, paradoxically, both emphasizes and assuages.

For Nel, the loss of Jude initiates a radical identity trauma, a disorientation of the complacent, socialized self; that she must first struggle with a disconcerting "emptiness" of the "thighs" leading to a nervous breakdown (objectified eerily in the image of her brain as a "[q]uiet, grey, dirty . . . ball of muddy strings . . . fluffy but terrible in its malevolence") perhaps suggests the totality of her dependence upon conventional sex roles. Jude is gone, but his tie provokes a disbelief so strong ("Could he be gone if his tie is still here?") that Nel seemingly hallucinates him into being, speaking to him as though he were visibly present (104–5).

Similarly, if ironically, Sula shares the lucid delusion of memory after her one "possessed" love, Ajax, leaves. Again, Morrison's language pinpoints both the reflective and creative functions of memory as it "realizes" a remembered being out of negation. Ajax "had left nothing but his stunning absence. An absence so decorative, so ornate, it was difficult for her to understand how she had ever endured . . . his magnificent presence. . . . His absence was everywhere, stinging everything, giving the furnishings primary colors . . . not only her eyes and all her senses but also inanimate things seemed to exist because of him, backdrops to his presence. Now that he had gone, these things, so long subdued by his presence, were glamorized in his wake" (134–35). The parallels between Nel's and Sula's memories, however, should not be overdrawn. Nel, whose marriage was grounded in inequality (82–83), entertains memories radiating from her "abandoned woman" complex that solipsistically "construct" a Jude so as to focus on *her*, and her pain. Sula, whose relationship with Ajax was a remarkably emancipated and "mutual" one, is perhaps not so surprisingly less egotistic in her memory, and imaginatively focuses more on the wonders of her gone lover than on any "injustice" done to her.

In literature as in life, memory acts as a cognitive and imaginative synthesizing connector of the lapses, gaps, absences, discontinuities, and ruptures of time. In *Sula*, a text structured with interstices and indeterminate spaces, memory repeatedly enacts a creative and creatively healing function. Furthermore, memory becomes a subjective method of communication with someone or something "not there." Appropriately, both Sula's and Nel's concluding statements in the novel are messages to each *absent* other across the breaches of space and time. Sula dies alone, but her dying comment—"Wait'll I tell Nel" (149)—invokes "the other half of her equation." Years later an enlightened Nel, at Sula's grave, appeals directly to the soul of her lost friend: "'Sula?' she whispered, gazing at the tops of trees. 'Sula? . . .' All that time, all that time, I thought I was missing Jude.' And the loss pressed down on her chest and came up in her throat. 'We was girls together,' she said as though explaining something. 'O Lord, Sula,' she cried, 'girl, girl, girlgirlgirl'" (174).

When Morrison states that her "language has to have holes and spaces so the reader can come into it," she is not signalling her abdication of moral consciousness or even of the writer's *authority* over a text, an intentionality which, particularly in the Afro-American literary tradition, is integrally identified with moral awareness. Morrison's elliptical technique invites participatory reading, and *Sula* may be a choice literary text to examine from the reader-reception perspective—"interpretations" of *Sula* inevitably inducing "creative" rather than limited, "predetermined" and formulaic readings—but that does not mean there are *no* "intentionalized," determinate "themes" in Morrison's novel. Characteristically, however, the most explicit "shaping insights" are framed as questions and speculations rather than statements. Such are the qualities of Sula's last remarks to Nel:

"How you know?" Sula asked.
"Know what?" Nel still wouldn't look at her.
"About who was good. How you know it was you?"
"What you mean?"
"I mean maybe it wasn't you. Maybe it was me." (146)

Sula haunts the novel and Nel through her clairvoyance as well as her oddly "masculine" carelessness. In Morrison's Bottom community no rigid science or protocol determined the blurring or maintenance of distinctions. For example, proper names and strict family lines are ignored in Eva's household and the boundary shifts between Nel's "goodness" and Sula's "evil." There is only insight, such as that suggested by Sula's question of Nel here, and by the institutionalized Eva's confusion-identification of Nel with her long-dead granddaughter Sula at the end of the novel (168–69). Certainly Nel has been protected from self-knowledge by a factitious, socialized "innocence" which allows her to categorize Sula as "bad" even as she enjoys using Sula as scapegoat and "other." That she herself may be as "evil" as Sula, and in fact more so because of her hypocrisy, strikes Nel at the conclusion, when she allows herself to understand the dark implications of her voyeuristic complicity in Chicken Little's death:

> What did old Eva mean by *you watched*? How could she help seeing it? She was right there. But Eva didn't say *see*, she said *watched*. "I did not watch it. I just saw it." But it was there anyway, as it had always been, the old feeling and the old question. The good feeling she had had when Chicken's hands slipped. She hadn't wondered about that in years. "Why didn't I feel bad when it happened? How come it felt so good to see him fall?" (170)

Nel's self-recognition here obviously mirrors Sula's earlier admission of her pleasure in watching Hannah burn to death. For the reader, Sula's claim to verifiable "goodness" derives from her relative lack of dishonesty in comparison with Nel's hypocritical virtuousness which impels her to visit Sula near the novel's end (138). But for the reader, for whom there is no socially recognizable "good" in Sula, her wholeness must be measured by the dictates of a subjective experientialism. "I have sung all the songs all the songs I have sung all the songs there are" she muses to herself, finally exhausted with experience (137). Like Camus in *The Stranger*, Morrison seems to be claiming for Sula a definition of "goodness" which connects more to an existential "inner" faith and integrity than with sociometric "good works" or charity. Morrison suggests that Sula's antinomianism demands for itself the title of a personalist "virtue" that is validated by the misperception and incomprehension of Nel and the Bottom community.

In *Sula*, Toni Morrison presents and confronts the reader with a text in which the perspectivism of memory and phenomenological perception— and interpretation—are in the foreground, and in which the necessary negations and "absences" of the text both enlarge the black female hero and deconstruct the expectation of politicized "determinacy." *Sula* therefore has its *politico*-cultural relevance as a text that simultaneously shatters boundaries and defines new dominions, but it preserves its unique status as a work which deals cognitatively and primarily with the psychology, sociology, and phenomenology of *relations* and relationships: it investigates the deep-structured sociological/anthropological connection between "pariahs" and collective morality (as in the presentation of the much-discussed functional relationship between Sula's "abnormal" behavior and its positive societal reactions in the Bottom), as well as with the necessary interrelation between indeterminacy and interpretation, an interrelation at the heart of both the reader's "conventional" enterprise *and* of the radiating metaphorical and philosophical power of *Sula*.

Notes

1. *Sula* (New York: Plume/N.A.L., 1982; rpt. of A.A. Knopf, 1973); further page references from this edition are made in the text.

2. Keith Byerman, *Finger the Jagged Grain; Tradition and Form in Recent Black Fiction* (Athens: University of Georgia Press, 1985), 193.

3. Michael Cooke, *Afro-American Literature in the Twentieth Century: The Achievement of Intimacy* (New Haven: Yale University Press, 1984), 210.

4. *Mystery and Manners*, ed. Sally and Robert Fitzgerald (New York: Farrar, Strauss, Giroux, 1961), 44.

5. See, for example, Robert Staples's *Introduction to Black Sociology* (New York: McGraw-Hill, 1976), especially the section of "Values," 76–77.

6. James Coleman, "The Quest for Wholeness in Toni Morrison's *Tar Baby*," *Black American Literature Forum* 20 (Spring–Summer 1986): 63.

7. Two such representative readings are: Renita Weems, "'Artists without Art Forms': A Look at One Black Woman's World of Unresolved Black Women," in *Conditions Five The Black Women's Issue* 11 (Autumn 1979): 45–58; and Barbara Smith, "Toward a Black Feminist Criticism," in *But Some of Us are Brave: Black Women's Studies*, ed. Gloria Hull et al. (Old Westbury: Feminist Press, 1982), 167–75.

8. *Black Women Writers at Work*, ed. Claudia Tate (New York: Continuum Press, 1983), 118.

9. Karen Stein, "Toni Morrison's *Sula*: A Black Woman's Epic," *Black American Literature Forum* 18 (Winter 1984): 146–50.

10. An edifying symposium on this theoretical issue is presented in *New Literary History* 15, no. 2 (Winter 1984); see especially Richard Wollheim, "Art, Interpretation, and the Creative Process" (241–53), and Wolfgang Iser, "The Interplay Between Creation and Interpretation" (387–95).

11. Tate, *Black Women Writers at Work*, 125.

12. Ibid., 128.

13. Cooke, *Afro-American Literature in the Twentieth Century*, 111.

14. Tate, *Black Women Writers at Work*, 117.

15. Frank Kermode, "Secrets and Narrative Sequence," in *On Narrative*, ed. W. J. T. Mitchell (Chicago: University of Chicago Press, 1981), 79–97.

16. Robert Stepto, "Intimate Things in Place: A Conversation with Toni Morrison," in *Chant of Saints: A Gathering of Afro-American Literature, Art and Scholarship*, ed. Michael Harper and Robert Stepto (Urbana: University of Illinois Press, 1981), 226-7.

17. Ibid., 219-20.

18. Bettye J. Parker, "Complexity: Toni Morrison's Women—An Interview Essay," in *Sturdy Black Bridges: Visions of Black Women in Literature*, ed. Roseann P. Bell, Bettye J. Parker and Beverly Guy-Sheltall (New York: Anchor/Doubleday, 1979), 254.

19. Stepto, "Intimate Things in Place," 215.

20. Parker, "Complexity: Toni Morrison's Women," 254.

21. See, e.g., Stepto, "Intimate Things in Place," 218 and *Sula*, 42-45.

22. Stepto, "Intimate Things in Place," 218.

Song of Solomon

Genealogical Archaeology or the Quest for Legacy in Toni Morrison's *Song of Solomon*

Genevieve Fabre*

Over the past decade, black women writers have clearly dominated the literary scene in Afro-American letters. A new, innovative force, their works are opening areas of exploration and experimentation and setting the tone for further developments. Black women are breaking new grounds with jubilant awareness, producing novels, poems, plays and essays, with incredible speed and high spiritedness. Eager to claim a voice and a space of their own, they are defining their common goals and concerns and their own artistic canons.

Black women writers and scholars, however, do not view the present renaissance or outburst as an isolated phenomenon; they see it more as part of a long and continuous tradition that has existed after slavery, an oral tradition that offers a wealth of verbal forms and skills, and a written one where each act of writing has been a political, historical, and artistic event. Works of slave or free women; of women abolitionists or of organizers of the post–Civil War era; of scholars, poets, and novelists of the Harlem Renaissance; and of blues singers, are being rediscovered and are receiving careful attention. The names of Phyllis Wheatly, Linda Brent, Frances Harper, Nella Larsen, Jessie Fauset, Zora Neale Hurston, and many others are no longer to be ignored, and are becoming familiar to wider audiences.

The early struggle of black women to achieve literacy (an authorial voice), closely associated with the quest for freedom, has paved the way for the present battles and empowerment. As Toni Morrison says: "their strategies of survival became our maneuvers for power."[1] This continuity between past and present is crucial and must be maintained. It creates bonds, kinship, mutual obligations, and a shared communal history of struggle for artistic expression that is a form of power. Contemporary black women writers are calling for a revision (an inversion of concepts, myths, images) and reexamination of important issues concerning their situation in American society and culture. As persons who have experienced life not only as blacks but also as women artists who have

*This essay is a shortened revised version of a talk given at the Salzburg Seminar in American Studies, June 1985, on "New Perspectives in American Literature," and is published here by permission of the author.

inherited the gift to "speak in tongues," they feel they can illuminate and authenticate parts of the black experience that have been ignored or misrepresented. Recorded from their perspectives with daring honesty and uncompromising outspokenness, the "souls of black folks" can be framed into new words and songs, shaped into new configurations; "coming" as Morrison says "from the rim of the world" and "rustling with life," to become "the touchstones by which all that is human can be measured."[2]

Black women writers call attention to the distinctiveness of their experiences and vision that differs as broadly from that of some black male writers as it does from that of whites, and which has never been adequately recognized. They claim the Afro-American tradition but "insist on their own name and central place." They do not strive for separatism but for the recognition of the singularity of their identity and of their expressive gifts. They wish to free themselves from the prescriptive tenets of a black aesthetic whose canons have been defined mostly by male critics. They also set themselves apart from white feminists who argue that sexism is more important than racism, who have ignored the particular fate or concerns of their black sisters and often used them as mere tokens for their cause. As blacks, women, and artists, their components are indissociable. None can be discarded without impairing the total vision which determines their artistic strategies, shapes their stylistic tone and profile, the pitch of their voices, and their symbolic imagination. Finally black women writers expose the inadequacies and the "signs of omission" of mainstream ideological discourse. They lay down a number of challenges to the purveyors of literary history, and questioning their monolithic and absolutist pronouncements, they call for an honest, sustained, and more perceptive analysis of their work. Their writings, deliberately disruptive and disturbing in their bold investigations, are part of a struggle against all forms of authority. In the process of interaction with a hostile environment their discourse takes shape, and their artistic consciousness evolves as a rejoinder. "Their gaze so lovingly unforgiving, stills, agitates, stills again."[3] Triumphing over interdiction, they reveal the limits and the constraints of a system that has excluded their voices, and that should take greater heed of the problems of alterity and acknowledge the essential significance of *difference*. In a culture, a country that has always looked for a unifying language, for myths to express its national mind and ethos, but one that is also aware of its pluralistic nature, the chorus of black-women voices joined by many other minority or "third world" women—Chicanas, Hispanics, Asiatics, American Indians—forces a new dialogue. This dialogue, which points at tensions, at inexhaustible wealth and contradictory multiplicity, orchestrates different degrees of otherness and creates a potential for an artistic experience and the development of a new national literary consciousness, no longer indifferent to difference. One is struck, in reading/hearing black women, by their insistence on the exploration of the legacy. Throughout their writings and talks, these women are expressing in eloquent and pressing ways their claims to a legacy that is distinctively theirs, and affirming their authority as participants, interpreters, and perpetuators. As witnesses for the future, they insist on their responsibility to build a heritage to be passed on to the new generations. The search for the legacy often presented as a ceremonial appropriation that follows a ritualistic pattern, dealt with in remarkably different ways by Alice Walker (*In Search of Our Mother's Gardens*)[4] or Audre Lorde (*Sister Outsider*),[5] who set the principles for an inquiry into the dialectics of black womanhood in the essay, or in a fictional work by Toni Morrison (*Song of Solomon*),[6] celebrates narrative and parable that dramatize an archetypal journey across ancestral territory.

The main call in Walker's book is the "daughters" in an attempt to build intricate emotional and *artistic* bonds and a definite lineage: "we must know our mothers's names, . . . [their] words, . . . [their] actions, . . . [their] lives."[7] Her own impulse is more to recollect and reconstruct forgotten lives, if necessary "bone by bone" (an image we find also in *Song of Solomon*), to retrieve them from oblivion and neglect. Walker's spirited visit to her mother's gardens—the concept of garden, an organizing metaphor, has replaced Virginia Woolf's idea of a room of one's own—is itself a pilgrimage pursued with filial piety and care, with a sense of will and direction: "in search of my mother's garden, I found my own."[8] Embracing her maiden name in tribute to one of her ancestors who "walked" through the continent, Walker reenters the garden of the past with a sense of reverence and wonder for places, she reinvents the lives of the women who call her from history. She creates her own garden, a blend of symbolic properties, peopled with ancient spirits, studded with images that capture the unique quality of her heritage as artist, as black, as woman, and as southerner.

In her reevaluation of black womanhood, Walker is anxious to set some guidelines for those who will record the legacy. Their writings should move away from sociology—from a discourse that emphasized the image of black women as victims—to a greater concern for the ambiguities, the dilemmas, and contradictions. "It must be away from the writing of explanation and further into mystery, poetry and prophecy."

Song of Solomon is precisely one of these incursions into "mystery, poetry and prophecy." The experience of legacy is treated with many ironic overtones that point to certain paradoxes, and to the fundamental complexities of the quest. Other novels have done this—*Invisible Man,* for instance, through the numerous adventures of a nameless hero examines the intricate legacy of the past and of history. Yet, *Song of Solomon* strikes a different and perplexing note, perhaps because it deliberately avoids chronological development and linear structure. Its drifting and unin- formed hero is caught in the ambiguities of a quest that presents itself as a succession of riddles; each recorded incident, act, or word is a new adventure that further complicates the overall puzzle. And the legacy—an ever elusive reality—takes on many serious or trivial forms: a name, a birthmark, a bag of bones, or a song. Each is presented as a possible clue or a new mystery. The deciphering of the enigma is seen as a game in which the character and reader are jostled from one puzzle to the next. Answers are presented piece by piece through hints that create further suspense, and this accounts for the structure of this enigmatic narrative: a pattern of revelation and deception, of recognition and denial.

The legacy is spelled out through stories that are often fables, or jokes, *lies* as Zora Neale Hurston would call them. Each story re-creates a particular patch of the past, but also reveals a new mystery and then calls for another story. In different places, by different characters, the same story is picked up, retold, expanded into further complexity and mystery. It is as though there is a crucial deficiency in each telling, so each generates the other, as though the assertion each makes raised new questions. And all queries converge toward Pilate the depository: "She who heard the voice and sang the song." The accumulation of stories, the call and response pattern, their gradual merging into the single story of the hero's ancestry, create an interesting structure. The legacy is that of voices to be listened to, voices that replace that of the narrator, each offering its own fragmented perception of the truth, while the author dramatizes the gap between the telling and what is being told.

Morrison's protagonist is entrusted with the task of putting bits and pieces together, of de/re/constructing chronology and genealogy. The use of Milkman is ironic; this male hero is unimaginative and uncommitted, a reluctant confidant, a poor listener who does not pay attention to words, asks the wrong questions, and offers erroneous interpretations. He is ill equipped for the quest: an imperfect inquirer into a heritage that is cumbersome to him. Pressed as he is by many questions set by those who entrust him with the secrets of their lives, his blunders paradoxically enrich the message. Revelations about the past bear no clear meaning to him at the time when they are uttered. Yet each becomes a part of his own history and must be put together in quilt fashion, like scraps to be seized before the wind carries them away, or to be stored like the mysterious stones his aunt has collected throughout her life.

By entrusting her own narrative to many voices (and basing its structure on many stories), Morrison acknowledges the debt that any black writer has to the oral tradition, the true legacy of black people. She reminds us that the storytelling tradition, so strong in black culture, is still alive. In homes, on street corners, in barbershops, stories are devised and told as statements, familiar historical realities, or as forms of entertainment, a thing to be created and enjoyed. Stories bear witness to the past, to the struggle of black people to survive in their triumphs and the familiar, reality and fantasy; creating both history and myth. The stories in *Song of Solomon* are about naming and misnaming, and about birth and death. Names are an essential part of the legacy, and names have stories which, incongruous, preposterous as they are, must be cared for.

Morrison calls attention to the importance of naming as a ritual in black people's lives. Blacks received dead patronyms from whites—through a trick illiteracy played on them, allowing the literate to mess up their names. In the Dead family—thus misnamed as a result of some white official's ignorance—first names were given by illiterate fathers who took a fancy to the shape for a letter or to a sound. Thus, people and places receive their names—names are "disguises, jokes or brand names"[9]—from yearnings, gestures, flaws, events, mistakes, weaknesses. Names endure like marks or have secrets they do not easily yield. Only when the whole story is told, the mystery unveiled, can the full meaning be grasped. *Song of Solomon* is strewn with such words, offered as riddles or as clues to the legacy: Song, Solomon, Shalimar, Sugarman . . . Part of Milkman's task is to trace the history of each name and to search for the one name that is real, the ancestor's name.

Milkman's name itself is a joke, but it is also his fate. The child who was breast-fed too long is doomed to become the subject of other people's fantasies: his mother's, Hagar's, Guitar's. His rechristening (by a man who is an important community figure in the book, a newsbreaker who cannot be entrusted with any secret) is the first of a series of baptisms. Interestingly, this ludicrous nickname makes Milkman an improbable perpetuator of his father's legacy. It unexpectedly sets him free from the legacy of the "Dead" house, from the dead side of his family. It estranges him from a father outraged to see his son renamed for reasons unknown to him, one that brings a tinge of shame on his reputation. Macon Dead himself fights against the odds of his own name—Dead—and tries to retrieve Milkman as his rightful heir. In his manly world where women exist only in the shadow or in the margin of life, his son belongs to that centrality where power and property can help build the legacy to be handed down from one male generation to the next.

The history of his name places Milkman in an ambiguous situation. The legacy—the true legacy that Milkman will acknowledge only late in his life—is sharply contrasted with the heritage his father has shaped for him. Significantly, while the latter is controlled by the authority of the men, the former is placed under the care of an unconventional feminine world. Milkman will waver in his quest between the world his father wants him to build—urging him on a straight path that ultimately will prove a dead end—and the sinuous line that the women, mostly his aunt, invite him to follow, a path that will take him on "the journey *back*," the journey *home*. Pilate, Macon Dead's sister, who "has been given the worst possible name, that of "Christ killing Pilate," is nevertheless the one who knows that the sanctity and magic of names is not to be disregarded. Her name is her sole legacy and must be saved from oblivion. That name, because it is the only word her father ever wrote, will go from the family Bible to a little box that she hangs from her ear. The box belonged to her mother who died before she was born. Pilate's unusual name therefore becomes appropriate for this woman who had an unusual childbirth "inching her way into life out of a still silent indifferent cave of flesh,"[10] without a navel, the strangest woman in town, reconstructing in the margin of the city a communal world rooted in ancestral lore.

With her reverence for the legacy, her secrecy and defiance, she becomes Milkman's pilot, the guiding force, the pedagogue who introduces him to the mysteries of life and death, and of blackness ("You think dark is just one color, but it ain't . . . . There are five or six kinds of black. Some silky, some woolly. . . .")[11]; with her pebbly voice, she spells for him the secrets of the world. This woman with no navel has to be taken seriously. She also has literally to invent herself. Her many gifts as natural healer, skilled wine maker, singer, conjure woman and soothsayer, truth giver, bear witness to the extent of the legacy of black womankind. She initiates Milkman into the wisdom and beliefs and souls of his people, and challenges his indifference and ignorance.

Thanks to Pilate, the uncomfortable boy foresees a future, is given a sense of purpose. His first visit to Pilate's house initiates his journey into the legacy: "in the winehouse of this lady who had one earring, no navel and looked like a tall black tree," amid the pervading odor of fermenting fruit and pine, Milkman is reborn. Pilate and her house, in sharp contrast to his father's house of death, bring a promise, suggest the possibility of flight. It is the seedbed of cultural activity. Symbolically it is for Milkman the threshold, both margin and *limen*, which represents the liminal phase of his rites of passage, the precursor of a real and permanent change that will involve a long and exacting pilgrimage.

"Black women can fly." This statement is emphatically made by black women in their writings. Pilate is the embodiment of that image. But the flying is in Morrison's text not just a metaphorical expression of black women's spirituality, it is rooted in ancient belief and folklore. Pilate has inherited the gift to fly—which, according to certain legends, was only given to those who knew the secret word. The absence of a navel isolates her, ensuring both fear and respect, but it also brings her close to the flying ancestor. It sets her free from conventional relationships, free to define the values according to which she will live, to design a life of her own, and to interpret on her own terms and unequivocally the particular legacy of her people. It also designates her as a mythical outsider, a sort of messiah. It is through her that the oracle will speak. Stories of names are thus inextricably woven into life stories. Significantly, many stories in *Song of Solomon* are also about birth and death, these essential rites of passage, about difficult and improbable beginnings and premature and violent endings; and they all share the same weird, uncanny, and awesome character. Birth is the one ritual that is closest to death and as "unnatural." There is the story of

Milkman's birth after he has been saved from his father's scheme of destruction, "his father trying to stop him dead before he was born," of Pilate's incredible birth after her mother's death, a birth that gives her a unique body. There are the cruel and violent deaths of fathers: Pilate and Macon's, shot off a fence; Guitar's father sliced in two by a sawmill. And in the background we have the endless accounts of many other deaths that occur daily in front of churches or in the streets. These stories of unnatural birth and deaths can be read as variations on the fate of a family whose name is Dead, but also as metaphors on the black condition, on an existence where nothing is to be taken for granted or *granted*. In a world where whites wish to see black people dead, where blacks "ain't supposed to die a natural death," it is not surprising that any birth looks like a miracle, that death is the subject of so much talk, predictions, threats or jokes, and of ritualized care. The dead bodies appearing and disappearing among the living, wait to receive the proper burial. And the living can become either wholly dedicated to the dead—as Ruth or Pilate are to their fathers—or to some death game. In their fight for survival blacks cannot escape the white man's strokes or the murderous fantasies of their brothers and sisters. They can either play the numbers game—with Guitar and his Brotherhood, The Seven Days Friends—and make even the number of deaths among whites and among blacks, or they can try to conjure death through some old trick, by playing humorously or imaginatively with it. No wonder so many stories are ones of craziness. Put together, they create a crazy quilt with a sense of pattern. The craziness is more on the women's side, whose voices echo Ryna's ancestral scream, all plead for the dead to return, "Sugarman don't leave me no more." The community watches silently, and with no surprise, these familiar scenes of madness. They record these sounds in children's rhymes. And the craziness of the black world is only matched by the insanity of the white world's devices.

Milkman discovers how much of the legacy revolves around this uncertain balance between life and death, how much wisdom and craziness are drawn from the familiarity with death. In Morrison's story everyone seems to be preying upon the other, each character is both a predator and a potential prey. Milkman's relation to Guitar develops into this sort of game. Guitar, the initiator (who first brought him to Pilate's house), the interpreter of his dreams, fears and wishes, is also the experienced trickster cunning and violent: the avenger. This double of Milkman is both friend and adversary. "Could you save my life or would you take it?" Morrison tells us that all human relationships boil down to these two fundamental questions. In her story, Guitar, the master of ambiguity, is the only exceptional person who could answer yes to both. The alternative, one is told, is either destruction or salvation. In the end, in his final leap, Milkman wheels into his friend's arms, surrendering to or freeing himself from Guitar's obsessive pursuit. *Song of Solomon* thus unfolds between two leaps. Characters are left on the edges from which they can either lose their balance and fall, or "surrender to the air and ride it."

Between Mr. Smith's fateful leap and Milkman's flight in the air, the protagonist's awkward yet persistent exploration of the legacy is in many ways archetypal. The journey, as in many other quests in American literature, must be redemptive of past flaws and weaknesses, and retributive. It must do justice to the dead and to the living. Milkman's journey is a succession of leaps and falls, of attempted deaths and incomplete rebirths, of blunders and triumphs, of moments of vulnerability or exhilaration. The real goal of his journey is disguised even to himself. He leaves the Dead house to free himself from "the wings of other people's nightmares." He leaves, cursed by one of his sisters who exposes his ignorance, vacuous and indifferent to other people's feelings. He sets off to find the gold that will buy his freedom—faithful both to the mercantile spirit of his father, and to the historical heritage of slaves, striving to buy their freedom.

Morrison deftly underlines the ambivalent character of each of Milkman's decisions or steps, which are at the same time an escape from and a recognition of the legacy. As he progresses into his journey, however, his resistance and estrangement weaken. Committed to paying his dues, he finds himself immersed in a heritage he can no longer deny. As he is acknowledged as one the tribe by those who have known his ancestors, he rises in fuller recognition of the meaning of kinship, of the rich filiation of several generations. He travels back in space and time to the woodlife of Pennsylvania and the wilder backwoods of Virginia, to the days of slavery when blacks moved in wagons toward the promised land. He gets closer to home, to the South, and to Africa wherefrom the Flying Ancestor, the one with the real name, came.

The journey, however, is full of pitfalls and trials. It takes him, the city bred, farther away from civilization, into close connection with the asocial powers of life and death, with the cosmos or chaos. Milkman's errand into the wilderness becomes a mock story of survival, a joke. Through the last stages of the quest, he feels alternately aloof, unconcerned, off center or, on the contrary, involved and caring. During moments of vacuity the very question "is it important for you to find your own people?" becomes itself aimless, and Guitar's vengefulness and suspicion deprive him of the only person he could trust. But when, on the other hand, moments of revelation occur, they are like new baptisms: as when in the heart of nature he "walks the earth," or when he watches the skinning of a bobcat, or again when he falls into the arms of the only person who does not threaten his life, a woman called Sweet.

In the deceptive creeks and woods or among country people where his presence—a black man with a white heart—is first an offense, the tests and trials become necessary rites of passage. They further purify him and initiate him back into the tribe. The spatial distance that he has to cover gives a measure of his original estrangement and disconnectedness. Morrison, who follows the conventional pattern of lyric epic adventure quest story, combines motifs from that tradition with those that belong specifically to Afro-American history and myth. Her narrative that makes the movements through time and space so artistically visible and responsive to each other is not just another version of a prototypical story: it is immersed in the Afro-American experience, informed by the sensibility, and the imagination of black people. In spite of Milkman's inadequacy and bewilderment, and of the ambiguities, and the wrong speculations, the quest must be pursued and completed. Sounds, words, upon which Milkman stumbles, will be his guides: a moan like a woman's voice, a children's song, names of people, his people, names of places named after his people, offer him the final clues he needs to reconstruct the whole message, to resurrect dead lives and fading memories.

Deciphering the song that the children are singing, thus keeping the story alive, Milkman finds new meanings for old words. The Byrd's house with its appropriate name delivers the last clue to the riddle, and this revelation must be shared with Pilate to whom it had initially been entrusted. She must be told about her mother's name, her father's wish to be buried where he belongs: at Solomon's leap where his own father "sailed off into the sky like an eagle." The wish, if fulfilled, will create history and complete the myth.

In the last swift scene, each gesture and act, unreal as they are, assume perfection and finality. They are the reenactment of familiar rites and rituals, and Milkman's leap, the fulfillment of a dream, is an act of faith in the legacy, an act of communion with Pilate, and with his flying ancestor. Milkman's and Pilate's names can enter the legend, for a new story to be written, a new song invented, that will record the story and secrecy of their lives and deaths. Thus, deeds generate songs, songs generate deeds in an uninterrupted act of creation. The long voyage in the land of the ancestors, exploring their dreams and frustrations, their failures and triumphs is also the story of the genesis of a culture and of a people who, living on the edge of life and death, have managed to create that culture and to keep it alive. *Song of Solomon* is a beautiful statement on the survival of the legacy and on the legacy of survival; on the power of memory, collective memories kept alive through names, stories, words, and songs; on the power of music that accompanies all the rituals of life, from birth to death, and through which feelings and the totality of experience are expressed. Transmitted orally from mouth to mouth and ear to ear, the legacy endures. Its secret is revealed but its secrecy remains. The song that weaves its way through the book is the sacred text: a proclamation available to all, and the repository of secrets. In its way of encoding messages as spirituals did, of yielding and keeping its secrecy, it becomes also the epitome of all narrative.

The strength and richness of that oral tradition is the legacy that black writers have inherited. Armed with pen and paper, and a long fight for literacy, they can now write. But they should do so with the same respect for the word and the devotion that Old Macon Dead showed when he wrote the only word he ever did, or that Pilate showed when she stored that word in her little box. From Zora Neale Hurston to Morrison, black women writers have felt a sense of responsibility toward the heritage—a legacy of beliefs, creeds, customs, and rituals—but also of endurance and humiliation, bereavements and victories—that must now endure through their writing. The leap into the air is a fit metaphor for the secret and hazardous act of writing, an act of faith and communion, the fulfillment of a promise and a pledge.

Notes

1. Toni Morrison, "A Knowing Deep," *Essence* (May 1985): 230.

2. Ibid., 230.

3. Ibid.

4. Alice Walker, *In Search of Our Mothers' Gardens* (New York: Harcourt Brace Jovanovich, 1983).

5. Audre Lorde, *Sister Outsider* (New York: Crossing Press, 1984).

6. Toni Morrison, *Song of Solomon* (New York: Alfred A. Knopf, 1977).

7. Walker, *In Search*, 276.

8. Ibid., 243.

9. Morrison, *Song of Solomon*, 330.

10. Ibid., 28.

11. Ibid., 40.

Song of Solomon: Rejecting Rank's Monomyth and Feminism   Gerry Brenner*

Around Milkman, the hero of her much-admired *Song of Solomon*, Toni Morrison wraps various collective fictions: a riddling *nursery rhyme* that presages his birth and, later chanted by children, leads him to discover his heritage; *fables*, like the one his father, Macon Dead, tells of the man who rescues a baby snake only to be poisoned to death by its bite; *fairy tales*, like "Rumpelstiltskin," "Jack and the Beanstalk," and "Hansel and Gretel"; a common black *folktale*, like "People Who Could Fly" (as collected by Julius Lester);[1] and family *legends*, like that of Milkman's great-grandfather's ability to fly. Even through family names and nicknames Morrison underscores a preoccupation of all four of her novels:

*Reprinted, with permission, from *Studies in American Fiction* 15 (1987): 13–24.

for better and worse, humans use and make fictions to give their lives meaning and significance. Underlying these commoner fictions, however, is Otto Rank's powerful monomyth, the myth of the birth of the hero. Its features—with only minor glossing—attach to Milkman and categorically lay claim to his place among the heroes from whose stories Rank extrapolates his monomyth: Moses, Oedipus, Perseus, Gilgamesh, Tristan, Romulus, Jesus, and Lohengrin—to name but half.[2] Despite Morrison's shrewd use of the monomyth on Milkman's behalf, she skillfully mocks him and the novel's other men. Offsetting his and their deflation is a subtle spectrum of praiseworthy women, prime among whom is the novel's only character of a heroic stature, Pilate.[3] "Marvelous" details circle her with a mythic nimbus that—combined with the humane values by which she conducts her life—rejects the sexism of Rank's monomyth and the expectations of feminists.

The nine parts of Rank's monomyth map the standard saga of the hero.[4]

The hero is the child of most distinguished parents, usually the son of a king. Milkman's father, the city's most affluent black property owner, stands as virtual king. His "lemon-yellow" mother, Ruth, sole daughter of the wealthy, "most respected," and "the most important Negro in the city" (22).[5] Dr. Foster has equally regal stature. To this pair Morrison adds Milkman's even more-distinguished forefathers. Grandfather Macon Dead (aka Jake Solomon), was an extraordinary man who, in sixteen years, made "one of the best farms in Montour County." In his fellow blacks' eyes he stood for "the farmer they wanted to be, the clever irrigator, the peach-tree grower, the hog slaughterer, the wild-turkey roaster, the man who could plow forty in no time flat and sang like an angel while he did it"; his farm "colored their lives like a paintbrush and spoke to them like a sermon" (237). And great-grandfather Solomon/Sugarman—virile progenitor of 21 sons and renowned for his ability to fly—is commemorated in nursery rhyme and his launching site, Solomon's Leap. [Milkman's nocturnal hunt with the elders of Shalimar begins and ends, not by happenstance, at a defunct gas station still presided over by a man who is no one less than *King Walker*.]

His origin is preceded by difficulties, such as continence, or prolonged barrenness, or secret intercourse of the parents due to external prohibition or obstacles. After finding his wife lying naked on the bed—and sucking the fingers—of her dying father (which he interprets as perverse, if not incestuous), Macon Dead abandons conjugal relations with her. A decade later his sister Pilate dissolves his abstinence with herbs whose powers bring him, puzzled, back to Ruth's bed for four days, effecting Milkman's conception. His attempts at aborting the fetus are thwarted by Pilate and Ruth, ensuring that Ruth's "aggressive act [is] brought to royal completion" (133).

During or before the pregnancy, there is a prophecy, in the form of a dream or oracle, cautioning against his birth, and usually threatening danger to the father (or his representative). Milkman's birth is heralded by the suicidal leap from the top of Mercy Hospital by an insurance salesman wearing blue wings who lands on a velvet rose-petal strewn and snow-blanketed pavement; his "flight" is accompanied by Pilate's song of Sugarman/Solomon: *"O Sugarman done fly away/Sugarman done gone/ Sugarman cut across the sky/Sugarman gone home."* Born the next day, Milkman becomes the first black child born in Mercy.

As a rule, he is surrendered to the water, in a box. Modernizing the monomyth, Morrison changes the element from water to air, thereby sustaining both the folktale's belief in a group of blacks who could fly and her hero's lineage; for in addition to the belief that Solomon could fly, even Milkman's grandfather, when shot to death, "was blown off a fence five feet into the air." The suicide's oracular leap from Mercy (his note declaring that he would "fly away on my own wings") signals the birth of Milkman, as though he, like his grandfather, drops from the sky. Because of the hero's potential threat, the father traditionally maims the infant before abandoning him; the result, the limping hero, is mirrored in the uneven length of Milkman's legs: "he acquired movements and habits to disguise what to him was a burning defect" (62).

He is then saved by animals, or by lowly people (shepherds) . . . Milkman is repeatedly saved by lowly women: Pilate, Ruth, Circe, Sweet, and Susan Byrd—of whom more anon.

. . . [A]nd is suckled by a female animal or by an humble woman. Macon's rejection of Ruth's affection demotes her from "queen" to humble woman, for which loss she compensates by suckling her son into his fourth year, the discovery of which yields his nickname of Milkman.

After he has grown up, he finds his distinguished parents, in a highly versatile fashion. Milkman's quest to Danville, Pennsylvania, and to Shalimar, ("pronounced *Shalleemone*") Virginia, results not in the gold his father led him to expect he'd find, but in the treasure of discovering his lineage, of having to unravel the knotted mysteries that hid from him the legendary lineaments and mythic prowess of his ancestors. "Versatile fashion" generously allows for Milkman's episodes with Sweet, Circe, and Susan Byrd, as well as his nocturnal hunt with the four elders of Shalimar.

He takes revenge on his father, on the one hand, and is acknowledged on the other. Milkman's journey and discoveries further free him from his father's grasping anality and fixation on respectability; this implies his revenge in the forms of his total repudiation of Macon Dead's obsessive capitalism, his esteem of Pilate's regard and values (eschewed by his father), and his scorn for the hate-steeped, vindictive racism of a surrogate father, Guitar. Acknowledgement comes with the special favors of Circe, Sweet, and Susan Byrd; with Hagar's death, symbolically lamenting the permanent loss of her lover; with Guitar's fanatic resolve to slay him as a scapegoat; and with Pilate's journeying with him to bury the bones of her father atop Solomon's Leap.

Finally he achieves rank and honors. Milkman accepts the heritage of his ancestors and lays claim to rank among them with his novel-ending plunge from Solomon's Leap, having earned such rank by solving the mystery of the bones Pilate long carried with her and hung from the ceiling of her home for three decades.

Although Morrison follows each of the road signs along the map of Rank's monomyth, she obscures that map by blurring the dates of the novel's events and, more important, undercuts its conventional celebration of the role of the hero in our culture.[6] For shrewdly she mocks the novel's men, especially its alleged hero. She finds little value in Ruth's father Dr. Foster, the image-proud black professional. Despite his stature as "the most important Negro in the city" (22) and his reputation among some whites as a "miracle-doctor" (65), he does little to better the plight of his fellow blacks, regarding himself as having risen above them. The wealth he accumulates goes into four different banks, into a "great big house," into expensive clothing in which to dress his only daughter, and into the two-horse carriage that makes him the "second man in the city" (71) to own one. His son-in-law Macon Dead vilifies him as incestuous toward his daughter, contemptuous toward his grand-daughters (because born without their mother's lemon-yellow skin), and hypocritical toward the "Negroes in the town [who] worshipped him": "He didn't give a damn about them, though. Called them cannibals" (71). Biased though Macon's view is, even Ruth owns her father's arrogance and destructiveness (124).

Morrison more savagely mocks Macon Dead, the acquisitive black. Property-owner and land-developer, his ruthlessness with delinquent tenants, his fixation on caste and respectability, his intractable notion of Ruth's relationship with her father, and his greed in encouraging Milkman and Guitar to steal what he assumes is gold in his sister's suspended green tarp—all tally to label him Freud's classic anal-retentive personality: parsimonious, obstinate, and compulsively orderly. Guitar, the vindictive racist whose membership in the brotherhood of the Seven Days feeds racial hatred, gets Morrison's scorn, too. Self-denying though he is, ready to sacrifice personal pleasure for the cause of the secret society, Morrison aligns him with Macon and Dr. Foster as one more pathetic—if not neurotically hollow—man, no model of manhood for white or black.

Nor is Milkman. Titular hero though his fit with Rank's criteria makes him, he too is an intolerable egotist.[7] True, he strikes out at his father, presumably in defense of his mother. But more typically he "almost never thought about her" (69). And after a 14-year relationship with Hagar, he naively believes—at 31 years of age!—that he can decently end it by sending her money in a thank-you note. Indeed, as Guitar tells him, he's not a "serious person" (104), and as Pilate tells both Ruth and Hagar, Milkman "wouldn't give a pile of swan shit for either of you" (138).

But what of his heroic quest? On the face of it Milkman's adventures in Danville and Shalimar, which make up the bulk of the novel's second half, surely heed the rule that the hero's discovery of "his distinguished parent[age]" be in "a highly versatile fashion." It is with rich invention that Morrison unfolds the ordeals of Milkman's journeys. He withstands the stench of the dog-befouled, decaying Butler home where the supposed-dead, supra-100-year-old Circe embraces him and plays gothic cicerone to his ancestry. He overcomes the mortifyingly minor mishaps of his trek to the cave where he expects to find gold. He survives the knife-and-broken-bottle fight in Shalimar. He aborts Guitar's homicidal attempt on his life during the coon-become-bobcat hunt with King Walker's elders. And he wrestles with the nursery rhyme, whose meaning his visits with Susan Byrd help him finally decipher.

Material though this all is for a hero's adventures—and for the epiphanies and knowledge expected of such a hero—its subtext is satiric.[8] Beneath all of these episodes resonates a malice-tinged chuckle, delight in humbling the hero. Watch his face twist as he tries not to inhale the foetid dog-stench during his interview with Circe. See his composure go slack when she scolds him: "You don't listen to people. Your ear is on your head, but it's not connected to your brain. . . . If you think I stay on here because I loved [Mrs. Butler], then you have about as much sense as a fart!" (249). And look at his mouth, pulling wide with fastidious disgust during his search for the gold: after removing his shoes and socks and rolling up his cuffs to ford the shallow stream between him and the cave in the distance, he gets a complete dunking; and then, in the cave, he soils himself on the bat-shit on its walls and the dirt of its floor—on which he must crawl in darkness, groping to find and feel all around the wide hole in which the gold allegedly waits. The aftermath to this cloacal interlude restores little dignity, for he returns to Danville like some vaudeville character, his flopping sole tie-tied to his shoe. Milkman survives the knife-and-broken-bottle skirmish in Shalimar; but the episode documents less his combative prowess than his stupidity, insensitive to the blacks whose culture he has intruded. And his nocturnal hunt with the elders who gather at King Walker's finds him as unfit for a test of physical endurance as Susan Byrd's crosstalk and the school-children's nursery rhyme find him slow at feats of intellectual penetration.

Should the satiric subtext slip past her readers, Morrison repeatedly invites a fundamental question of her hero: does he do anything to warrant that honorific label? Alas, little. Like Dr. Foster, Macon Dead, and Guitar, Milkman has the potential to become a hero—though perhaps not a Rankian one. But just as their self-centered, goal-dominated ambitions reflect warped forms of self-aggrandizement, so, too, do Milkman's journey and discovery of his parentage end in attempts at self-glorification. Indeed he learns some truth about his past. And he shares that truth with

Pilate, to whose credit it is that her father's bones, which she has unwittingly honored for threescore years, will be given fit burial on Solomon's Leap. But Milkman's discovery of his lineage is little more than an intoxicant to gratify his wish for some grandiose illusion—that in his gene pool lies the birdlike ability to soar. Upon that illusion he acts in his novel-ending leap into the arms of his assailant, the psychopathic Guitar.[9]

Morrison's prose seems to celebrate that illusion, enough so that most readers mistake her irony for endorsement.[10] But beneath the positive thrust of her imaginative prose and the seemingly upbeat ending of her novel lies Morrison's disdain for Milkman because of what he fails to learn on his journey—that in his gene pool also swims the congenital habit of desertion. The nursery rhyme changed by the Shalimar schoolchildren indicts Solomon as feckless father for abandoning the woman from whose womb he has fathered 21 sons, Ryna: "O Solomon don't leave me here/ Cotton balls to choke me/Solomon don't leave me here/Bukra's arms to yoke me" (307). Likewise did Jake Solomon desert his adoptive mother, Heddy Byrd, whom he left to go north with Sing, as did Macon Dead desert both his sister in the cave and his wife to her own bed; Milkman's desertion of Hagar, then, honors the tradition of the man's prerogative—to escape domestication, to fly from responsibilities, in the name of self-fulfillment or self-discovery or self-indulgence. Waking to find himself tied up on Pilate's cellar floor, Milkman realizes that Hagar's death must account for Pilate's act of knocking him senseless with a wet bottle when he returned from Shalimar: "Sweet's silvery voice came back to him: 'Who'd he leave behind?'" He even recalls Jake Solomon's commandment to Pilate, "'You just can't fly on off and leave a body.'" But Milkman assigns himself no culpability: "What difference did [Hagar's death] make? He had hurt her, left her, and now she was dead—He was certain of it. He had left her" (336). So when Milkman leaps at the novel's end into Guitar's arms and certain death, his act is but one more gesture of irresponsibility; he flies, indeed, from the burdens of doing something meaningful in life, preferring the sumptuous illusion that he will ride the air.

By appropriating Rank's monomyth, tailoring her hero to fit its criteria, and then bringing us close to see the incongruity of her 32-year-old wearing a suit leagues larger than he, Morrison continues the ambiguous and ambivalent analysis of myths on which all of her novels pivot. But if she holds her hero up to a set of criteria only to ridicule him—albeit subtly— she also resists the temptation to use her novel as a feminist platform for celebrating wholesale its women. Rather she alternates the current of her attitude towards them, portraying a spectrum from pathetic to praise-worthy. Most pathetic is Hagar. As if it weren't enough to carry the biblical burden of her name—concubine to patriarchal Abraham, mother to outcast Ishmael, and handmaiden to jealous Sara—she is utterly resourceless in a crisis. Forsaken by Milkman, she becomes obsessively jealous, impotently vindictive, and, most pathetic of all, deluded with the notion that the acquisition of allegedly beautifying commodities will magically repossess Milkman.[11] Less pathetic is Magdalene called Lena, doomed to spinsterhood by her father's pretensions and her own resignation to her role as her mother's guardian: "I didn't go to college because of [father]. Because I was afraid of what he might do to Mama" (217). In Morrison's spectrum Lena's ascendancy over her niece Hagar is due to her refusal to accept her role meekly. Discovering that Milkman has told their father of First Corinthians' affair with a man far beneath the caste of the Deads—a delinquent tenant, to boot—she confronts Milkman in the scene that ends the first part of the novel. Forceful and partially gratuitous (certainly signaling some personal anger in Morrison's own life), Lena's speech gathers women's deepest domestic resentments against men, heroes or not, berating Milkman for his pampered arrogance, his notions of domestic noblesse oblige, his obtuse chauvinism, and his utter insensitivity to his sisters' suppressed lives:

> "Our girlhood was spent like a found nickel on you. When you slept we were quiet; when you were hungry, we cooked; when you wanted to play, we entertained you; and when you got grown enough to know the difference between a woman and a two-toned Ford, everything in this house stopped for you. You have yet to wash your underwear, spread a bed, wipe the ring from your tub, or move a fleck of your dirt from one place to another. And to this day, you have never asked one of us if we were tired, or sad, or wanted a cup of coffee. You've never picked up anything heavier than your own feet, or solved a problem harder than fourth-grade arithmetic. Where do you get the *right* to decide our lives?" (216–217)

Like Hagar's overreaction to the loss of Milkman, Lena's deep-seated resentment against men underscores Morrison's disdain of heroes and hero-worship.

Ruth Foster Dead seems little more than a weak replica of her biblical namesake, exemplar of dutiful, self-abnegating obedience, certainly no candidate for praise. Yet Ruth's small-scale concerns show her carving some minimal means of sustenance and significance for her life: "content to do tiny things," she nurtures "small life that would not hurt her if it died: rhododendron, goldfish, dahlias, geraniums, imperial tulips" (64). More, she knows how to avenge herself on her husband: "it may have been that suspicion of personal failure and rejection (plus a smidgen of revenge against Macon) that made her lead her husband down paths from which there was no exit save violence. . . . but of helplessness" (64). Ruth's minor, domestic triumphs over her pigheaded, repressive husband encourage First Corinthians' rebellion against the ingrained snobbery of her father's expectations. Secretly she gets a job as a maid and, at 45, begins an affair that leads to a marriage that emancipates her from domestic bondage, even though it might enslave her to another.[12] Deserving greater praise is Circe. Overcoming the infamy of her classical namesake and her identity as lifelong slave to ruthless gentry, her sedentary, cloistered passivity has led neighbors to assume her dead. Among them she is legendary, both for her midwifery (she "Delivered everybody," her only loss in childbirth being Sing) and for her role as avenger: "any evening up left to do, Circe took care of" (235). But little do her neighbors know how committed she is to "evening up." Milkman's visit discovers that she survives in the old Butler mansion, breeding Weimaraners to bring on the home the ruination and rot that characterized its owners, moral swine, in Circe's eyes.

But it is on Pilate that Morrison devotes her celebratory prose. Despite the stigma of her name and her own reputation and appearance as a "raggedy bootlegger," Morrison assigns her uncanny powers. Miraculously born, she springs to life from the womb of her already-dead mother, Sing, and has no navel to show for her birth, spooking all who later discover her scarlessness. Bereft of father, abandoned by brother, and routinely ostracized by blacks who learn of her lack of navel, her odyssey of 23 years before arriving in Michigan with daughter and granddaughter makes child's play of Milkman's journeys. Intuitively sensing the harm to Ruth of Macon's decade-long abstinence, Pilate concocts an aphrodisiac that brings him to Ruth's bed. Her voodoo doll halts his attempts to abort Ruth's pregnancy, and her song to the rhyme of Sugarman/Solomon outside Mercy Hospital accompanies the blue-winged angel's descent to a snow-blanketed pavement strewn with red-velvet rose petals, the event that presages Milkman's birth. She rescues not only her daughter Reba from a beating by a casual lover (93–94), but also Milkman and Guitar from arrest by "her Aunt Jemima act" (211), vouching that their theft of her green tarp of bones was but a joke on an old lady, quoting chapter and verse from the Bible, and virtually shrinking to make her act credible. Around her have gathered fabulous beliefs: that she has "the power to step out of her skin, set a bush afire from fifty yards, and turn a man into a ripe rutabaga" (94). And as though by some preternatural sense, she had returned to Danville three years after the murder of her father and unwittingly gathered up his bones, bones which she properly buries, just before she is slain. Despite the comic tilt to the nimbus that hovers over her (sometimes her mind arrived "at the revelations of a three-year-old" [149]), undeniable is her nurturant power, the quality shared by several of the novel's women—Circe, Sweet, Susan Byrd, and Mary, the barmaid/part-owner of "the bar/lounge that did the best business in the Blood Bank" (84).

For feminists expecting Morrison to fashion some outsized heroine of Wagnerian stature, Pilate is as much a disappointment as Milkman should be for critics who find heroic lineaments in him. As one feminist articulates the case against Pilate, she "originates" nothing, lacks "conscious knowledge," and has an "oddly garbled" "sense of mission."[13] Yet Pilate is a "culture bearer," someone whose primary function is to sustain the durable human values of the past, not to be a trend-setter who innovates newfangled values or models or standards.[14] No rural throwback who lives on the margins of modern society, Pilate inherits our celebrated American tradition of individualism, and she challenges and rejects her society's values by living in its very midst, refusing to retreat from it. Indeed, her actions repeatedly show that she chooses to reject the idea of "originating" something, a masculine goal that leads to such dehumanizing gods as exploitative capitalism (Macon Dead), racist vindictiveness (The Seven Days), commercial enslavement (Hagar), and escapist fantasy (Milkman). Abandoned by brother and lovers, shunned by neighbors, she overcomes adversity and rejection without recrimination or self-pity. Resourceful and independent, she scorns civilized creature comforts, ekes out a satisfying life for herself, Reba, and Hagar, and protects herself and those she cares for in times of crisis—as when she rescues Reba from the abusing lover. No passive woman, she intercedes when occasion warrants, helping the desperate Ruth to conceive and deliver Milkman. But unlike her predecessor—the meddling, managerial, and matriarchal Eva Peace of *Sula*—after Milkman's birth it only takes her brothers' signal for Pilate to walk away from his house bearing no resentment, jealousy, or wish for sibling harmony: she had "respect for other people's privacy" (150).

"Wide-spirited," she lays no guilt-trip on Milkman, never telling him of her role in his birth, never insinuating any debt he owed her. Nor does Pilate meddle in her granddaughter's life, despite the consequences and the criticism she has received for not guiding Hagar more than she does.[15] But Pilate knows well the hazard of trying to teach others her values, shows by the example of how she lives what it is that she values, letting the results be what they will; besides, the responsibility to raise Hagar is primarily Reba's, not Pilate's. And, finally, since no amount of parental guidance guarantees the values one's offspring will acquire, to fault Pilate for Hagar's death exposes the judgmental attitude of someone looking for a scapegoat. Despite Pilate's refusal to be her homonym, a pilot, her lack of meddlesomeness in how Hagar lives her life reflects no indifference on her part, as her behavior at Hagar's funeral shows. To Reba's spontaneous obbligato she chants "Mercy," sings "the very same reassurance she had promised her when she was a little girl," speaks to each person at the funeral, calling Hagar "My baby girl," and then, "Suddenly, like an elephant who has just found his anger and lifts his trunk over the heads of the little men who want his teeth or his hide or his flesh or his amazing strength, Pilate trumpeted for the sky itself to hear, "'And she was loved!'" (323).

Lack of "conscious knowledge," presumably a major flaw in Pilate's character, also seems to ask that she fit some masculine, rational model. But it matters not whether the bones she has carried to Michigan are those of husband (as she tells the policemen), of murdered white man (as she believes), or of father (as Milkman informs her). What matters is her regard of the bones as symbols of an obligation to a past event and a human relationship. She misunderstands her father's "posthumous communication," "Sing. Sing." For she hears it as his injunction for her to sing, rather than as his crying out his wife's name. But singing, "which she did beautifully, relieved her gloom immediately" (148), showing that her ignorance of one meaning of her father's words did not render worthless another meaning. More, it is arguable whether she lacks "conscious knowledge," for whether by intuition, induction, or deduction, she knows of Hagar's hunger, of Macon's attempts to abort Milkman, of the imminence of Ruth's delivery, and of Milkman's and Guitar's need of her false testimony at the police station. Finally, Pilate repeatedly addresses the rudimentary problems that face her existence, solving them with intelligence and "a deep concern for and about human relationships" (150): "she tackled the problem of trying to decide how she wanted to live and what was valuable to her. When am I happy and when am I sad and what is the difference? What do I need to know to stay alive? What is true in the world? Her mind traveled crooked streets and aimless goat paths, arriving sometimes at profundity, other times at the revelations of a three-year-old" (149).

Her mission, far from "oddly garbled," can be dealt with briefly. Her mission is exemplary, because it is nothing less than to live her life in manifest repudiation of the grasping ambitiousness and obsessive desires of those around her who end up as grotesques, fanatics, neurotics, or fantasists. Pilate hungers not for family dynasty, for domestic respectability, for the authority of some Big House Mammy, or even for others' regard. Her heroism resides in her self-acceptance and self-content, the heroism of performing routine responsibilities without fretting about whether she is "macon" something of her life. Add to that her old-fashioned, simple ethic of love: "Watch Reba for me," she tells Milkman with her last breath. "I wish I'd a knowed more people. I would of loved 'em all. If I'd a knowed more, I would a loved more" (340).

History, literature, and life ask us to bestow adulation upon heroes elevated by fictions that burnish their images and airbrush their defects. And Morrison understands our human need to augment our lives with heroes capable of expressing the deeper wishes and ambitions and possibilities of our kind. But she also mocks the bizarre caricatures that humans become in imitating such heroes, pities the warped behavior that emulation of them results in. And while for some it may not be enough to model oneself after Pilate, better that than after someone silly enough to thrill to the notion that the capacity to fly is important.

Notes

1. *Black Folktales* (New York: Grove Press, 1970), 147–152.
2. Most studies of *Song of Solomon* remark Morrison's use of myth, the majority using the term loosely or citing such general features as those of Jung's or Campbell's departure-

initiation-return cycle: Jacqueline de Weever, "Toni Morrison's Use of Fairy Tale, Folk Tale, and Myth in *Song of Solomon*," *Southern Folklore Quarterly* 44 (1980): 131–144; A. Leslie Harris, "Myth as Structure in Toni Morrison's *Song of Solomon*," MELUS 7 (1980): 69–76; Norris Clark, "Flying Black: Toni Morrison's *The Bluest Eye, Sula* and *Song of Solomon*," *Minority Voices* 4 (1980): 51–63; Jane S. Bakerman, "Failures of Love: Female Initiation in the Novels of Toni Morrison," *American Literature* 52 (1981): 541–563; Charles Scruggs, "The Nature of Desire in Toni Morrison's *Song of Solomon*," *Arizona Quarterly* 38 (1982): 311–335; Dorothy H. Lee, "*Song of Solomon:* To Ride the Air," *Black American Literature Forum* 16 (1982): 64–70; and Cynthia A. Davis, "Self, Society, and Myth in Toni Morrison's Fiction," *Contemporary Literature* 23 (1982): 323–342. The exception to such general use of the term is Wilfred D. Samuels, "Liminality and the Search for Self in Toni Morrison's *Song of Solomon*," *Minority Voices* 5 (1981): 59–68; but Samuels' discussion, which details the particulars of the *rites of passage* identified by Lord Raglan's *The Hero* and two more recent books on the matter, loses Morrison's novel in a forest of scholarly—if not pedantic—apparatus.

3. Both Bakerman, in "Female Initiation," and Davis, in "Self, Society, and Myth," find Pilate too flawed for such a role, pp. 554–558 and pp. 337–341, respectively. And Scruggs, "The Nature of Desire," finds her pathetic, p. 321. But see Nellie McKay, "An interview with Toni Morrison," *Contemporary Literature* 24 (1983): 418–422, for Morrison's own valuation of Pilate.

4. For Rank's essay, first published in 1914, see *The Myth of the Birth of the Hero and Other Writings*, ed. Philip Freund (New York: Random House, 1959), 14–96. The summary of traits, boldfaced in my text, appears on p. 65.

5. All quotations in my text are from the Signet 1978 paperback edition of *Song of Solomon*, page numbers parenthesized.

6. In her interview with Nellie McKay, Morrison makes a statement which may make readers duly skeptical of my argument that she appropriates Rank's monomyth: "Other kinds of structures are imposed on my works, and therefore they are either praised or dismissed on the basis of something that I have no interest in whatever, which is writing a novel according to some structure that comes out of a different culture" (425). Perhaps this statement is in response to Samuels' essay and the "twenty-two elements" of Lord Raglan's heroic pattern or *rites of passage* which guide his discussion. Whether she has any interest in Rank's monomyth, of course, is a matter I leave my readers to decide.

7. Samuels, Scruggs, Lee, and Davis, above, argue the authenticity of Milkman's heroic stature, although Davis, pp. 333–337, chafes at doing so.

8. Scruggs argues differently, attributing to Milkman two epiphanies and the completion of his "moral education," pp. 331–332. Also acknowledging his pair of epiphanies is Elizabeth B. House, "'The Sweet Life' in Toni Morrison's Fiction," *American Literature* 56 (1984): 196.

9. In her interview with Nellie McKay, Morrison maintains that Milkman's novel-ending act does "something important" with what he has learned (428): "Milkman's hope, almost a conviction, has to be that he can be like [Pilate]" (421); for he "is willing to die at the end, and the person he is willing to die for is a woman [Pilate]" (419). With all due respect to the author's interpretation of her character, it seems that her intention to convey her idea of Milkman's motives either failed to be achieved by her prose or came aground upon the counter-intention of her possibly unconscious hostility toward him. More than she herself may realize, her statement in McKay's interview may apply to this discrepancy: "In all the history of black women . . . we have been both the ship and the harbor. . . . We can do things one at a time, or four things at a time if we have to" (413: second ellipsis McKay's).

10. Bakerman also notes that "Milkman's quest is ironically successful" (554).

11. See Susan Willis, "Eruptions of Funk: Historicizing Toni Morrison," *Black American Literature Forum* 16 (1982): 34–42, for Hagar's "bourgeoise reification: and commodity consumption."

12. Bakerman, "Female Initiation," regards First Corinthians as the only woman in the novel who achieves a slim "chance for even modified happiness" (563).

13. These criteria are from Davis, 339. Bakerman also finds against Pilate, claiming that she's ill-equipped for success, a failure (556); but her discussion of the shortcomings of Pilate, Hagar and First Corinthians are not overtly feminist.

14. The term "culture-bearer," like that of "wide-spirited," below, is Morrison's even though she does not use the first to describe Pilate; see McKay, "Interview," pp. 415, 418, respectively.

15. To Bakerman "The failure of Pilate's life foreshadows Hagar's tragedy" (556).

"Life life life life": The Community as Chorus in *Song of Solomon*

Kathleen O'Shaughnessy*

The community as a formal chorus is an important element in Toni Morrison's fiction. Her third novel, *Song of Solomon*, combines the ritual elements of traditional African dance and song with a commentary on the characters' actions. As in ancient Greek drama, the effect is one of heightened audience or reader participation. In *Song of Solomon* the chorus is composed of individuals and groups in the community who act as both observers and participants. We can trace their influence on the main character, Milkman Dead, as he journeys from North to South in search of gold and his ancestral past. Milkman at first simply reacts to the values and demands of the black community in his native Michigan, but he is slowly drawn into the world of his kinsmen in Danville, Pennsylvania. By the time he reaches Shalimar, Virginia, his involvement with the community is direct and physical. His linear journey from North to South is, therefore, paralleled by a movement through increasingly smaller social circles that instead of suffocating him, lead him to transcend death in his final flight and to embrace the life of humanity.

A number of critics have noted the characteristic use of the community in Morrison's work or what Dorothy H. Lee calls the author's "preoccupation with the effect of the community on the individual's achievement and retention of an integrated, acceptable self."[1] Cynthia A. Davis claims the "misnaming" in the novel occurs because "the right to create a recognizable public self" has been denied,[2] while Barbara Christian recognizes the use of community as place or setting.[3]

Morrison's purpose, however, goes beyond depicting the community as the sum of the sociological forces at work on her characters. Her ultimate aim is to reach a community of readers and involve her audience as participants. In her article "Rootedness: The Ancestor as Foundation,"

*This essay was written specifically for this volume and is published here for the first time by permission of the author.

Morrison states her goal is "To make the story appear oral, meandering, effortless, spoken—to have the reader *feel* the narrator without identifying the narrator. . . ."[4] Her method, she says, is "To use, even formally, a chorus. The real presence of a chorus. Meaning the community or the reader at large, commenting on the action as it goes ahead."[5]

Morrison's rationale for this method is that black music, the traditional medium of black art, no longer performs its "healing" functions for the black community because it has been assimilated into the music of white society.[6] In an interview with Thomas LeClair she said the novel was a way ". . . to do what the music did for blacks, what we used to be able to do for each other in private and in that civilization that existed underneath the white civilization."[7] This function of the novel is particularly necessary now for Afro-Americans because ". . . parents don't sit around and tell their children those classical, mythological archetypal stories that we heard years ago."[8] By using the chorus as ritual dance, song, and commentary, Morrison accentuates that archetypal quality and extends her audience beyond the actual communities through which Milkman journeys to include a larger community of readers.

The role of the chorus as a dance motif is not so clearly seen in Part 1 of the novel as it is in Part 2. This lack results primarily from thematic uses of dance and song, which appear with increasing frequency as Milkman gains a greater knowledge of his past and of himself as he travels South. A second reason stems from the nature of the ritual dance and its traditional role in African society, where it is often an integral part of the daily life of a community in which "Each member of a society understands his role as one unit that is part of a whole."[9] In the black community in Michigan where Milkman spends his first thirty-one years, he is ultimately alienated from every group and individual with whom he comes in contact, particularly from his family. As he tells Guitar: "Daddy wants me to be like him and hate my mother. My mother wants me to think like her and hate my father. Corinthians won't speak to me; Lena wants me out. And Hagar wants me chained to her bed or dead."[10]

We can see one major example of a choral dance, however, in the opening scene of the novel when Robert Smith attempts to fly from the roof of Mercy Hospital, which the townspeople call Not Mercy Hospital. Smith is the insurance agent, who as a member of the militant Seven Days group, has done much to insure an end to the lives of others. The community gathers and as Smith flaps his blue wings before his suicidal leap, beneath him Ruth Foster goes into labor while her daughters chase the red velvet roses they have so carefully sewn. The movements have a ritual quality, the dance of death with the blue wings on the tower contrasted with the chase of the rose petals, symbols of both love and blood against the white snow. The baby, later known as Milkman Dead, is born figuratively dead, cut off from knowledge of his past, which he will not learn until he is an adult.

The crowd in this scene acts as witness to both the man's suicide and the baby's birth. At the moment of Smith's fall a woman wrapped in an old quilt, whom we later learn is Pilate, sings "O Sugarman done fly/O Sugarman done gone/Sugarman cut across the sky/Sugarman gone home. . . ."[11] The lines foreshadow the children's dance and song of Solomon in Shalimar, as well as Pilate's and Milkman's deaths. This "structural interdependence of music and dance"[12] is basic to traditional African culture; its use helps Morrison extend her audience at Smith's suicide to encompass the community of readers.

Throughout much of the first part of the novel we see ritual movement without song, accompanied by a silence that is associated not with meditative contemplation or inner peace, but with loss and alienation from the community. This separation is first apparent in the Dead family's Sunday afternoon rides. Through the town's eyes we see both the family's distance from the community and the lack of sound. There is no gunning of engines nor screeching of brakes to call out to passersby. The locals' name of "Macon Dead's hearse"[13] is appropriate, for the slow-moving Packard takes the Dead family nowhere in particular.

Cars have an almost instrumental quality in the novel. Macon Dead's Packard is heavy, lifeless, a hearse, trapping those inside, isolating them from participation with the community. Porter's Oldsmobile is drummed by Corinthians in her attempt to eliminate that isolation. "She banged her knuckles until they ached to get the attention of the living flesh behind the glass, and would have smashed her fist through the window just to touch him. . . ."[14] Not until Milkman has proved himself by his active involvement with the townspeople of Shalimar does he receive help in fixing the fan belt of his broken-down car.

The silence in the Northern section is also evident in the seeming incongruity of names with musical references. Guitar does not play music, but as chief spokesman for the Seven Days, he does play on the members' desire for vengeance. Although none of Morrison's characters are purely representative, and we see Guitar's humanity in his friendship with Milkman and in his pity for Hagar, it is as the advocate of a group espousing racial hatred disguised as love that Guitar is mainly presented. Silence surrounds the other members of the Seven Days as well. There is the mute Empire State, stricken dumb by his "graveyard love"; the two Tommys, who can talk only of what was; Porter, who can't "carry" love; the silent desperate Smith; and Nero, whose name suggests the emperor who fiddled while Rome burned. The members have little communication with each other and even less with their anonymous victims. As Guitar explains to Milkman: "We don't even tell the victims. We just whisper to him, 'Your Day has come.' The beauty of what we do is its secrecy, its smallness. The fact that nobody needs the unnatural satisfaction of talking about it."[15] The Seven Days is a perversion not only of justice, but also of the essential interaction between members of a community.

One of the most powerful uses of song and ritual dance in Part 1 centers around Hagar's stalking of Milkman and the keening of Pilate and her "Mercy" song at Hagar's funeral. Although the funeral scene occurs in Part 2, Hagar never travels South, and her death and the accompanying pain that Reba and Pilate suffer are closely related to the themes of alienation, loss, and death in the Northern section. The last time Hagar tries to kill Milkman as he waits for her in Guitar's apartment, Milkman is still and Hagar silent. The choral quality of the hunter's chant is within Milkman's head: "Either she will kill me or she will drop dead. Either I am to live in this world on my terms or I will die out of it. . . . One or the other. Me or her. Choose. Die, Hagar. Die. Die. Die."[16] The butcher knife breaks his skin, but on the second attempt Hagar is paralyzed, the stalk is over and the death dance is immobilized.

Guitar, who finds Hagar and takes her home, realizes she is without any sense of community to guide her, for Pilate and Reba could give her love, but not the ability to live in the world. Guitar's thoughts take on the choral quality of the female voices his sisters grew up hearing, but Hagar did not: "Put something on your head. You gonna catch your death a cold. Ain't you hot? Ain't you cold? Ain't you scared you gonna get wet? Uncross your legs. Pull up your socks. . . ."[17]

At Hagar's funeral we see one of the most poignant uses of song in the novel, a ritual combined with dancelike movement, orchestrated by Pilate. She interrupts the minister's sermon with her shout of "Mercy!" It becomes a whisper and then she "transformed the plea into a note. In a clear bluebell voice she sang it out."[18] The refrain is answered by Reba's soprano of "I hear you."[19] As they sing with Pilate in the front of the chapel and Reba in the back, their litany effectively circles the congregation. Then Pilate sings the lullaby "Who's been botherin my sweet sugar lumpkin?" She repeats the phrase "My baby girl" over and over until like an angry elephant "Pilate trumpeted for the sky itself to hear. 'And she was loved!'"[20] Pilate and Reba's slow movement about the chapel and their songs, although intensely personal, emphasize the universal grief of a mother mourning her dead "baby girl."

In Danville, Pennsylvania, Milkman enters the smaller society of his distant relatives. Rev. Cooper and the old men of the town circle around Milkman as though he were a long-lost kinsman returning to the tribe. As Milkman hears the stories about his grandfather Jake and the old men's envy for his farm, which Jake had built from scratch into one of the best in Montour County, Milkman realizes his father's desire to own land, perverted as it has become, had its literal roots in the nobleness of his grandfather. As a counterpoint to the female voices of the community who could not protect Hagar, we hear a chorus of male voices on the tradition of working the land. The language is that of a preacher urging his followers: "Grab it. Grab this land! Take it, hold it, my brothers, make it, my brothers, shake it, squeeze it . . . kick it, kiss it, whip it, stomp it . . . buy it, sell it, own it, build it, multiply it, and pass it on—can you hear me? Pass it on!"[21]

The chorus functions in the Pennsylvania section not so much in terms of literal song and dance, as in the role of the storyteller's circle, bringing back into the group the one who had been lost. Milkman responds by his first, if inept, attempts at reciprocating. He visits Circe and offers her money. She refuses, telling him he already helped her: "You came in here and pretended it didn't stink and told me about Macon and my sweet little Pilate."[22] After Milkman's discovery that there is no gold in the cave and his walk through the woods, where he symbolically tears and sheds his clothes, he circles back to civilization and is picked up by a driver who refuses his offer of payment: "My name's Garnett, Fred Garnett. I ain't got much, but I can afford a Coke and a lift now and then."[23] When Milkman returns to town he helps a man move a huge crate. The irony that Guitar witnesses the action and later uses it as evidence that Milkman found the gold and shipped it out does not undercut the kindness.

By the time Milkman reaches Shalimar the images of dance and song are much more apparent. The entire community of the rural Virginia town takes part in Milkman's discovery of his identity through the untangling of his past. The young men do this with the fight, the old men with the hunt, the women with the provision of the reward in the person of Sweet, and the children with their song and dance of Milkman's genealogy.

The young begin to fight Milkman after he unwittingly insults them, first, with his comment about the women in the town, and second, with his casual dismissal of the men at Solomon's store. He does not ask their names nor give them his, but asks only for information and help, wanting to take from them. The older men's test comes in the long hunt scene with its ritual dance that goes beyond the traditional hunt of the dogs chasing the bobcat. Milkman becomes aware of the subtle communication between man and animal and realizes the animals' sounds are not only a form of language, but also a kind of music: "All those shrieks, those rapid tumbling barks, the long sustained yells, the tuba sound, the drumbeat sounds, the low Liquid *howm howm*, the reedy whistles, the thin *eeeee's* of a cornet, the *unh unh unh* bass chords. It was all language."[24]

After Milkman survives Guitar's attempt on his life (made with a wire, befitting the player who is named for a stringed instrument, but who makes not music but death), we hear Milkman's thoughts, memories of Guitar's statements about life, interwoven with the description of the men, skinning and gutting the cat. The effect is to emphasize the brutality of Guitar's ideas through the choral phrasing:

> Luther reached into the paunch and lifted the entrails . . . "It is about love. What else but love? Can't I love what I criticize?" Then he grabbed the windpipe and the gullet, eased them back, and severed them with one

stroke of his little knife. "It is about love. What else?" They turned to Milkman. "You want the heart?"[25]

Without thinking, Milkman plunges both his hands into the cat's rib cage. Although the idea is presented thematically by the parallel stalking of Milkman by Guitar and of the cat by the men and dogs, clearly Morrison uses the ritual skinning and the choral quality of the language to show us that the eventual victor will be the one with the heart.

The reward of Milkman's new understanding is sweet, personified by the woman of the same name. The language with its harmony describing their actions following lovemaking, shows the responsibility Milkman now gladly undertakes. The repeated juxtaposition of "he" and "she" draws the wider circle of readers into the universal sweetness that comes from shared caring and giving: "He made up the bed. She gave him gumbo to eat. He washed out the dishes . . . She kissed his mouth. He touched her face. She said please come back. He said I'll see you tonight."[26]

The children's dance of the song of Solomon, which seems little more than a kind of "ring-around-the-rosy" when Milkman first enters Shalimar, is an obvious example of how the community, represented by its children, works as a chorus and transmitter of genealogy. The children form a circle, and "A boy in the middle, his arms outstretched, turned around like an airplane, while the other sang some meaningless rhyme: 'Jay the only son of Solomon/Come booba yalla, come booba tambee/Whirl about and touch the sun/Come booba tambee. . . .'"[27] The ritual shouting of the nonsense words, the twirling, and the last line of "Twenty-one children the last one Jay!" certainly echo the theme of flying and its connection with death.

The children's dance of the song of Solomon is a key to Milkman's discovery of his link with Jay or Jake, his grandfather, the son of Solomon, whose flight back to Africa is commemorated in the song. There is a direct connection between song and dance, which is reminiscent of Robert Smith's attempt to fly in the opening scene, as well as a foreshadowing of Milkman's leap at the end of the novel. However, it is a children's game, a ritual empty of meaning to the performers. Milkman is able to puzzle it out only after his new awareness following the hunt and his relationship with Sweet.

The litany of family names is echoed in Milkman's bus trip back North. The cataloging starts with specific names of relatives and members of the communities in the North and South, then includes those with no clear reference in the novel: "Names that bore witness: Macon Dead, Sing Byrd, Crowell Byrd, Pilate, Reba, Hagar . . . Small Boy, Sweet, Circe . . . Dough Belly, Rocky River . . . Bo Diddley, Cat-Iron . . . and Dat Nigger."[28] These final names extend the community to include all blacks and involve the reader in seeing he is a member of a larger community.

The language becomes even more rhythmic as Milkman considers Guitar. The sinister quality of Guitar's plan is apparent in the ironic use of the measured restatement of the death notice that Milkman receives when he first arrives in Shalimar: "Guitar is biding his time. Guitar is biding his time. Your day has come. Your day has come. Guitar is biding his time. Guitar is a very good Day. Guitar is a very good Day. A very good Day, a very good Day, and biding, biding his time."[29]

Milkman returns home a changed person, but learns that the world has not changed because of his new awareness. Although he cannot undo the past, he attempts to interact with the community he had had little part of before and persuades Pilate to return with him to Shalimar to bury her father's bones.

The ritual dance and song is evident in the final scene of the novel when Pilate and Milkman walk up to Solomon's Leap. They bury the bones and with it Pilate's earring with her name inside, the one word her father wrote. Pilate is shot and in her dying scene we hear the ritual singing that occurred at Hagar's funeral, except that Milkman is now the one who sings, at Pilate's specific request. Although "Milkman knew no songs, and had no singing voice that anybody would want to hear . . . he couldn't ignore the urgency in her voice."[30] He sings Pilate's song, the chorus Pilate sang at Smith's suicide when Milkman was born, and the same song Milkman heard in Shalimar. Instead of "Sugarman" or "Solomon," however, Milkman sings "Sugar girl don't leave me here."[31] His is not the wailing lament of Pilate and Reba's "Mercy" song, but a song of direct involvement between speaker and listener, and it holds the promise of flight to another world.

Ironically, it is on top of Solomon's Leap that Milkman is confronted with the closest circle of the community as represented by Pilate and Guitar, the diametrically opposed leaders of the two fringe groups from his native Michigan. The circles of social groups around Milkman and his interaction with them have, in dancelike fashion, become increasingly smaller throughout the novel. He has moved from an alienation from the community in the North through the slow awareness of self and his place in the smaller group of his people in Pennsylvania, to the final direct involvement with the men, women, and children of Shalimar. What keeps the ever-enclosing circles from suffocating Milkman is his ability to transcend the community, to follow the lead of Pilate, who is ultimately his pilot, in her affirmation of life and love. Pilate's only regret at death is that she didn't know more people, for if she had, she would have loved more.[32] Her philosophy is directly opposite that of Guitar, who would kill the innocent out of a perverted sense of love for an abstract concept.

Milkman's last action is an echo, literally of Robert Smith's act in the opening scene. Milkman's jump, however, unlike Smith's of desperation, is reminiscent of the boy in the middle of the circle dance of Solomon's song. Milkman calls to Guitar: "You want my life? . . . You need it? Here."[33] As he leaps, Milkman transcends the literal community and flies away like Solomon, though perhaps not as heroically. Milkman's problems are not all solved, and he is still responsible for Hagar's death. Yet, Milkman is able to see Guitar as his true "brother," not as a militant member of the Seven Days, but as one who ". . . knew what Shalimar knew; if you surrendered to the air, you could ride it."[34] In Milkman's leap there is the pure motion of flight, a dance to the heavens, witnessed by the rocks and hills near Solomon's Leap and Ryna's Gulch, where "Life life life life" is the chorus that echoes to those of us in the community beyond.

Notes

1. Dorothy H. Lee, "The Quest for Self: Triumph and Failure in the Works of Toni Morrison," *Black Women Writers 1950-1980: A Critical Evaluation*, ed. Mari Evans (New York: Anchor, 1984), 346.

2. Cynthia A. Davis, "Self, Society and Myth in Toni Morrison's Fiction," *Contemporary Literature* 23, no. 3, Summer 1982, 327.

3. Barbara Christian, "Community and Nature: The Novels of Toni Morrison," *Journal of Ethnic Studies* 7.4, 1980, 65.

4. Toni Morrison, "Rootedness: The Ancestor as Foundation," in *Black Women Writers (1950-1980)*, ed. Mari Evans (New York: Doubleday, 1984), 341.

5. Ibid.

6. Ibid., 340.

7. Thomas LeClair, "A Conversation With Toni Morrison: 'The Language Must Not Sweat,'" *New Republic* 184 (21 Mar 1981), 26.

8. Morrison, "Rootedness," 340.

9. Lee Warren, *The Dance of Africa: An Introduction* (Englewood Cliffs: Prentice Hall, 1972), 9.

10. Toni Morrison, *Song of Solomon* (New York: NAL, 1977), 5.

11. Ibid.

12. J. H. Kwabena Nketia, in *The Music of Africa* (New York: Norton, 1974), states that music is rarely found not associated with dance or drama in traditional African society (206), for the primary emphasis is on "music as a social activity" (2). Likewise, the dance's chief purpose is to facilitate social communication and help release emotion from the music (207).

13. Morrison, *Solomon*, 32.

14. Ibid., 200.

15. Ibid., 159.

16. Ibid., 130.

17. Ibid., 310-11.

18. Ibid., 321.

19. Ibid.

20. Ibid., 323.

21. Ibid., 238.

22. Ibid., 250.

23. Ibid., 257.

24. Ibid., 281.

25. Ibid., 285.

26. Ibid., 289.
27. Ibid., 267.
28. Ibid., 234.
29. Ibid., 324.
30. Ibid., 340.
31. Ibid.
32. Ibid.
33. Ibid., 341.
34. Ibid.

Tar Baby

The Fabulous World of
Toni Morrison: *Tar Baby*

Eleanor W. Traylor[*]

Today, around the schools, they speak of *cultural transmission*. Back then before I went to school, we called it *Grandma say* and *Grandpa say*. In the Pear Orchard—which, to me, was the blackberry patch as well as the peach and fig tree grove or the cornfield or the yard of morning glory, honeysuckle, tiger lily, sunflower, mimosa tree, and elephant ear or the garden of cabbage, collards, peppers, tomatoes, watermelon, and butter beans—was Grandma's house. Grandpa had built it, before he died, out of sentient oak, and he had built the pigpen and the chicken coop and the outhouse, had planted the cornfield and placed the big black pot right square in the middle of the backyard.

On Mondays, my Grandma and me (then) I (now) washed and boiled and starched white sheets and pillowcases handworked in Grandma's embroidery; we scrubbed large gingham aprons and tiny dresses (with underpants to match) and doilies and linen napkins that Grandma made on a washboard that sounded like the sea. We washed Miss Darlene's clothes separate from ours. Our clothes bubbled in the big black pot filled with bluin' water where Grandma churned them with the flatwood battlin' stick 'til they sloshed out cleaner than new.

On Tuesdays, we damped down and rolled smooth the starched-crisp wash that my Grandma flat-ironed to first-wear perfection. And the sound of Tuesday was the crackle of Grandma's spit-fingers testing the surface of the smoothin' iron heated in charcoal just "pert" for the heavy starched ginghams and blued-out sheets. And the smells of Tuesday were the sweet odors of starch and charcoal fire and hot, wet, clean, pure steam on damped-down brighter-than-bleach starched clothes.

Wednesday was weeding day in my Grandma's collard-rich garden behind the big black pot square in the middle of the backyard, but not if it rained. If it rained, Wednesday was piecing day. The piecing trunk stood at the foot of Grandma's carved brass bed dressed in the North Star quilt that she had made. On piecing day, we laid out the millionteenth scraps of flour-

[*]Reprinted from *Confirmation: An Anthology of African American Women*, ed. Amiri Baraka (LeRoi Jones) and Amina Baraka (New York: Quill, 1983), 333–52. © 1983 by Amiri and Amina Baraka. Reprinted by permission of William Morrow & Co., Inc.

135

sack prints, muslins, burlap, lace, monk's cloth, linen, crepe de chine, velvet, wool, silk stockings, and gingham that Grandma saved to make her rugs and doilies and quilts and dresses with matching underpants for me. And on piecing day, the silence between my Grandma and me, broken only by the sound of raindrops on a shingled roof, was an immensity of space in which we were inseparable forever. Unlike washing or ironing or weeding day or even Friday baking-day evening, when Miss Cora came from 'cross the road and she and Grandma sat and rocked on the front porch and I swung in the oak tree swing that my Grandpa had built for my Daddy just off the front porch where the grown folks could watch, piecing day was different. It was different even from Saturday cleaning day and early morning store-boughten shopping or even Sunday when, in church, I never sat in the children's section, for everyone knew me not as a child but as Grandma's *Grand*. Those days, not piecing day, were days of *Grandma say* and Grandma's songs and me saying, "Grandma, you 'member 'bout the time when . . ." and her saying, "One day when I was a tiny thing like you . . ." And that is when I knew about all the things that they now call folklore, folktale, legend, fairy tale, myth. To me, those things are what my Grandma told me in our yard, on our porch, in her kitchen, and at night before we fell asleep.

"He got stuck," she said. Brer Rabbit got stuck on Farmer Brown's tar baby. I think now that she meant me to understand that I should never get stuck. And if I ever did, I should be smart enough, as the rabbit was, to plea-bargain or battle my way back to the Pear Orchard, which was really the rural section of Thomasville, Georgia, a legion time ago, but which, for me, is the place where on piecing day, my Grandma and I together in an enormity of silence laid out the patchwork designs that yet dress my mother's bed and mine and laid out the patchwork design that is now my life.

Like the rain of color drenching the patchwork collages of Romare Bearden, the crystalline images governing the brilliant fiction of Toni Morrison invite us to absorb experience with multitextured vision. Both the writer and the painter reschedule our imagination and alter the way we see by contracting the distance between the familiar and the strange, finding the point of juncture. What is apparent on the canvases of Bearden is certainly obvious in the novels of Toni Morrison. For instance, "the evocations and associations in Bearden's works are indeed so strong, and so deliberately and specifically and idiomatically either downhome rural or up-north urban, that his preoccupation with imagery from Afro-American experience . . . appears to be surpassed only by his commitment to the esthetic process."[1] That process for Bearden is one that "gives his painting the quality of a flat surface painted by hand."[2] That process for Morrison is one that gives her novels the quality of the signifyin' oral tale of Afro-American folk tradition. A flat surface painted by hand is, of course, a wall, much like the historical and mythological walls that Aeneas saw everywhere in the ancient-modern city of Carthage or like the wall painted in 1967 by the OBACHI painters of Chicago or like the walls of our grandparents' houses in south Georgia decorated in newsprint. Bearden's story-murals are made for homes whose walls, no longer restrictors of rooms, could open outward upon the history of the world. Likewise, a tale recounted from mouth to mouth personalizes experience, making it not the possession of any teller but the possession of the whole wide community whose tale it is, much as the blues singer's task invites the world to dance.

The fate of Brer Rabbit, the imported wise scamp of the Afro-American bestiary, and the evocation of the title *Tar Baby*, is not quite the fate of the poor hapless river on Isle des Chevaliers. That island, the primary setting of the story told in *Tar Baby*, "three hundred years ago, had struck slaves blind the moment they saw it" (p. 8).[3] On that island, signifying a virgin world, civilization by forced labor had disturbed the balance of nature and "the land, clouds and fish were convinced that the world was over, that the sea-green green of the sea and sky-blue of the sky were no longer permanent" (p. 9). This perception is precisely what had blinded the first one hundred slaves who looked upon the land. "A rain forest already two thousand years old and scheduled for eternity" had been felled to accommodate "magnificent winter houses on Isle des Chevaliers" (p. 9). But the forest had shielded the river and equalized the rain, and now with the earth "hollowed . . . where there had been no hollow," the poor river had "crested, then lost its course, and finally its head. Evicted from the place where it had lived, and forced into unknown turf, it could not form its pools or waterfalls, and ran every which way" (p. 9).

The tale of the hapless river, crashing "headlong into the haunches of hills with no notion of where it was going, until exhausted, ill and grieving, it slowed to a stop just twenty leagues short of the sea: becoming "a swamp . . . a shriveled fogbound oval seeping with a black substance that even mosquitoes could not live near" (pp. 9, 10), foreshadows one half of the story of *Tar Baby*. A variant of the "tar baby" tales featuring the fabulous escapades of Brer Rabbit, by turns a practical joker, a braggart, a wit, a glutton, a ladies' man, and a trickster whose essential ability to outwit eviction and flourish in unknown turf prefigures the other half. Thus, a new fable, the tale of the river, and an old one, the fable of Brer Rabbit and the tar baby, play point counterpoint, and weave, like fine patchwork, threads of a multitude of stories, legends, and tales into the fabulous collage. *Tar Baby* is a modern fable of society in which humanity, like the faces on a Bearden scape, is Black.

A man standing on the deck of a ship is the image opening Toni Morrison's *Tar Baby*; the scene calls to mind a similar one from a book written 194 years ago. The man, whose name we learn to be Son, about to jump ship in *Tar Baby*, is reminiscent of a man called Equiano in *The Life of Olaudah Equiano* or *Gustavas Vassa, the African* (1789). Equiano's tale is a slave narrative recounting the historical and mythical, the terrifying and mighty passage of the African from the oldest world to the newest. Standing on the deck of a slave ship, the young Equiano recalls his beloved homeland, contemplates means of escape from the dreadful ship, and concludes that he will learn to "navigate" circumstances that would otherwise destroy him. In *Tar Baby*, Son, a refugee, jumps ship and swims to Isle des Chevaliers, the highly symbolic setting (a virgin world raped by the machinations of man) in which the primary action of the story told in *Tar Baby* takes place. Son arrives on the island, climbs aboard a docked houseboat, searches for food, finds too little, spies a great house not far from the houseboat, and enters it. Thus, the quick brushstroke that opens *Tar Baby* introduces Son, the Brer Rabbit of the story, and outlines, by suggestion, the details of the earlier tale in which the rabbit, foraging for food, enters the fenced-in garden-world of Farmer Brown, the self-appointed keeper of the bounty of the world. Having been introduced in the first six pages, a prologue to the novel, Son, though we are ever conscious of his presence, does not reappear for eighty more pages, during which we learn the ways of Farmer Brown.

This re-created Farmer Brown of Toni Morrison's *Tar Baby* is called Valerian Street. His name is interesting; it derives from the Latin proper noun Valerius, the name of a Roman clan, a number of families connected by a common descent and the use of the same name. One relative of the noun Valerius is *valeo* meaning "to be vigorous," "to have force," "to be strong," "to be worth." Yet another meaning of the same word is "to bid farewell"; it may also be an expression of scorn. According to *Cassell's New Latin Dictionary*, the expression from Cicero "*si talis est deus, valeat*" means "let me have nothing to do with him" and "*quare valeant ista*" means "away with them"! Moreover, Valerian, a farmer, was Roman emperor from A.D. 253 to 260. In *Tar Baby*, Valerian Street is a retired, resigned, no longer vigorous or forceful industrialist, a former candy manufacturer who has inherited and brought to corporate success his family's candy business. Now he has "bought an island in the Caribbean for almost nothing; built a house on a hill away from the mosquitoes and vacationed there when he could and when his wife did not throw a fit to go elsewhere. Over the years, he sold off parts of it, provided the parcels were large and the buyers discreet" (p. 53). Of Valerian Street, we learn that "his claims to decency were human: he had never cheated anybody. Had done the better thing whenever he had a choice and sometimes when he did not" (p. 54). In his prime, "he married Miss Maine" (p. 53), a beauty queen whose name is Margaret and who, he discovers, after years of marriage, has never been and has no possibility of becoming a woman.

In her own mind, Margaret, Miss Maine, wife of Valerian Street, fancies herself an envied beauty as in the fairy tale "Beauty and the Beast," or as Cinderella rescued by a slightly aging (for Valerian is almost twenty years older than she) wealthy prince, or as the uneasy queen of "Snow White and the Seven Dwarfs" who keeps asking the mirror, "Who is the fairest of them all?" For Margaret, though it has not been her intention, is a failed wife and mother. Although her beauty, during her childhood, was a source of pain to her as it made her victim of the begrudgeful, yet her beauty has been her sole claim to personhood since her parents, scared a little by her beauty, "stepped back and let her be. They gave her care, but they withdrew attention. Their strength they gave to the others [of their children] who were not beautiful; their knowledge, what information they had they did not give to this single beautiful one. They saved it, distributed it instead to those whose characters had to be built. The rest of their energies they used on the problems of surviving in a country that did not want them there" (pp. 556–57).

Thus Margaret, when she met Valerian, was completely won by him when the first thing he said to her was "You really *are* beautiful," and she asked him, "Is that enough?" and he replied, "Beauty is never enough . . . but you are" (p. 83). Thinking that at last she is loved for *herself*—a *self* that has never developed—she is disabused when married to the elegant, worldly businessman, Valerian Street, and expected to supervise a great house in Philadelphia (so unlike in many ways, but in certain others very like, the trailer home that she was born into), command the respect of servants sophisticated and capable beyond her comprehension though not much older than she, and be the mother of a baby boy. The task is beyond her capability; she expected to be Valerian's valentine, a constant sweetheart: "Margaret lived for the concerts Valerian took her to, and the dinners for two at restaurants and even alone at home" (pp. 58–59). Nevertheless, when Ondine, the wife of Sydney—they are "the colored couple" who efficiently manage the Street household—explains to Margaret the characters in *Search for Tomorrow*, Margaret makes the only real friend that she has ever known. But "Valerian put a stop to it saying that she should guide the servants, not consort with them" (p. 59). Yet, "Valerian was never rude to Ondine or Sydney, in fact he pampered them. No, the point was not consorting with Negroes, the point was her ignorance and origins. It was a nasty quarrel . . . It frightened Margaret—the possibility of losing him" (p. 59). So it is that when Margaret's first and only child is born, a son, Michael, she loves him, of course; she knows that his birth binds the adoring Valerian to his family. But Margaret, the beautiful child-lady, is resentful of the attention that now she must share with the beautiful baby and cannot resist pricking him, from time to time, with pins or burning him with cigarettes or cutting his flesh, ever so gently, with knives. Valerian learns of this, as we do, years after it has happened. He learns of it on Isle des Chevaliers at Christmas dinner when Ondine can no longer suppress her rage at Margaret and at the circumstances in the Street household and shouts, "You baby killer! I saw you! I saw you! . . . I used to hold him and pet him. He was so scared . . . All the time scared. And he wanted her to stop . . . so bad. And every time she'd stop for a while, but then I'd see him curled up on his side, staring off. After a while . . . he didn't

even cry . . . A little boy who she hurt so much he can't even cry"
(pp. 208–209).

The servants of Margaret and Valerian Street, Ondine and Sydney
Childs, are like members of the family. They have nourished and made
stable the Street residences for over thirty years. Indeed, they are so
immersed in the ways of the Street family, that, except for their
accomplished science and style, unremarkable in either Valerian or
Margaret, and except for their link with Jadine, their niece, they appear to
have had no other nascence. Jadine, the daughter of Sydney's dead sister,
has been raised by Ondine and Sydney since she was twelve. Even earlier,
Jadine would live with them "at Valerian's house" in the summer. When
they had sent her away to school, "they had gotten Valerian to pay her
tuition while they sent her the rest" (p. 49). Ondine and Sydney are "good as
gold" people whose distinction in life has become their servanthood. They
live in a suite of their own within the Streets's magnificent house on Isle des
Chevaliers; they are both guardians of the family and the extension of the
family ways. They know Margaret and Valerian so well that they not only
anticipate their needs and wants but prescribe them. Their own personal
rituals—ablutions, eating habits, little ways of being and doing—are in
perfect rapport with the Streets'. They even respond to the other two
servants, residents of the island, as the Streets do. Gideon and Therese,
natives of Isle des Chevaliers, do the menial chores of the Street household
while Ondine is the cook and Sydney is valet-butler. The Streets and the
Childses call Therese and Gideon "Mary" and "Yardman"; they do not
know their names—they do not inquire. To Ondine and Sydney Childs,
Mary and Yardman are shiftless, trifling "niggers" to be dealt with
accordingly, for they are proper Philadelphia Negroes in the terms of
Dr. Dubois. Indeed, Ondine and Sydney, as they are, are more *valeo* than
Valerian: they are stronger than he, who now spends his days sitting in a
greenhouse on a tropical island listening to the radio, for agile industrious-
ness has kept them vigorous except for Ondine's arthritic knees and feet;
they are more than worthy of their hire and the Streets have rewarded
them; they are assured of better than social security as long as they are with
and in the family. Like Pauline Breedlove of Morrison's *The Bluest Eye*,
Ondine and Sydney work hard, are reliable, aim to please and do. Unlike
Pauline, they do not shoo away their niece, Jadine, as Pauline shoos away
her daughter, Pecola, in order to lavish attention upon the blue-eyed child
of the family she serves, yet Ondine and Sydney give Jadine over to
Valerian and Margaret, who guide her choices and mold her ways and steer
her thinking in the manner in which they wish to guide and mold and steer
their own son, Michael, who rejects them.

Jadine, a "copper Venus" (p. 115), has grown up to become a high-
fashion model who is also a "graduate of the Sorbonne . . . an accomplished student of art history . . . an expert on cloisonne . . . An American
now living in Paris and Rome, where she had a small but brilliantly

executed role in a film" (p. 116). At twenty-five, Jadine is confident of her conclusions concerning the nature of things: "Picasso," she tells Valerian, "*is* better than an Itumba mask. The fact that he was intrigued by them is proof of *his* genius, not the mask makers'" (p. 74). But, after all, she has been taught in the schools what *real* culture is. Assured and confident of the fruits of her assumptions, her choices, her way of life, and her successes, Jadine's self-confidence has been deeply wounded only once. In Paris, at a "Supra Market," shopping for a party celebrating her having been "chosen for the cover of *Elle*" magazine, having received "a letter from a charming old man saying your orals were satisfactory to the committee," and being wooed by "three gorgeous and raucous men . . . in Yugoslavian touring cars" (p. 44), Jadine sees a woman,

> a woman much too tall. Under her long canary yellow dress Jadine knew there was too much hip, too much bust. The agency would laugh her out of the lobby, so why was she and everybody else in the store transfixed? The height? The skin like tar against the canary yellow dress? The woman walked down the aisle as though her many-colored sandals were pressing gold tracks on the floor. Two upside-down V's were scored into each of her cheeks, her hair was wrapped in a gelee as yellow as her dress . . . She had no arm basket or cart. Just her many-colored sandals and her yellow robe . . . The woman leaned into the dairy section and opened a carton from which she selected three eggs. Then she put her right elbow into the palm of her left hand and held the eggs aloft between earlobe and shoulder. She looked up then and they saw something in her eyes so powerful it had burnt away the eyelashes.
>
> She strolled along the aisle, eggs on high, to the cashier, who tried to tell her that eggs were sold by the dozen or half-dozen—not one or two or three or four—but she had to look up into those eyes too beautiful for lashes to say it . . . The woman reached into the pocket of her yellow dress and put a ten-louis piece on the counter and walked away, away, gold tracking the floor and leaving them all behind. (pp. 45–46)

In this woman, Jadine catches a glimpse of an essence, a beauty, an assurance, a womanliness, an indwelling elegance, a nurture, an authenticity that she had never known before and certainly not achieved. Jadine follows the woman with her eyes, unable to mask her admiration and even awe, but just as the woman disappears, "she turned her head sharply around to the left and looked right at Jadine. Turned those eyes too beautiful for eyelashes on Jadine and, with a small parting of her lips, shot an arrow of saliva between her teeth down to the pavement . . . below" (p. 48). Hence on Isle des Chevaliers, visiting her "Nanadine" and Uncle Sydney for Christmas at L'Arbe de la Croix, the house of Valerian and Margaret Street, Jadine still ponders the splendid woman holding three eggs aloft in a market in Paris. She sought the woman's approval with her eyes, but the woman spat a rejection that shook Jadine's self-assurance for the first time in her life until she meets Son, the Brer Rabbit whom she, as tar baby of Toni Morrison's modern fable, ensnares.

In a scene recalling Richard Wright's *Native Son*, Morrison's Son, hiding in Margaret Street's walk-in closet, is discovered. Son's entry into the Street household, his reentry into the action of the fable, dissolves all pretensions. Attitudes, buried deep, emerge; hidden fears erupt; Margaret, the aged beauty, is convinced that Son has come to rape her; Ondine and Sydney are outraged at the invasion of "niggerdom"; Valerian, managing style, topples under pressure; and Jadine, embarrassed, contemptuous, and insulted, is now Beauty both terrified by and interested in the Beast. Son has entered the house looking for nourishment. Wet, filthy, and hungry from his sea-change, Son, like the rabbit, has inadvertently entered the bounteous garden-world of Farmer Brown, emperor of abundance. The collision-encounter between Son and the inhabitants of L'Arbe de la Croix and the outgrowth of that form the heart of the tale told in *Tar Baby*.

Tar Baby is a fable, and a fable, for one thing, is a story in which values are juxtaposed and exposed. In the world that a fable creates, persons, places and things assume strange contours bearing large, small, or no resemblance to persons, places, and things in the world we call reality. Wit, humor, subtlety, irony, and verbal color—exquisite finesse—are the materials that shape the fabulous, which, on canvas or in story, presents an image of a world. The world painted by the opulent palette of Toni Morrison, grand fabulist of our time, is a world as much afflicted by bad ideas as blessed by good ones. Yet the fabulous genius of Morrision does not accuse her world so much as it exposes and defines its moral, emotional, and spiritual quagmire and points to its source of renewal and regeneration. The people who inhabit the world created in *The Bluest Eye* (1970), *Sula* (1973), *Song of Solomon* (1977), and *Tar Baby* (1981) represent the ideas that daily bombard them, for these are solidly twentieth-century people. And what that means, in one sense, is that they receive ideas, good or bad, more rapidly than any other people in human history ever have. They are the inheritors of the industrial age, where by means of stupendous technology, ideas, like medicines, are unleashed, many times insufficiently tested, upon the populace and found only later to be fatal.

The people of this fable-world imbibe toxic ideas like Pauline Breedlove of *The Bluest Eye* swallowing whole the nineteen-twenties extravaganzas of movieland and hating herself, her husband, and her child by comparison. Or like Sula of the novel by that name or First Corinthians of *Song of Solomon* or Jadine of *Tar Baby*, they are miseducated by cant; by historical, cultural, and political bias or ignorance of schoolish books; by insidious daily-diet propaganda sponsored by moneymongers; by the pretensions of those who live in the valleys and islands of abundance in this world; by the surrender to pretensions of those who could but do not call upon mother wit and an ancestry endowing them with extraordinary sensibility to double-sight and pierce the core of bad ideas; by foolish slogans rampant in this world convincing many that "if you White, you right; if you Black, stand back or catch up"; by the perennial lusts of a world where "every/body/wants/to be/boozie woozie." An affliction of bad ideas, like a rain of bile, pours down upon the natural landscape and the people of the story-world of Toni Morrison. The deluge makes "the daisy trees marshal for war . . . winds do not trade . . . bees have no sting . . . no honey" and "the avocado tree . . . folds its leaves tightly over its fruit" (*Tar Baby* passim). People caught in the storm of bad ideas lose their direction and become bemused like Shadrack of *Sula*, or become dangerous to the life of their neighborhoods like Soaphead Church or Geraldine, who scorn little Pecola of *The Bluest Eye*, or unhinged like Hagar of *Song of Solomon*, or disconnected from their life-engendering source like Jadine, or bedazzled like Son of *Tar Baby*. Still worse, others, like Valerian Street, whom many wish to become, are beyond the hope of life at its urgent sources—joy, pain, love, struggle:

> He had not known because he had not taken the trouble to know. He was satisfied with what he did know. Knowing more was inconvenient and frightening . . . He had made it up. Made up the information he was waiting for. Preoccupied himself with the construction of the world and its inhabitants according to this imagined message . . . And all he could say was that he did not know. He was guilty, therefore, of innocence. Was there anything so loathsome as a willfully innocent man? . . . An innocent man is a sin before God. Inhuman and therefore unworthy. No man should live without absorbing the sins of his kind, the foul air of his innocence, even if it did wilt rows of angel trumpets and cause them to fall from their vines. (pp. 242–243)

Unlike Valerian, Son is not guilty of the crime of unseasonal innocence—a state of spiritual ignorance and vacuity, self-barricaded willfulness, allowing only what one desires to pass for what is. Son, born and raised in Eloe, Florida, knows both the briar patch and the fruit of life. In Eloe, more a neighborhood than a town, people know that life is a nourishing root, sometimes gall and sometimes sweeter than coolest well water at a dogday noon. Such people are the source of nourishment and of renewal in the fable-land of Toni Morrison. They are shelters from the storm of bad ideas that afflict that world; they are not self-righteous, nor are they free from error; they think neither too little of themselves nor too much; they know both anguish and joy—neither overwhelms them; they can hear and taste and touch and see a lie two hours before it manifests, yet they themselves may lie; but they never call it truth. They do not separate character from ability or industry from fraternity or individuality from communality. To them, a person is more than what he or she does; a person is not merely the sum of his or her work or achievement or talents—those are expected of any human being according to his gifts. No, the people who are sources of nourishment and clear vision in this world measure a person in a different way. They measure a man in a certain way: a man is a good man, over all he says and does, if he understands something crucial to his *man-ness*—his own and that of his tribe—and understanding that acts or does not act, knows or can be instantly reminded of the boundaries of his *can-ness*. Understanding makes him deft, on beat, in time, graphing arcs of movement—soul, mind, body—more arduous and adroit than "grace under pressure"[4] or "purity of line."[5] No, the motion of such a man is more like the invisible ripple of still wings in high flight. The men who teach Milkman in *Song of Solomon* are such men; Gideon of *Tar Baby* is such a man; and in Sydney reside those qualities and their opposite. Guitar of *Song of Solomon* and Son, the journeymen of *Tar Baby*, have the makings of such men.

The people who are sources of nourishment in this fable-world also measure women in a certain way; a woman is a good woman, over all she says or does, if she knows something crucial to her *woman-ness*—her own and that of her tribe. Knowing that, she moves or does not move; if perplexed, she can instantly be reminded of the inscape of her *is-ness*. Knowing makes her easy, still resilient, alchemic, salient, protogenic. The motion of a woman who *knows* is very like the sea: tidal, undulating, mirroring the sun or cloud, whichever sustains life at any moment. The people who are guides and measures of moral probity in a world as much afflicted by bad ideas as blessed by good ones are the progenitors of and heirs to the fundamental ethos of African American sensibility untainted by pretension, unpolluted by the storm of bilious thought that pummels the world in which they live.

Son issues from such people; he knows them on sight. Even in the midst of his own transgression, he is able to purify his spirit in the storm. But for eight years, he has traveled far from Eloe. He has fought in Vietnam and seen his world from different shores. He has worked at sea and mingled with all manner of men, but mainly he has been a refugee from transgression caused by transgression and

> in those eight homeless years he had joined that great underclass of undocumented men. And although there were more of his kind in the world than students or soldiers, unlike students or soldiers they were not counted. They were an international legion of day laborers and musclemen, gamblers, sidewalk merchants, migrants, unlicensed crew-men on ships with volatile cargo, part-time mercenaries, full-time gigolos, or curbside musicians. What distinguished them from other men (aside from their terror of Social Security cards and cedula de identidad) was their refusal to equate work with life and an inability to stay anywhere for long. Some were Huck Finns; some Nigger Jims. Others were Calibans, Staggerlees and John Henrys. Anarchic, wandering, they read about their hometowns in the pages of out-of-town newspapers. (p. 166)

Son, arriving on Isle des Chevaliers at Christmastime, is a starving man in search of nourishment. He is offered the bounty of Christmas food at the table of Valerian Street; he is not nourished by it. Rather, it is Son, the man in search, who brings a nourishment to the house that it has, heretofore, not known. He unlocks the mental dungeon of Sydney and Ondine; he reveals to Valerian Margaret, who is forced to crack her mirror; he offers Valerian the gift of introspection. Son, in turn, finds his meal, his potion and his portion, at the island home of Gideon and Therese, menial servants in the House of Street. But Son finds something else. In the household of the Streets, Son, a man benumbed by a deluge of experience, rediscovers feeling. He discovers desire—intense and delicious. This, he feels, is love inspired by the "copper Venus" of the house. Son is not an ignorant man; he is, like Guitar of *Song of Solomon*, a bedazzled man. Bedazzlement in a world of storm is a common malady afflicting the best of men. The "big white fog"[6] hanging curtainlike over such a world creates illusions that pass for reality. Guitar of *Song of Solomon*, like Bigger Thomas of Richard Wright's *Native Son*, enraged by the deluge of bad ideas that afflicts his world, attempts to murder the deluded. But to rid the land of the deluded is itself an illusion—a bedazzlement. For the fog that is ubiquitous can be cleared only within the mind, the spirit of those who inhabit the storm-ridden world. And the way to that clearing is through the guides, the sources of nourishment in this world. Son, the Brer Rabbit of *Tar Baby*, sees in Jadine the appearance of something real. He is bedazzled.

If the fable wrought in *Song of Solomon* is about a man, Milkman, overweaned but potentially vivifying, who must make a "journey home" to find his bearings in his world, and if the fable wrought in *The Bluest Eye* is about a community whose greatness is its ability to send forth children of the light, of little Claudia, but whose blight, by surrender to pretension, makes possible its derangement of a lovely child—Pecola—and if the fable wrought in *Sula* is about the offspring of that same community who somehow do not fully comprehend its glory and range askew, then *Tar Baby* is about a woman, Jadine, who, disconnected from the life potential of her origins, has lost the crucial is-ness of her tribe. "She has forgotten her ancient properties" (p. 305). That loss has cast her adrift as in a wide world alone, and even when she meets the issue of the tribe, now lost to her, though she feels the authenticity of its is-ness and though it awakens in her what has slept before, she cannot manage the motion—tidal, undulating, protogenic—of the knowing women of her tribe.

The communion, the sweet and bitter wine, that Son and Jadine taste together is contained in the very cup of trembling. Those who have tasted from that cup know its baptism. That communion and its affliction are the deep pulse of the heart of *Tar Baby*. The beat of that pulse must be experienced in the blood. On the page, we have not seen its like since the story of Teacake and Janie in Zora Hurston's *Their Eyes Were Watching God*. But in that story, Janie and Teacake are both deep within their shared ancestral source. The distance between Son and Jadine is an immensity not of the flesh, not even of the heart, but of the soul of things. Son is a man whose journey far from home, has undernourished him; he sees in Jadine the *look* of home absent of its is-ness. Despite his effort, his diluted strength cannot endow it. In Son, Jadine has found the source from which she is disconnected; the woman in the yellow dress has seen the disconnection and forsworn it. The women of Eloe, for Son, honoring custom and his heart, have brought her to them, have seen the disconnection and rebuked it. These women, like those of *The Bluest Eye*, *Sula*, and *Song of Solomon*, young, middle-aged, and old (among them the mother of Claudia, the Maginot Line; Nell, Eva; Pilate, Circe, the woman whose is-ness revitalizes Milkman; also Therese and, in her way, Ondine) despite any flaw, know the crucial thing Jadine does not. She has seen it in the woman in the yellow dress, and she has drunk of it from Son. She cannot find it in herself. She is, perhaps, an unwilling Delilah sucking at the Samson strength of Son. But more and more terribly, Jadine is the embodiment in language of the carcinogenic disease eating away at the ancestral spirit of the race at the present time. It is that disease at which the pen-knife of Toni Morrison cuts.

Jadinese is the disease of disconnection, whose malignancy causes a slaughter of reality. The disease has a long history, and, in America, has manifested itself often and variously in the life, in the government, and in the literature of the country. Disconnection is the disease from which all who live in the land suffer. Some admit their malady; they may, if they wish, become whole. Others are deluded and call their illness health, for they live invincibly in a slaughter of reality. From time to time, some experience a shock from which, if they recover, they gain recognition and seek wholeness. All American writers have been tortured by the national disease. Some have been victims of the malady of disconnection and have themselves been carriers. Others have been diagnosticians, anatomists, or surgeons. And some have achieved, through the practice of letters, epiphany—a vision of wholeness. Thus, from the birth date of the literature of the country, American writers may be fully understood and finally judged by the record that they have left either of their own affliction or of their perception of the anatomy, symptoms, and effects of the national disease—a slaughter of reality—or by their vision of wholeness and by the implicit audience that their efforts have specifically addressed: those who acknowledge their malady; those who are invincibly deluded (in which case, the writer is representative); or those who may from time to time experience a shock from which, if they recover, they gain recognition and seek and may achieve, like the writer, wholeness.

The presence of the disease of disconnection resulting in the slaughter of reality can be seen in the literature as early as *A True Relation of . . . Virginia* by Captain John Smith, published in 1608 and called the birth of American literature. In that epistle-journal, language slaughters reality, as when the captain, speaking gratefully of his reception by the Great Powhatan, father of Pocahontas, "who kindly welcomed me with good words, and great platters of sundry victuals, assuring me his friendship. . . ."[7] and who provides him not only the very soul of hospitality but the example of the ways and abundance and opportunities of life in the New World, calls his—the captain's—reception "barbarous."[8] For the captain is the child of the Old World sensibility and must appropriate its language, though it is inept for the task of reporting the reality of the abundant and welcoming sensibility of a grand New World.

By the publication in 1782 of *Letters From An American Farmer* by St. Jean de Crevecoeur, the problem of unreality is firmly planted in the American soul and in the literature that reveals it. "What then is the American, this new man?" asks Crevecoeur in the third letter of his volume. He answers:

> He is either an European or the descendant of an European, hence that strange mixture of blood, which you will find in no other country. I could point out to you a family whose grandfather was an Englishman, whose wife was Dutch, whose son married a French woman, and whose present four sons have now four wives of different nations . . . the Americans were scattered all over Europe; here they are incorporated into one of the finest systems of population which has ever appeared. . . .[9]

In this epistle of Crevecoeur, perception slaughters reality, for twenty-three years before his *Letters* appear, a narrative was published whose existence troubles the very terms of Crevecoeur's definition. The publication is called *A Narrative of the Uncommon Sufferings & Surprising Deliverance of Briton Hammon, A Negro Man . . . Servant to General Winslow* (1760). Yet Crevecoeur claims, "None among us suffer oppression either from government or religion."[10] Stranger still, in his fourth letters, a description of slavery and an attack, Crevecoeur observes "the horrors of slavery, the hardship of incessant toils . . . those showers of sweat and of tears which from the bodies of Africans daily drop and moisten the ground they till."[11] What may appear contradictory to a beholder is not at all to Crevecoeur or to the sensibility of which he is representative, for in his essay "Manners of the Americans" in *Sketches of Eighteenth Century America*, championing the social freedoms that the American enjoys, having escaped "the absurd ordinances" of the Old World, Crevecoeur says of him (emphasis added)

> *Thus this man* devoid of society learns more *than* ever to center every idea within that of his *own* welfare. *To him all that appears good, just, equitable, has a necessary relation to himself and family. He has been so long alone that* he has almost forgot the rest of mankind except it is when he carries his crops on the snow to some distant market . . . *this introduces him to all* the little mysteries of self-interest *clothed under the general name of profits and emoluments. He sells for good that which perhaps he knows to be indifferent* . . . Fearful of fraud *in all his dealings and transactions*, he arms himself, therefore, with it. *Strict integrity is* not much wanted *as each is on his guard in his daily intercourse, and this mode of thinking and acting becomes habitual.*[12]

Here, *individualism*, which Emerson was to accept and fully exonerate in "Self-Reliance" (*Essays, First Series*, 1841) but which Melville was to fully condemn as solipsism in his character Ahab in *Moby Dick* (1851), is the conundrum, as early as Crevecoeur, slaughtering reality in the American place.

By 1845, most of the viral elements involved in the disease affecting the heart of the country are announced in its literature. Terrible oppositions struggle in, say, Franklin and Jefferson, as well as between them and, say, Adams and Hamilton. But in *The Life of Olaudah Equiano or Gustavas Vassa, the African* (1789), another convolution has assumed shape. That narrative raises the question of authenticity. It begins with the author's account of himself as he knows himself within the context of his now lost homeland. He is on the high seas, imprisoned in the belly of a slave ship. His account of himself pivots between a revelation of his own identity and that of an identity assigned to him by the captain and the crew of the ship. Inside and outside, or the opposition between the authentic and the imposed blurring reality—and aiding its slaughter—is another convolution of the national disease. But the insight of Equiano, in a shock of recognition occurring midway through the narrative, is, for him and us, sufficient antidote. He says, "I must learn to navigate."[13] And with the publication of *Narrative of the Life of Frederick Douglass, an American Slave* (1845), the measure of the disease of disconnection in the American sensibility is fully taken. To go behind *Narrative* and to come forward in time, examining the materials, the design, and the story substance of American writing to the present is the crucial connection (restoring disconnection) that the criticism of American literature must make.

The Afro-American novelist has consistently attempted connection. Posing at least two cultural traditions and offering a third dimension of synthesis, novelists from William Wells Brown to Ralph Ellison have offered paradigms of wholeness. That offering is a phase of literary history awaiting the critic's full report. Within the wake of the consummation that is Ellison's *Invisible Man* (1952), another phase begins. And from the publication of James Baldwin's *Go Tell It on the Mountain* (1953) to the present time, the history of the Afro-American novel demands a scholarship that must teach itself its duties.[14] Toni Morrison and her contemporaries, exposing the present awful and crucial effects of disconnection, and simultaneously working at possibilities of wholeness in new forms born of old traditions that they and they alone fully possess, await the most serious and fully conscious—whole—investigation that the soul of the critic can mount.

Exquisitely told, *Tar Baby* is a story about nourishment—the devastation caused by its lack and the regenerative power of its presence. It is the story of a man in search of nourishment and of a woman whose nourishing power, cut off from its source, has been defused. It is the story of a world where pretension wars with authenticity and where people who live in that world must choose, for there are guides. And those guides, throughout the fabulous fiction of Toni Morrison, are legion. They are, for instance, women who, like those to whom *Tar Baby* is dedicated, are representative of a culture, of a time, of a magnificence perpetually present in human history. *Tar Baby* is dedicated to

Mrs. Caroline Smith
Mrs. Millie McTyeire
Mrs. Ardelia Willis
Mrs. Ramah Wofford
Mrs. Lois Brooks
—and each of their sisters
—and each of their sisters,
all of whom knew
their true and ancient
properties

The women of the dedication are the grandmother, mother, aunts, and sister of the writer; these, then, are the guides to whom the narrative voice of the writer is accountable. Thus, it is not the narrative voice alone that measures sensibility in the story told in *Tar Baby*. Neither is it the narrator who makes crucial judgments, for, after all, what is judged in the world of the story is the behavior of a woman—of women. That judgment implies a definition exceeding the grasp of any narrator alone. Only the cultural integrity from which the storyteller draws is able to adjudicate, much less to authenticate, crucial aesthetic and moral judgments. So the women of the dedication join, as guides, the woman of the "burnt eyelashes" and Therese and the women of Eloe, as well as, by implication, the chorus of women of the Morrison canon. These women, by allusion, figure the warrior women, the market women, the calabash-carrying women, the queen women, the life-bearing, culture-bearing women of their own ancient origins. In their songs, their tales, their reference, these women acknowledge women of other cultures whose paradigms they either approve or reject. Just so, the adroit brush of the narrator shades a faint outline of the Clytemnestras, Cassandras, Penelopes, Helens, Hekubas, Andromaches, Medeas, Sapphos, Salomes, Judiths, Deborahs, Esthers, Cinderellas, Goldilockses, or latter-day Revlon girls: women who sink a culture or save it, who delude it or provide it clarity. *Tar Baby* is a sublime story of a people whose experience, ancestral and present, has prepared them to circumnavigate deluge, and their humanity, the source of nourishment in the world in which they live, like the faces on a Bearden scape is Black.

Sometimes at dusk of evening
When Lightning Bugs would glow,
My Grandma told me stories in the dark.
And now at dusk of evening

When city lights burn bright,
I live
The very stories that she told.

Notes

1. Albert Murray, "The Visual Equivalent of the Blues," in *Romare Bearden: 1970–1980*, ed. Jerald L. Melberg and Milton J. Block (Charlotte, N.C.: The Mint Museum, 1980), pp. 17–28.

2. Ibid.

3. All quotations from Toni Morrison's *Tar Baby* (New York: Alfred A. Knopf, 1981) are cited only by page number.

4. A phrase used by Ernest Hemingway to describe exemplary behavior in *The Sun Also Rises* (New York: Charles Scribner's Sons, 1926).

5. Another Hemingway phrase descriptive of exemplary behavior in ibid.

6. A phrase of Richard Wright's dominating the landscape of *Native Son*, and the title of Theodore Ward's suggestive play of 1940.

7. Captain John Smith, *A True Relation of . . . Virginia* (Boston: Charles Deane, 1866), pp. 33–38.

8. Ibid.

9. St. John de Crevecoeur, *Letters From An American Farmer* (London: E. P. Dutton, 1912), p. 43.

10. Ibid., p. 151.

11. Ibid., p. 155.

12. St. John de Crevecoeur, *Sketches of Eighteenth Century America*, ed. H. L. Boudin et al. (1925; reprint, ed., New York: Arno Press, 1969).

13. Arna Bontemps, ed., *Great Slave Narratives* (Boston: Beacon Press, 1969).

14. Full explication of this point is attempted in my study *The Presence of Ancestry: Traditions in Recent Afro-American Fiction* now in progress.

The Briar Patch as Modernist Myth: Morrison, Barthes and Tar Baby As-Is
Craig H. Werner°

Toni Morrison remakes (post)modern myths. Shifting gradually from the conventional modernist use of myth as structure in *The Bluest Eye* to the postmodern meta-mythology of *Tar Baby*, Morrison recapitulates the literary/historical movement from T. S. Eliot's classic essay "Ulysses, Order and Myth" (1923) to Roland Barthes's "Myth Today" (1957). Exploring the complex genealogy of the tar baby myth in both Afro- and Euro-American culture, Morrison's fourth novel highlights the link between

°This essay was written specifically for this volume and is published here for the first time.

Barthes's theory of myth and the Afro-American folk tradition that precedes, echoes, and revises it. Specifically, Morrison shares Barthes's concern with the "double function" of myth as something that both "makes us understand something and imposes it on us."[1] While Morrison seems aware of French literary theory—one of the characters in *Tar Baby* is named Foucault—her understanding of the way myths impose dehistoricized meanings derives more directly from Afro-American culture. Attuned to both folk and literary traditions of double-voicing (masking, signifying, lying), Morrison apprehends myth both as a tool of Euro-American power and as a reservoir of historical knowledge capable of resisting that power.

In "Myth Today" Barthes revises Eliot's influential presentation of the high modernist concept of myth as a manifestation of universal values. Commenting on Joyce's "mythic method"—his use of a "continuous parallel between contemporaneity and antiquity"—Eliot issued a pronouncement that proved at least as influential as Joyce's "discovery" itself. Eliot described Joyce's use of myth as "simply a way of controlling, of ordering, of giving a shape and significance to the immense panorama of futility and anarchy which is contemporary history."[2] This statement claims what Eliot called the "mythical method" for the elitist strain of modernism which viewed the contemporary world and especially popular movements with disdain. Recognizing the linguistic assumptions and political implications of such an approach, Barthes emphasizes the peculiar nature of "myth" as both sign and signifier. As "sign," a myth derives its significance from a continuing and unfixable set of historical processes. When uprooted from this process, however, myths become signifiers, encoding and serving as a shorthand version of the historical process. As Barthes realized, the transformation of sign into myth simplifies history by repressing process and excluding alternative meanings. Myth posits "meaning [as] *already* complete, it postulates a kind of knowledge, a past, a memory, a comparative order of facts, ideas, decisions."[3] Recognizing the political implications of this process, Barthes observes that the most influential myths encode the understanding of whatever group possesses the economic, political, or military power to silence dissent. Sharing Barthes's awareness of the way in which myth imposes meanings on experience, Morrison focuses *Tar Baby* on the processes through which individuals confront the resulting tensions. Morrison does not simply present an Afro-American version of Barthes's theory of myth; to do so would be to endorse indirectly the limitations identified by Wole Soyinka and Sunday Anozie in their discussion of Barthes in relation to the African continuum. His myth of the impoverished language of the oppressed, for example, collapses when confronted with historical evidence. Still, Barthes's limitations are neither extreme nor, given his personal history, incomprehensible. More important, his insights complement, and, for some audiences, clarify the folk wisdom embedded in Morrison's works.

Is-ness, Masking, and Tar Baby as Mascon

Morrison's Afro-American ancestors and relatives, in both the folk and literary communities, have explored two basic responses to the power of Euro-American myth: masking and an insistent focus on what George Kent calls "is-ness." Both responses reflect a clear awareness of Barthes's basic insights concerning myth. As Jean Fagan Yellin's *The Intricate Knot* and Winthrop Jordan's *White Over Black* demonstrate, Afro-Americans have for centuries encountered racial myths that deny the reality of their experience.[4] Presented as unarguable expressions of the meaning of a historical experience ascribed to a distant past, Euro-American racial myths are not subject to interrogation. In naive form, these myths present Afro-American character in terms of simple stereotypes: the mammy, the black beast, and so forth. In more sophisticated form, they reinterpret the kinetic Afro-American cultural patterns of ascent and immersion[5] as myths of endurance.[6] For blacks faced with unquestioning white endorsement of such myths, survival depended on two factors, both implicit in the mythic awareness Barthes desires: 1) an awareness of the power system enforcing the myths, a system largely unconscious of its own myth-making processes; and 2) the ability to use this awareness to resist (and when possible subvert) that system. Gauging their actions to accord with white expectations, blacks frequently assumed stereotypical masks to distract attention from events that Euro-American observers—unaware of even the most obvious human motives denied by the myths of animalistic blacks—had in effect trained themselves not to see.

The Afro-American tradition encourages awareness of both sign and myth. To accept a myth without excavating its reservoir of repressed history, from an Afro-American perspective, would be to accept the obliteration of one's identity. Kent describes the resulting insistence on immediate experience, understood to include ideas about and apprehensions of that experience, in his brilliant volume *Blackness and the Adventure of Western Culture*: "From the animal tales to the hipsterish urban myth-making, folk tradition has *is-ness*. Things are. Things are funny, sad, tragic, tragicomic, bitter, sweet, tender, harsh, awe-inspiring, cynical, other-worldly, worldly—sometimes, alternately expressing the conflicting and contradictory qualities; sometimes, expressing conflicting qualities simultaneously. Thus a Brer Rabbit story is full of the contradictions of experience—an expression of the existing order of the world and Brer Rabbit's unspecific sense of something 'other.' And there are times in Brer Rabbit stories during which the existing order and Brer Rabbit's 'other' have almost equal validity."[7] The is-ness of the folk tradition generally and the Brer Rabbit stories in particular resists Euro-American myth. As Bernard Wolfe demonstrates in his classic essay "Uncle Remus and the Malevolent Rabbit," the animal tales encode a worldview profoundly incompatible with Joel Chandler Harris's plantation mythology.[8] The racial animosity and sexual tensions of the tales subvert the pastoral surface, pointing to the complex racial history repressed by the frame. The is-ness of Afro-American experience survives, although it cannot be articulated directly for fear of white retribution. Asserting a high level of Barthean mythic awareness for the folk tradition, Houston Baker emphasizes that forms like the blues and animal tales mediate between competing myths through a highly developed meta-language: "blues and its sundry performers offer interpretations of the *experiencing of experience*"[9] (emphasis added).

The Afro-American artist attempting to tap this metalanguage enters into a complex process involving 1) a structural awareness of Euro-American myths, 2) a focus on the is-ness of Afro-American experience that acknowledges the mediating power of these myths, and 3) an awareness of the potential and limitations of counter-myths, which may either reclaim elements of the repressed history or impose new repressions. Afro-American writers seeking to create effective counter-myths typically employ some version of the masking strategy. In Barthean terms, the artist presents his/herself in a way that appears to accord with the myths of the predominantly white audience. Drawing on a wider sense of both the historical and the contemporary is-ness, however, the artist seeks to manipulate the audience's responses, inserting "masked" messages that subvert the myth and/or communicate with the (predominantly black) segment of the audience aware of the repressed history encoded in the mask the white audience accepts as reality. For the black audience, this generates a counter-myth that asserts an alternative to the historical understanding of the dominant myth. At their most effective, such counter-myths encourage the black audience to refine its own myth-making capacities in order to discredit the racist power structure. From Charles W. Chesnutt and Hurston through Ralph Ellison and Morrison, Afro-American writers have insinuated their counter-myths into the dominant discourse by appearing to endorse myths they in fact seek to subvert. The plantation tradition trappings of *The Conjure Woman*, the exoticism of *Mules and Men*, the universalist rhetoric of *Invisible Man*: all manipulate Euro-American myths of Afro-American character and/or universal literature while calling the premises of those myths into question. Frequently, as in Hurston's *Moses, Man of the Mountain* and Chesnutt's "Baxter's Pro-crustes," Afro-American writers carry out explicit pre-Barthean inquiries into the mythic process.

Such encounters with and revisions of Euro-American myth involve several risks. On the one hand, the writer must maintain an awareness of the historical basis of the counter-myths which, however useful, are no more adequate than the Euro-American myths they challenge. During both the Harlem Renaissance and the Black Arts Movement, some counter-myths assumed the power to impose a myth (or ideology) of Afro-American experience which, while preferable to Euro-American racist myths, repressed the historical experience of many segments of the community. A second potential problem stems from the difficulty of maintaining clarity while interacting with the Euro-American power structure. The creation of effective counter-myths requires mastery of what Stepto calls the "literacy" of the Euro-American world, including the myths that represses Afro-American experience. Because such literacy increases access to the material rewards of the dominant culture, the Afro-American individual may come to accept some of its myths, in effect losing the "tribal literacy" that Stepto sees as necessary to intraracial communication.[10] The great difficulty lies in protecting the sense of is-ness while obtaining the knowledge and tools necessary for the construction of counter-myths capable of altering (even minimally) the oppressive power structure.

The Afro-American counter-myth of Brer Rabbit and the tar baby focuses on just such problems. Both mythic signifier and irreducible sign, the tar baby invokes the energy Stephen Henderson associates with the Afro-American "mascon": "Certain words and constructions seem to carry an inordinate charge of emotional and psychological weight, so that whenever they are used they set all kinds of bells ringing on all kinds of levels. . . . These words, of course, are used in complex associations, and thus form meaningful wholes in ways which defy understanding by outsiders. I call such words 'mascon' words . . . I use it to mean *a massive concentration of Black experiential energy* which powerfully affects the meaning of Black speech, Black song, and Black poetry."[11]

The tar baby story has gathered a large amount of such energy as it has been related in a wide variety of contexts. Whatever the setting, the constituent elements and plot structure alter only minimally. Brer Rabbit (or a similar trickster figure) encounters a tar baby that has been placed in the road by a white farmer or other animals. When the tar baby fails to respond to his greeting, Brer Rabbit slaps and/or kicks it, becoming more and more entangled until he is finally immobilized. When his captors begin to torment him, Brer Rabbit regains his freedom by convincing them that he dreads being thrown into the briar patch. Manipulating their cruelty and their shallow apprehension of his character, he thus effects his escape and runs off taunting them that the briar patch is his home. In addition to this plot, each version of the story involves one other element basic to its meaning as sign: the frame. This frame may be either textual—the scholarly apparatus of a folklore anthology or Harris's plantation setting—or contextual—the specific circumstances in which the oral tale is related.

The mascon energy of the tar baby accrues largely from its complex genealogy in African, Afro-American, and significantly Euro-American discourse. Assuming new meanings as its context shifts, tar baby metamorphoses repeatedly from sign to myth. Encoding several layers of repressed historical experience, each new version of the myth influences the consciousness of the individuals who, even though they accept the myths that they inherit, gradually assign them new meanings as signs that can be transformed into further myths. The tar baby myth has passed through at least four such transformations. Originating (although the concept of an origin is simply another myth in Barthean terms) in Africa, the tale assumes early meaning in trickster cycles that developed prior to extensive contact with Europeans. As an Afro-American folktale, it revoices the African myth as a response to slavery. Retold in Harris's *Uncle Remus*, it enters the mythology of the plantation tradition. A fourth transformation occurs in the Walt Disney movie *Song of the South*. Morrison's novel represents only the most recent stage in an ongoing genealogical process. Each level builds on previous levels without totally comprehending them, although Morrison approximates a comprehensive meta-mythic perspective. Most versions of the tale adapt previous versions as if their meaning were transparent: the tar baby myth becomes a signifier rather than a sign pointing to history. The most obvious example occurs in Harris's *Uncle Remus*. Presenting Uncle Remus as the wise but childlike darky of plantation mythology, Harris seems unaware of the explosive racial anger encoded in the tales Uncle Remus tells. Similarly, Afro-American tales, framed by slavery, project a more positive view of the trickster than their African sources; the violence and dishonesty prob-lematic in a context where authority comes from within the community are necessary tools for survival in the United States. Aware of the shifting meanings of the myth, Morrison reexamines its genealogy and considers its significance in the context of contemporary Afro-American culture. Developing in the context of an oppressive Euro-American culture, Morrison presents the African myth of the trickster in a generally positive light; his violence and dishonesty are simply necessary tools for survival.

The tar baby myth provides Morrison with a field of mascon energy within which numerous potential meanings coexist. As racial allegory, the myth can be understood in the following terms: white folks (the farmer, Brer Bear) set traps (the tar baby) for black folks (Brer Rabbit). The best response is to ignore them entirely. Once involved, it is best to pull out slowly since struggling only worsens the situation. Once captured, one should use what one knows about whites—their cruelty and their ignorance of black experience (the briar patch)—to create an effective mask that will allow for escape. While traces of this meaning persist in most Afro-American versions of the tale, each element remains open to a multitude of interpretations. The tar baby could evoke materialism or the white stereotypes of blacks (it is black, stupid, lazy and smells bad). Similarly, the briar patch can be read as a figure for Africa, the African aspect of DuBois's "double consciousness," the black community, the woods of the black belt, and so forth.

The presence of a Euro-American mythic frame substantially alters the meanings. Repressing the history of racial conflict that would call into question the racial harmony he associated with the (mythic) New South, Harris renders both Brer Rabbit and the tar baby as extensions of the childlike Uncle Remus. Placed in a nonracial frame, the tale can support readings as a fable of the maturing child confronting the power of the adult world; as a discussion of the problems of surviving in an amoral context; or, in Jungian terms, as a confrontation with repressed psychological impulses.

What seems to attract Morrison in the tale is precisely this multiplicity, the undifferentiated quality of the tar baby that can support numerous meanings. Generally consistent with Barthes's theory, the consideration of individual mythic processes in *Tar Baby* seems a logical outgrowth of Morrison's previous novels. Many critics have noted Morrison's use of myth, citing the Philomela/Persephone myth in *The Bluest Eye*,[12] the scapegoat myth in *Sula*, [13] the Gullah[14] and biblical[15] myths in *Song of Solomon*, and her continuing interest in Joseph Campbell's "monomyth."[16] Focusing on individual novels, however, obscures the increasing complexity of Morrison's approach to myth. Although *The Bluest Eye* asserts the destructiveness of unquestioning acceptance of the Euro-American myth of beauty, Morrison's use of the Persephone myth to structure and clarify the meaning of Pecola's experience is generally consistent with Eliot's idea of the "mythic method." By *Song of Solomon*, however, she has begun to develop the meta-mythic sensibility that will emerge fully in *Tar Baby*. Juxtaposing the myths of the flying African and the Native American "bird" clan with the Euro-American myths of Icarus and the Cavaliers (the Byrd clan), Morrison suggests the multiplicity of repressed historical experience. Morrison's point in *Song of Solomon*, as Susan Willis observes in her brilliant essay "Eruptions of Funk: Historicizing Toni Morrison," is that while Afro-American history may be repressed by the reifying myths, it is not destroyed.[17] Where *Song of Solomon* emphasizes Milkman's developing understanding of this repressed history, *Tar Baby* expands the focus to involve a multitude of individuals engaged in similar processes. Morrison's panoramic presentation of the complex is-ness of Afro-American experience focuses on the way individuals—both blacks and the whites who frame their world—express and reflect on the tar baby myth, in the process reasserting its historical genealogy and renewing its mascon energy.

Tar Baby

In *Tar Baby*, Morrison adapts the folk sensibility to the is-ness of contemporary Afro-American experience. Rather than employing a traditional myth or creating a counter-myth to give order, Morrison explores the is-ness as a texture of competing myths and understandings of myths. The style and texture of *Tar Baby* emphasize multiplicity. When Valerian and Son think of the Isle des Chevaliers, Morrison's description highlights the split between Euro-American myth and Afro-American history/counter-myth. Valerian interprets the island as a bastion of European culture, a stay against chaos: "Somewhere in the back of

Valerian's mind one hundred French chevaliers were roaming the hills on horses. Their swords were in their scabbards and their epaulets glittered in the sun. Backs straight, shoulders high—alert but restful in the security of the Napoleonic code." Son thinks of the island in terms of the oppressive racial history (the jettisoning of blacks and horses from a slave ship) repressed in Valerian's myth (the jettisoning of slaves and horses from a slaveship) he has learned from the island's black inhabitants: "Somewhere in the back of Son's mind one hundred black men and one hundred unshod horses rode blind and naked through the hills and had done so for hundreds of years."[18] Given the reality of Valerian's economic power, a comprehensive understanding of the island requires an awareness of both perspectives.

Focusing on the novel's four male-female pairs, who present a continuum spanning the Afro- and Euro-American worlds, Morrison investigates a variety of ways of understanding myth. At one extreme, Therese and Gideon are content inhabiting the mythic blackness of the islands; at the other Valerian and Margaret occupy positions in a later-day version of the plantation myth. Poised uneasily between these extremes, Sydney and Ondine attempt to maintain their economic security in Valerian's household while preserving the core Afro-American values of family loyalty and personal dignity. Morrison's primary focus, however, is on Son and Jadine, the only characters she presents explicitly in terms of the tar baby story. Whatever their specific history, whatever racial myths they accept, Morrison's characters consistently seek to evade the painful aspects of their experience and retreat to some version of an encompassing myth of "safety." For Morrison, the myth of safety itself becomes the tar baby, the trap capable of ensnaring even the most wily of tricksters. In *Tar Baby*, any element of experience can become such a snare when uprooted from history. A fixed conception of masking, a total rejection of contact with whites, a romantic myth of the briar patch home: all can become traps.

Of all the characters in *Tar Baby*, Therese and her nephew Gideon view myth from the perspective most closely aligned to the early versions of the tar baby tale. Therese, especially, perceives the white world, in which she includes assimilated blacks such as Sydney and Ondine, as a tar baby to be avoided at all costs. She refuses to work inside the house, assuming an evasive mask whenever she comes into contact with its inhabitants: "[Her] hatreds were complex and passionate as exemplified by her refusal to speak to the American Negroes, and never even to acknowledge the presence of the white Americans in her world" (110). While her refusal to look at Americans reinforces white myths of black stupidity, Morrison observes that "What they took for inattentiveness was a miracle of concentration" (111). This disengagement from the white world contributes to Therese's economic survival. Gideon describes the masking strategy: "When they say to let Therese go, I say okay. But I bring her right back and tell them it's a brand-new woman" (153). Accepting the myth that all blacks look alike, the white world (including Sydney and Ondine) accepts the mask as reality, creating an absurd myth of an island populated by a multitude of Marys to avoid questioning the more basic myth of black simplicity. Although the details repress historical complexities, Therese constructs counter-myths consistent with her cultural situation. Her disturbingly accurate myth of America supports her resolve to avoid contact with the tar baby: "Therese said America was where doctors took the stomachs, eyes, umbilical cords, the backs of the neck where the hair grew, blood, sperm, hearts and fingers of the poor and froze them in plastic packages to be sold later to the rich" (151).

The problem with such an extreme position, from Morrison's perspective, is that it limits the effectiveness of the Brer Rabbit strategy, which demands knowledge of *both* black and white histories. Without Gideon's knowledge of whites, for example, Therese would have lost her job much earlier. Still, Gideon shares Therese's basic attitude. Tricked into returning to the island briar patch, he has no desire to return to the American tar baby: "He could not understand why Son wanted to return to the country too terrible for dying" (218). Like Mary/Therese, Gideon remains invisible to the Americans, who call him "Yardman." Unlike his aunt, Gideon takes pleasure in using his invisibility to manipulate whites. Revelling over Son's presence in the house, he joins Therese in creating a counter-myth of Son as "part-Brer Rabbit, part African spirit" (106). At times Gideon himself assumes the role of Brer Rabbit. Perceiving her black "servant" in terms of Euro-American racial myth, Ondine assumes Gideon is illiterate. However, as he tells Son, his "stupidity" is simply a mask: "I don't let on over there that I can read. Too much work they give you. Instructions about how to install this and that. I make out that I can't read at all" (154). Generally sympathetic to Gideon and Therese, Morrison also portrays their limitations. Distanced from the Euro-American world, they cannot effectively resist its power. When Therese begins to create a counter-myth around Son's relationship with the black Americans, Morrison points to her limitations: "She had forgotten the white Americans. How would they fit into the story? She could not imagine them" (111).

Including the white Americans in her own version of the myth, Morrison's treatment of Margaret and Valerian concentrates on the experiences that lead Euro-Americans to create the myths of blackness that render individual blacks invisible. These racial myths, Morrison indicates, are complexly interwoven with the more encompassing myth of "safety." Shared by both Margaret and Valerian, this myth necessitates the repression of unpleasant experiences that are projected onto black scapegoats. Retiring to his pastoral greenhouse, Valerian creates a modern version of the plantation myth. Like the writers who envisioned the antebellum South as an unjustly maligned world of benevolent patriarchs, gracious ladies, and contented slaves, Valerian presents his myth as a natural signifier: "Every effort had been made to keep it from looking 'designed'" (11). Valerian plays the kindly master with Sydney and

Ondine, humoring what he sees as their idiosyncrasies and assuring Margaret that "I have always taken care of them" (31). Beneath this benevolent surface, however, Morrison identifies a rigid adherence to convention, a use of myth that controls behavior and represses historical realities. When Margaret and Ondine begin to develop a friendship, Valerian imposes the values of the plantation myth: "Valerian put a stop to it saying she should guide the servants, not consort with them" (59). Morrison extends this motif in a specifically postmodern fashion when she describes the relationship between Valerian's social and literary attitudes: "He read only mail these days, having given up books because the language in them had changed so much—stained with rivulets of disorder and meaninglessness" (14). For Valerian, anything that challenged his comfortable myths was "meaningless." He does not hesitate to enforce this illusion through the economic power always present, but rarely acknowledged, in the plantation myth. When Therese and Gideon violate his rules, he fires them. When he responds to Sydney's question "Everything all right, Mr. Street?" by saying "I am going to kill you, Sydney" (33), he unintentionally reveals the historical reality behind the plantation myth.

If Valerian constructs myths to ward off meaninglessness, Margaret is unable to repress her knowledge of the ambiguous relationship between signified and signifier: "Like a blank frame in a roll of film, she lost the picture that should have accompanied the word" (32). Despite this underlying uneasiness with the meanings she has been taught, Margaret derives much of her vocabulary from conventional Euro-American myth. When she stumbles upon Son hiding in her closet, she falls back on racist clichés, referring to him as a "gorilla" (129), "literally, literally a nigger in the woodpile" (83). Still, Margaret senses the insufficiency of Valerian's plantation myth. Comparing the myth that asserts white control with her actual experience, she challenges Valerian's interpretation of Sydney and Ondine's roles: "They tell *us* what to eat. Who's working for who?" (23). Similarly, she identifies the core of Valerian's insecurity when she says: "You're scared. Scared Kingfish and Beulah won't take care of you." After Valerian responds that he has always taken care of his loyal servants, Margaret comes close to the slave-system premises of the plantation myth: "And they will do the same for you. . . . They are yours for life." Unable to accept the implications of her insights, however, Margaret retreats to the safety of the myth admitting "They're loyal people and they should be" (31).

Both Margaret and Valerian endorse myths of blackness not because they are racists but primarily because such myths support the myth of safety, in which they are heavily invested. Morrison traces the racial implications of Valerian's desire for safety to his childhood relationship with a black washerwoman. In standard plantation myth style, the isolated white child seeks out the black adult for human companionship. After his father dies, Valerian's first impulse is to deny the painful reality. Only when he speaks to the black woman, whom he remembers "like a pet" (140), does he begin to realize the significance of death: "The woman looked up at him and paused for an awkward silence in which he suddenly understood the awfulness of what had happened" (141). Unfortunately, neither Valerian nor the people around him accept the is-ness of the situation. Rather, they project the reality of death onto the black woman and, as Valerian will do later with Therese and Gideon, dismiss her from their presence: "They let the woman go and Valerian never again had to say 'He's dead today'" (142). Playing a minor role in Valerian's psychic drama, blacks provide an outlet for psychological impulses excluded from the pastoral myth.

Margaret's willingness to accept racial myths can also be traced to her desire for safety. Although she comes from a "poor white" family, she accepts Valerian's values to escape from the (not purely economic) uncertainties of her family history: "The safety she heard in his voice was in his nice square fingernails too. And it was that, not his money, that comforted her" (83). The primary difference between Margaret and Valerian lies in Margaret's inability to repress her personal history indefinitely. She experiences a kind of release when Ondine reveals that she had abused her son when he was a baby. No longer forced to project her own evil impulses onto blacks, she can begin to accept herself and to pursue a more normal relationship with her son (278). Valerian, on the other hand, cannot extricate himself from the tar baby of safety. When Ondine, like the washerwoman, challenges the harmonious surface of his family myth, he has no recourse. During the Christmas dinner, Sydney, Ondine, and Margaret remove masks which—held in place because the maskers feared his power—Valerian had come to accept as their true faces. Given the fact that, despite his intelligence, Valerian remains content with a superficial apprehension of his experience, it seems particularly ironic that he is attuned to some forms of double-voicing. When he tells Jadine to read *The Little Prince* as the key to understanding Michael, he cautions her to "pay attention not to what it says, but what it means" (73). Still, he is unable to apply this knowledge to his life. When his family myth collapses—in part because he listened only to what Michael was capable of saying—Valerian cannot cope with the meaninglessness that is part of Margaret's everyday reality: "He achieved a kind of blank, whited-out, no-feeling-at-all" (235). Inhabiting a mythic landscape, accustomed to repressing unpleasant realities, Valerian denies the is-ness of the world entirely: "No world in the world would allow it. So this is not the world at all. It must be something else" (234). Totally unaware of the Afro-American myths that might cast light on his situation, Valerian is hopelessly enmeshed in the tar baby he has created. Although it provides little solace, Valerian comprehends that his ahistorical myth-making process is responsible for his alienation: "[Valerian] preoccupied himself with the construction of the world and its inhabitants according to this imagined message. But he had chosen not to know the real message that his son had mailed to him from underneath the sink. And all he could say was that he did not know. He was guilty, therefore, of innocence. Was there anything so loathsome as a willfully innocent man?" (243).

Combining elements of Afro- and Euro-American mythic sensibilities, Sydney and Ondine occupy a particularly complex position in *Tar Baby*. Superficially, both play their expected roles in the plantation myth: Sydney cajoles and trades in jokes with Valerian while Ondine plays the nurturing "Mammy" when she defends her treatment of Michael saying "You can't spoil a child. Love and good food never spoiled nobody" (35). In addition, both echo white racial myths when they condemn "low class" blacks. Like Margaret, Sydney at first views Son as a black beast, a "stinking ignorant swamp nigger" (101), a "wife-raper" who should be shot or imprisoned (99). Similarly, Ondine perceives Son as a sexual threat to Jadine, an animalistic presence filled with "Wildness. Plain straight-out wildness" (192). Recasting racial myth in class terms, Sydney casts himself in the role of plantation master when he tells Son "My people owned drugstores and taught school while yours were still cutting their faces open so as to be able to tell one of you from the other" (163).

Despite such attitudes, however, Sydney and Ondine do not simply or unthinkingly accept white myth. Both employ Afro-American masking techniques; both are aware of the reality of Euro-American power. Sydney recognizes the shallowness of the good master's concern for his loyal servants: "You ever see him worry over [Margaret]?" he asks Ondine. "No. You don't. And he don't worry over us neither. What he wants is for people to do what he says do" (163). Somewhat closer to the early versions of the tar baby myth in her basic attitude, Ondine practices the psychological disengagement implicit in Sydney's observation. When Sydney continues to express his outrage over Valerian's treatment of Son, Ondine insists that he "drop that bone. Drop it before it chokes you" (102). Even though he finds it difficult to dissociate himself psychologically from the white world, Sydney endorses the tar baby principle as it applies to interracial social contact: "[White folks and black folks] should work together sometimes, but they should not eat together or live together or sleep together. Do any of those personal things in life" (210).

By no means unsympathetic, Sydney and Ondine nonetheless demonstrate the dangers of *any* involvement with the tar baby of racial myth. Having attained a substantial degree of literacy and personal freedom within the Euro-American world, they cast light on the difficulties involved in the ascent pattern which Stepto identifies as central to Afro-American culture. Their racial attitudes resemble those of the blacks who refuse to buy Valerian candy after moving from the south to the north: "They're *leaving* the South. When they move out they want to leave that stuff behind. They don't want to be reminded" (51). Even though they acknowledge some links with other blacks, Sydney and Ondine distance themselves from the majority of the Afro-American community, the illiterate unnameable "niggers" such as Son, Yardman, and Mary. Their escape from the tar baby of race exists only in their minds; from Morrison's perspective, they are totally entangled in the tar baby of racist myth. There is a tragic poignancy to Ondine's realization that, from Jadine's perspective, she and Sydney share Son's position in the mythic structure they taught her to accept: "Her niece, her baby, her crown had put her in the same category as that thing she ran off with" (282). Failing to balance Afro-American history and Euro-American myth, Sydney and Ondine find themselves cast into a blackness that makes a mockery of their desire for safety and support.

Morrison's concern with the is-ness of Afro-American life—an is-ness that involves Gideon and Therese, Margaret and Valerian, Sydney and Ondine—focuses on Son and Jadine, the only characters Morrison images specifically in terms of the tar baby story. All three direct allusions to tar baby cast light on the tension in their relationship. When Jadine enters the forest while waiting for Son, she begins to sink into a substance that "looks like pitch" (185). Frightened and feeling revulsion, Jadine taps the wisdom of the animal tales—which she ironically attributes to "girl scouts"—and realizes that to escape she must quit struggling. This scene prefigures her encounter with Son and the is-ness of the Afro-American world that Jadine knows only from a distance. Jadine's feelings about blackness are amorphous; she can both "black up" and "universal out" (64). She remains unsure whether to view blackness as tar baby to be avoided or briar patch to be embraced. They have not even crystallized into the semihuman form of the tar baby. The realities behind the Euro-American myths that influence Jadine's own perceptions remain obscure to her.

Presenting a sharp contrast to Jadine's racial attitudes, Son—a modern Brer Rabbit—feels at home in the black world and has little interest in the comfort and safety Jadine associates with the white world. Like Gideon and Therese, Son prefers to avoid contact with whites whenever possible. This apprehension of the folk wisdom does not, however, protect Son from the danger of entanglement in the tar baby. In his case, the tar baby is associated not with racial myth, but with women. When Son thinks of the story, he associates the trap directly with Jadine, whom he considers a "tar baby side-of-the-road whore trap, who called a black man old enough to be her father 'Yardman' and who couldn't give a shit who he himself was and only wanted his name to file away in her restrung brain so she could remember it when the cops came to fill out the report" (220). Later, Son reiterates this version of the myth directly to Jadine. Casting himself as Brer Rabbit and Valerian as the white farmer, Son condemns Jadine as an unthinking tool of the white world: "There was a farmer—a white farmer . . . And he had this bullshit bullshit bullshit farm. And a rabbit. A rabbit came along and ate a couple of his . . . ow . . . cabbages. . . . So he got this great idea about how to get him. How to, to trap . . . this rabbit.

And you know what he did? He made him a tar baby. He made it, you hear me? He made it!" (270).

Spoken in a moment of passionate anger, this version of the myth represses a great deal of Jadine's personal history. The repression reflects Son's own desire for safety; he creates a counter-myth that would justify evading the risk and pain associated with a mature love. In addition, Son's version of tar baby fails to address a problem more basic than Jadine's relationship with Valerian. When Jadine tells Son that she is unable to see lights, stars, or moon in the darkness behind her own eyes (214), she effectively endorses the underlying structure of Euro-American myth that associates blackness with absence. At times, Jadine senses that such perceptions identify her as, to some degree, a creation of the Euro-American education that veils important aspects of reality: "Too many art history courses, she thought, had made her not perceptive but simple-minded. She saw planes and angles and missed character" (158). When she visits Eloe with Son, she discovers that she has lost her ability to communicate with black people who do not share her background. In Stepto's terms, she has lost her tribal literacy: "She needed air, and taxicabs and conversation in a language she understood. She didn't want to have any more discussions in which the silences meant more than the words did" (259). Like Valerian, Jadine resists forms of communication that draw attention to the gap between signifier and signified; the forms basic to the Afro-American tradition. From the beginning, Jadine recognizes Son as a tar baby, a threat to her safety. When she first encounters Son, her first impulse is to dismiss him from consciousness, to retreat to the safety and simplicity of the Euro-American world: "With him she was in strange waters. She had not seen a Black like him in ten years. . . . The black people she knew wanted what she wanted—either steadily and carefully like Sydney and Ondine or uproariously and flashily like theater or media types. But whatever their scam, 'making it' was on their minds and they played the game with house cards, each deck issued and dealt by the house. With white people the rules were even simpler. She needed only to be stunning, and to convince them she was not as smart as they were. Say the obvious, ask stupid questions, laugh with abandon, look interested, and light up at any display of their humanity if they showed it" (126–27). This alienation from Afro-American tribal literacy renders Jadine vulnerable to individuals associated with the history repressed by the dominant myths: the African woman in yellow who spits at her and Son himself. Significantly, she finds it easy to dismiss ostensibly similar criticism from Michael whose concern with her roots derives not from an awareness of repressed history but from a myth of black primitivism. Conversely, Son continually challenges Jadine to acknowledge the realities repressed by her myths of blackness and of safety. Confronting her with her own sexual impulses, he subverts the myth that associates "funkiness" with blacks and animals. Son attempts to draw Jadine out of the safety of the white world, releasing the "night women" whom she encounters during the visit to Eloe. Although she retreats from some implications of the vision, Jadine begins to reach beneath the surface of the racial and sexual myths to the ambiguous history that has shaped her is-ness as a contemporary Afro-American woman.

At home in the Afro-American world, Son is in many respects the classic trickster; gauging all actions for survival value, he readily accepts the uncertainties that Jadine and Valerian resist. His understanding of world and self are formed in terms of relation: "He did not always know who he was, but he always knew what he was like" (165). Son recognizes that the effectiveness of his masks depends on an accurate understanding of his audience's understanding (myths) of "likeness": "The sex, weight, the demeanor of whomever he encountered would inform and determine his tale" (5). As he tells Valerian, his context determines his attitude toward any particular myth: "In a swamp, I believe" (93). For Son, masking is reflex response. Approaching all myths with caution, he attempts to keep his mind free to perceive the actual situation he understands to be shaped by a variety of mythic understandings.

Despite this awareness, Son contributes to the collapse of his relationship with Jadine by constructing a romantic counter-myth of blackness that represses aspects of black women's experience. Son's myth centers on his hometown of Eloe, Florida. Although he describes Eloe as "All black," Jadine quickly observes its dependence on white technology (172). Holding to the folk myth of the white world as a tar baby, Son creates a complementary myth of Eloe as briar patch. In his memory, Eloe provides an image of safety, offering release from the pressure of remaining constantly on guard against the traps of the white world. Like all myths of safety in *Tar Baby*, however, Son's myth collapses. Eloe cannot comprehend or support his relationship with Jadine. Morrison makes it clear that, despite Jadine's accusations, this is not simply a matter of sexism. Thinking of the women he knew when growing up, Son thinks that "Anybody who thought women were inferior didn't come out of north Florida" (268). Rather, the problem derives from Son's atypical desire to resist changes in the is-ness. Although his Brer Rabbit knowledge should discourage such simplification, Son removes Eloe from history, freezing his idea of the briar patch rather than adapting it to changes in sexual roles. After Jadine returns to New York, Son seeks to recapture the feeling of safety in her pictures of Eloe: "he opened the envelope and looked at the pictures of all the places and people he had loved. Then he could be still. Gazing at the photos one by one trying to find in them what it was that used to comfort him so, used to reside with him, in him like royalty in his veins. Used to people his dreams, and anchor his floating days" (294). With Jadine, however, Son is no longer floating; he has entered the deep waters.

His myth of safety in the briar patch evades the risk of his relationship with Jadine. By embracing a myth that dehistoricizes Jadine's complex history as a black woman, he increases the possibility of suffering the loss he most fears. Once again, Morrison implies that myths that attempt to evade reality by dehistoricizing experience are doomed to failure.

This is not to say that Morrison repudiates myth. As *Tar Baby* demonstrates, she perceives reality as a texture of competing myths that strongly influence individual and cultural behavior. In the context of Afro-American experience, almost all myths must be apprehended with a fully operating double consciousness to be comprehensible. Very few characters, however, have anything approaching an adequate understanding of both Euro- and Afro-American mythic processes. Several times, Morrison presents images that imply a full knowledge split between two characters. After Valerian fires Therese and Gideon, Morrison describes his encounter with Son as a meeting of different worlds: "The man who respected industry looked over a gulf at the man who prized fraternity" (205). Later, she writes of the tension between Son and Jadine in similar terms: "One had a past, the other a future and each one bore the culture to save the race in his hands. Mama-spoiled black man, will you mature with me? Culture-bearing black woman, whose culture are you bearing?" (269).

Morrison provides no pat answers. Like *Song of Solomon*, *Tar Baby* concludes with a new beginning or, to be more precise, new beginnings. Recognizing the inadequacy of the myths she has accepted, most particularly the encompassing myth of safety, Jadine takes control of her mythic environment. She determines to confront the repressed elements of her is-ness: her funky "animal" passion (associated with the "silver dogs") and the "night women" who reassert the repressed history of black women. Significantly, Jadine hopes to begin again in Paris; she realizes the impossibility of attaining safety through withdrawal: "She would go back to Paris and begin at Go. Let loose the dogs, tangle with the woman in yellow—with her and with all the night women who had *looked* at her. . . . No more dreams of safety. No more. Perhaps that was the thing—the thing Ondine was saying. A grown woman did not need safety or its dreams. She *was* the safety she longed for" (290). Morrison follows this resolve with the new myth of the female soldier ants and their queen, a myth that acknowledges sexuality, death, work, and dreams. Echoing Jadine's memory of Son, the concluding image of "the man who fucked like a star" (292) suggests that the new myth is grounded in history and confrontation. The new story, like all stories, remains subject to eventual deformation; at the end of *Tar Baby*, however, it is a sign of Jadine's growing resolve to confront her is-ness without evasion. The concluding lines, which echo Jadine's memory of "the man who fucked like a star" (292), suggest that she will not simply create a new second-order myth repressing the reality of her past experience. While the new myth, like all myths, remains subject to eventual deformation, for the moment it marks a nearly adequate attempt to incorporate the changing is-ness of Jadine's confrontation with the myriad tar babies.

Meanwhile, Son resumes his mythic identity as Brer Rabbit, a Brer Rabbit capable of benefiting from his increased experience of both tar baby and briar patch. His encounter with Jadine has taught him that danger—the tar baby as the white world, as love, as myth—is simply a part of the is-ness. Therese's myths of disengagement, however necessary to the historical development of the Afro-American community, are no longer adequate. Like Jadine, Son resolves to confront his deepest fear, the fear of loving a woman he is afraid to lose: "Already done and he was in it; stuck in it and revolted by the possibility of being freed" (301). When Therese delivers him to the Isle des Chevaliers at the beginning of his renewed search for Jadine, she challenges him to return to the black world, the briar patch represented by the blind horsemen in the hills. Son neither accepts nor rejects the challenge. No longer limited by a dehistoricized understanding of the Afro-American counter myth, Son/Brer Rabbit provides an image of process, of a flexible encounter with the is-ness of the island which includes myth and history, repressed Afro-American history and the Euro-American "plantation." Advancing into the unsafe unknown, Son/Brer Rabbit's footsteps echo the voices of the storytellers of the Afro-American tradition as he walks toward the ever-present, ever-changing tar baby that tempts him to remove his eyes from the woman who can help him forge a unified mythic consciousness: "The mist lifted and the trees stepped back a bit as if to make the way easier for a certain kind of man. Then he ran. Lickety-split. Lickety-split. Looking neither to the left nor to the right. Lickety-split. Lickety-split. Lickety-lickety-lickety-split" (306).

For Jadine, for Son, for Toni Morrison, the tar baby is everywhere. The briar patch remains to be seen.

Notes

1. Roland Barthes, "Myth Today," in *Mythologies*, trans. Annette Lavers (New York: Hill and Wang, 1956), 117. I am indebted to Judylyn Ryan's forthcoming paper on Zora Neale Hurston's *Moses Man of the Mountain* for suggesting the applicability of Barthes's theory to Afro-American practice.

2. T. S. Eliot, "Ulysses, Myth and Order," in *Selected Essays of T. S. Eliot* (New York: Harcourt Brace Jovanovich, 1975), 715–78.

3. Barthes, "Myth Today," 117.

4. Jean Fagan Yellin, *The Intricate Knot: Black Figures in American Literature, 1776–1863* (New York: New York University Press, 1972).

5. Robert Stepto, *From Behind the Veil: A Study of Afro-American Narrative* (Urbana: University of Illinois Press, 1979).

6. Craig Werner, "Tell Old Pharaoh: The Afro-American Response to Faulkner," *Southern Review* 19 (1983): 711–35.

7. George Kent, *Blackness and the Adventure of Western Culture* (Chicago: Third World Press, 1972), 53.

8. Bernard Wolfe, "Uncle Remus and the Malevolent Rabbit: 'Takes a Limber-Toe Gemmun fer ter Jump Jim Crow,'" in *Critical Essays on Joel Chandler Harris*, ed. R. Bruce Bickley, Jr. (Boston: G. K. Hall, 1981), 70–84.

9. Houston Baker, *Blues, Ideology, and Afro-American Literature: A Vernacular Theory* (Chicago: University of Chicago Press, 1984), 7.

10. Stepto, *From Behind the Veil*, 174–75.

11. Stephen Henderson, *Understanding the New Black Poetry: Black Speech and Black Music as Poetic References* (New York: William Morrow, 1973), 44.

12. Madonne M. Miner, "Lady No Longer Sings the Blues: Rape, Madness, and Silence in *The Bluest Eye*," in *Conjuring: Black Women, Fiction, and Literary Tradition*, ed. Marjorie Pryse and Hortense Spillers (Bloomington: University of Indiana Press, 1985), 176–91.

13. Dorothy H. Lee, "*Song of Solomon*: To Ride the Air," *Black American Literature Forum* 16 (1982): 64–70.

14. Susan Blake, "Folklore and Community in *Song of Solomon*," *MELUS* 7, no. 3 (1981): 77–82.

15. Craig Werner, *Paradoxical Resolutions: American Fiction Since James Joyce* (Urbana: University of Illinois Press, 1982).

16. Charles DeArman, "Milkman as the Archetypal Hero: 'Thursday's Child Has Far to Go,'" *Obsidian* 6, no. 3 (1980): 56–59; Leslie A. Harris, "Myth as Structure in Toni Morrison's *Song of Solomon*," *MELUS* 7, no. 3 (1980): 69–76; Lee, "To Ride the Air," 64–70.

17. Susan Willis, "Eruptions of Funk: Historicizing Toni Morrison," *Black American Literature Forum* 16 (1982): 34–42. The extended version of this essay in Willis's book *Specifying* (Madison: University of Wisconsin Press, 1986) is much less convincing than the original. Willis's specific discussion of *Tar Baby* is marred by her narrowly ideological understanding of Afro-American expressive traditions.

18. Toni Morrison, *Tar Baby* (New York: Alfred A. Knopf, 1981), 206. All further citations refer to this edition and will be noted parenthetically in the text.

GENERAL TOPICS

The Convergence of Feminism and Ethnicity in the Fiction of Toni Morrison

Carolyn Denard[*]

Feminism defined politically, according to Bell Hooks in *Feminist Theory from Margin to Center*, is "a movement to end sexist oppression."[1] Defined culturally, as Elaine Showalter points out in "Toward a Feminist Poetics," it is self-conscious interest in and celebration of the values, beliefs, ideas, and behavior uniquely, or traditionally characteristic of women.[2] Ethnicity, the concern with one's ancestral group membership, also has political and cultural definitions. Its political connotation is derived from the desire on the part of minority ethnic groups in a multi-ethnic society to end social oppression by the dominant ethnic group. Its cultural corollary is a self-conscious interest in and celebration of the separate values, beliefs, ideas, and behavior of all ethnic groups in society.

Usually a writer's self-conscious concern for these issues stems from a desire to correct the wrongs that have been historically levelled against women and minority ethnic groups. Feminist scholarship for example, addresses the reasons why or the ways in which power can and should be shared with women; or it celebrates the values, the beliefs—the culture—uniquely characteristic of women. Scholarship and artistic production concerned with ethnicity argues social and political equality and cultural pluralism, or it celebrates the separate values, beliefs, and behaviors of a particular ethnic group.

Among black women, who have historically suffered oppression because of both race and gender, there is usually a simultaneous concern for both these issues. They abhor both sexist and racist oppression. But because of their minority ethnic status, which keeps their allegiance to ancestral group foremost, most shun an advocacy of the kind of political, existential feminism embraced by many women of the majority culture. For black women, their concern with feminism is usually more group-centered than self-centered, more cultural than political. As a result, they tend to be concerned more with the particular female cultural values of their own ethnic group rather than with those of women in general. They

[*]This essay was written specifically for this volume and is published here for the first time by permission of the author.

171

advocate what may be called ethnic cultural feminism. And in so doing, they are able to address the rights and values of women without separating themselves from an allegiance to their ethnic group.

Morrison's development of the women characters in her novels parallels the way in which most black women combine their concern for feminism and ethnicity. Morrison exposes the damages that sexist oppression, both inside and outside of the ethnic group, has had on black women, but she does not allow these negatives to characterize the whole of their experience. She does not advocate as a solution to their oppression an existential, political feminism that alienates black women from their ethnic group. Morrison is more concerned with celebrating the unique feminine cultural values that black women have developed in spite of and often because of their oppression. For as ethnic cultural feminist, it is a feminism that encourages allegiance to rather than an alienation from ethnic group that she ultimately wants to achieve.

In her first novel, *The Bluest Eye*,[3] Morrison explores what she believes to be one of the most damaging components of sexist and racist oppression on black women: the perpetuation by the larger society of a physical Anglo-Saxon standard of female beauty as a measurement of self worth. Blonde hair and blue eyes, according to this standard, are considered the prerequisites for female beauty and virtue. A physical standard of beauty, Morrison believes, commercializes the virtue of all women, but because the inherent origin of the physical traits glamorized in this standard are Anglo-Saxon, it suggests that women who are not Anglo-Saxon are not beautiful and hence inferior.

Historically, the worst of this situation, says Morrison, has not been the white society's commercialization of an Anglo-Saxon physical standard of female beauty but the acceptance by blacks of this standard in regard to their own women; "The concept of physical beauty as a virtue," says Morrison, "is one of the dumbest, most pernicious and destructive ideas of the Western world, and we should have nothing to do with it. Physical beauty has nothing to do with our past, present, future."[4]

In the novel, the self-esteem of both Pauline and Pecola Breedlove is summarily destroyed by their and the black community's acceptance of the standards of feminine beauty glamorized by the majority white culture. They believe that the closer a woman is to Anglo-Saxon standards of beauty the more desirable she becomes. In lieu of white skin, they prefer yellow or light brown skin, if not blonde hair, long straight hair of any color, if not blue eyes, then sharply chiseled features that look more Caucasian than African. To have none of these was to be completely hopeless, the subject of constant ridicule and rejection. Pauline was not "pretty" by these standards, so she gave up on caring for herself and her family and settled down, she said, "to just being ugly."[5] More tragically, Pecola bemoaned the rejection her "ugliness" caused her and prayed for blue eyes as a solution:

Long hours she sat looking in the mirror, trying to discover the secret of the ugliness, the ugliness that made her ignored or despised at school by teachers and classmates alike. She was the only member of her class who sat alone at a double desk . . . Her teachers had always treated her this way. They tried never to glance at her, and called on her only when everyone was required to respond. She also knew that when one of the girls at school wanted to be particularly insulting to a boy, or wanted to get an immediate response from him, she would say, "Bobby loves Pecola Breedlove! Bobby loves Pecola Breedlove!" and never fail to get peals of laughter from those in earshot, and mock anger from the accused.[6]

Morrison shows Pauline and Pecola victims of the sexist and racist oppression of an Anglo-Saxon standard of female beauty. Neither woman voices a self-conscious protest against this condition because the focus of Morrison's criticism in her first novel is not the way in which black women should rebel against prevailing social standards of beauty, but on the society which makes such women victims.

Pauline and Pecola are the victims of both the sexist and racist oppression of an Anglo-Saxon standard of female beauty. The enemy of their oppression is not just men—black or white—but the entire majority culture that has perpetuated the standard in every channel available to them—from Saturday matinees to elementary school primers. The solution then, as Morrison suggests by implication, is not a political feminism that alienates black women from black men but a more self-conscious appreciation of the particular beauty of black women by everyone in the society. In the development of Sula and Jadine, the protagonist of her later novels, *Sula*[7] and *Tar Baby*,[8] Morrison explores the implications of a black woman's self-conscious objection to these oppressions. It is not, however, the physical standards of beauty that these later women feel most oppressed by and subsequently reject, but the subservient roles that black women have generally filled in society. They believe that community and societal roles traditionally expected of black women are too limiting. Too much of their time has historically been given over to the domestic work of making life comfortable for others, resulting in few chances for them to think about or to realize their own self-fulfillment: "I know what every Black woman in this country is doing," Sula says to Nel on her death bed, "dying just like me."[9] These characters especially resent the black woman's acceptance of this role for herself. Thus even at the risk of distancing themselves from other black women, they seek to assert a sense of self defined outside of the parameters set for women by the black community as well as by the society at large: "Your way is one . . . but it's not my way," Jadine admits to her aunt, "I don't want to be . . . like you . . . I don't want to be that kind of woman."[10]

Jadine and Sula are Morrison's objectors; they speak out against their oppression and criticize black women who serve these roles. But while

Morrison allows them full opportunity to voice their objections to what they view as the limited life of black women, she does not condone the existentialist position. Morrison suggests that a definition of self that excludes an ethnic cultural connection will for minority ethnic women finally be empty and meaningless. "Sula knows all there is to know about herself because she examines herself, she is experimental with herself, she's perfectly willing to think the unthinkable thing and so on. But she has trouble making a connection with other people and just feeling that lovely sense of accomplishment of being close in a very strong way."[11] In fact, rather than diminish the worth of the domestic roles that black women have served, Morrison accentuates the value of and the inner strength required to perform them. To reject a connection to these women, Morrison suggests, would be to negate the positive cultural values that have gone into making black women different from all other women. Thus the women who assume existentialist positions are always made to come to terms with their ethnic connection in the black community. They are either forced to return to the community or they are haunted by a feeling of betrayal of its feminine cultural values.

When Sula leaves her home town of Medallion, she is full of the hope that she will find a more fulfilling life than that of the women of her community. But Sula finally has to return to Medallion. Whatever new freedom she had hoped to find has not been realized. The passive resignation of the women of Medallion, she finds, is a lesser evil than the racism outside of it. In the 1940s, the "free life" that Sula desired, was not easy for black women to realize. There was a prescribed role for black women in the larger community that did not allow individual self-expression. The only black women who could enjoy the free-spirited life that Sula desires without consequence were "show business women"— those singers and dancers who travelled from town to town and lived outside the total value control of any one home community. Thus whatever rebellion she chooses to engage in was ultimately restricted to the boundaries of her ethnic community. And within its boundaries she willfully defies its values and conventions: she slept with her best friend's husband, she put her grandmother in a nursing home, she went to church suppers without underwear, and worst of all, it was rumored, she slept with white men. The people of her community ostracize her and they call her evil, but they do not harm her; they do not even totally reject her. For despite her evil ways, when Sula dies members of the community come quietly and collectively to her graveside to sing for one of their own a loving benediction.[12] Black women, as Morrison suggests in her development of Sula, always maintain, whether they desire it or not, a connection to their ethnic community. The larger society never totally accepts a desire on the part of blacks to assume an autonomous / existentialist identity and the black community never totally rejects them because of it. Separation, then,

Morrison believes is futile. Thus the connection to the ethnic community should be nourished instead of minimized.

Jadine is much like Sula. She, too, tried to defy the conventions of womanhood set forth by the black community. She rebels against the ways of her aunt and the black women of her past. Jadine sees these women as backward; like Sula, she sees no self-fulfilling value in the role that they serve. Because she is of a later generation than Sula, Jadine has greater opportunities to follow the nontraditional lifestyle that Sula desired with more success. She has a graduate degree from the Sorbonne; she is a successful model, she lives an upperclass European lifestyle, and she has none of the encumbrances of husband, home, and family. She is the contemporary "liberated" woman as it were. But for black women, Morrison suggests, and perhaps for all women whose ethnic group and culture has been discriminated against by the larger society, "liberation" must not bring with it alienation from the ethnic community. Thus rather than glorify Jadine's successes, Morrison centers the conflict in the novel around her unwillingness to accept alliance with the cultural traditions of her ancestors.

Jadine is constantly haunted by a sense of having lost a connection to the values and traditions of the black women of her past. The African woman in yellow spits at her during a shopping trip in Paris. The night women of her dreams taunt her with their nurturing breasts, and her Aunt expresses shame and disappointment over her lack of concern for her family. The point of these confrontations Morrison emphasizes is not to criticize Jadine for her accomplishments, but to caution women such as her not to forget the positive connections that they have to the women of their ethnic past: "No Black woman should apologize for being educated or anything else," says Morrison. "The problem" she explains, "is not paying attention to the ancient proprieties." Black women, Morrison explains, have had "the ability to be the ship *and* the safe harbor," to build the houses and raise the children, to be complete human beings who did not allow education to keep them from their nurturing abilities.[13] For black women to forget their ancient properties or to minimize their worthiness, Morrison concludes, "would be to diminish (themselves) unnecessarily."[14]

The feminist position that Morrison advocates for black women is one that aligns itself with the cultural values of the ethnic group—that validates the traditional beauty and strengths of black women. Thus the women that Morrison celebrates in her fiction are those who exhibit the traditional values of black womanhood. Drawing from the African myth of the "tar lady,"[15] Morrison calls the historical ability of black women to keep their families and their households together the "tar quality."[16] And it is in the development of these "tar women" that Morrison herself engages in the kind of ethnic cultural feminism that she advocates.

The older black women she described in *The Bluest Eye* provide an eloquent panoramic example of what Morrison considers the "tar quality" of black women who came

> edging into life from the back door. Becoming. Everybody in the world was in a position to give them orders. White women said, "Do this." White children said, "Give me that." White men said "Come here." Black men said, "Lay down." The only people they need not take orders from were black children and each other. But they took all of that and recreated it in their own image. They ran the houses of white people, and they knew it. When white men beat their men, they cleaned up the blood and went home to receive abuse from the victim. They beat their children with one hand and stole for them with the other. The hands that felled trees also cut umbilical cords; the hand that wrung the necks of chickens and butchered hogs also nudged African violets into bloom; the arms that loaded sheaves, bales and sacks rocked babies into sleep. They patted biscuits into flaky ovals of innocence—and shrouded the dead. They plowed all day and came home to nestle like plums under the limbs of their men. The legs that straddled a mule's back were the same ones that straddled their men's hips.[17]

These women held things together inside and outside the home; they understood the historical circumstances that limited their own potential as well as that of their men, yet they took that and created their own positive images. They took care of their families, loved their husbands, and were not preoccupied with physical standards of beauty as a measurement of self worth. They did not resent the roles they necessarily served in their families and their communities. Although their roles might be viewed by contemporary standards as limiting, they were the roles that sustained black family and community life.

Many such "tar women" exist in Morrison's novels. First there is Mrs. McTeer, the mother of the narrator in *The Bluest Eye*. She works, she manages the household, she cares for her husband and children, and she takes in boarders and the homeless. Morally upright, she is a good example for her children. Because she is black, Mrs. McTeer is subject to the same victimization as Pauline Breedlove. Her life could be viewed as dull and uneventful as Sula viewed the lives of the women in Medallion. But she does not succumb to self-pity or resentment. She realizes the value and the necessity of the role she serves for her family and community and therefore she does not allow her self-worth to be defined on the terms of others.

There is also Eva Peace, the mother and grandmother in *Sula*. Eva too, albeit through questionable means, takes care of her children and the homeless, and has, although she hates her exhusband, an ongoing relationship with men. She is not preoccupied with alien standards of physical beauty or measurements of self-worth. She reportedly had her leg run over by a train in order to collect insurance payments to care for her family. She is not a doting mother; she did not "play" with her children,[18] but she provded what was needed for them to survive.

Pilate, the memorable character of *Song of Solomon*,[19] is Morrison's mythical tar woman incarnate. Defying all Anglo-Saxon standards of physical beauty, Pilate is perhaps the most awesomely attractive of Morrison's women characters. She is tall and angular with short hair, smooth black skin, large brown eyes, and has no navel. She is clean but unkempt. She wears long dresses with unlaced brogans, knitted hats, and long quilts over her shoulders. Her physical idiosyncrasies, however, do not determine Pilate's self-worth or her value to her family and community. She raises and provides for her daughter and granddaughter alone. She helps the weak and saves those in trouble. Her home offers genuine comfort. Pilate has an inner calm. Her allegiance is to the women and men of her past and the values they taught her; she has no concern for the artificial standards set presently by her own community or by the larger society. Yet even in her insistence on what appears to be eccentric, individualist standards, Pilate is neither alienated from her community nor antagonistic toward it. In essence her values are like those of all tar women: a caring concern for home, family, and community. Pilate simply adheres to these values in a way that is historically and culturally uncompromising. Unlike Sula, the depth of Pilate's understanding of her role in the world and her connection to other black women before her frees her rather than imprisons her. She understands that when insisted upon and exercised to its fullest that there is power and freedom in the role traditionally thought to be subservient and limiting.

And finally there is Ondine, the assiduous cook and housekeeper in *Tar Baby*. Ondine cares for the child of the white family for whom she works, she sees to it that her niece gets a good education, she cooks and cleans in the Street household, and takes care of her husband. She has an historical commitment to family loyalty and to upholding good over evil. Ondine's value has been in the love and stability she has provided for her family. For her it is not physical beauty that is the measurement of self-worth for a black woman, but the degree and sincerity of her commitment to family. Ondine has been taught, as she tries belatedly to teach Jadine, that "a woman has got to be a daughter first." She has to care enough to care about those who cared for her, and as Ondine concludes, "if she never learns how to be daughter, she can't never learn how to be a woman . . . a real woman—good enough for a child; good enough for a man—good enough even for the respect of other women."[20] The responsibility of daughter-hood is the unspoken but expected role that black women define for each other. It is what Sula and Jadine reject, and what Pecola and Pauline, because they fall prey to victimization, never understand. Ondine and the women like her hold proudly and steadfastly to the values of black womanhood. They are the "tar women" whom Morrison applauds and whose value, she believes, should not be minimized by attention to the wrong value system or by existential longings and separate self-definitions.

They provide the consistency that holds their families and communities together.

Mrs. McTeer, Eva, Pilate, Ondine, and the old women of *The Bluest Eye* are the heroines of Morrison's fiction. They did not have societal support systems that paid them well or appreciated their beauty and the often dual role as homemaker and provider they assumed in their families. But somehow these women, even without any endorsement from the society, kept their vision and their energies focused on that which was worthwhile and sustaining. Morrison's emphasis on their selflessness and their strength is not to romanticize their limited opportunity for adventure or fulfillment outside the boundaries of their own communities. Instead it is to show the value and the difficulty of the role that they did serve. The ability of these women, Morrison believes, is too often ridiculed in negative matriarchal jargon that diminishes the context in which they perform them. Thus her role, as ethnic cultural feminist, has been to try to alleviate these prejudices and misconceptions and to seek ways to reinforce the value that racism and sexism would take away from the beauty, the work, and the cultural values of black women.

Notes

1. Bell Hooks, *Feminist Theory: From Margin to Center* (Boston: South End Press, 1984), 26.

2. Elaine Showalter, "Toward a Feminist Poetics," in *The New Feminist Criticism: Essays on Women, Literature and Theory*, ed. Elaine Showalter (New York: Pantheon Books, 1985), 131.

3. Toni Morrison, *The Bluest Eye* (New York: Holt, Rinehart and Winston, 1970; Pocket Books, 1972).

4. Toni Morrison, "Behind the Making of *The Black Book*," *Black World*, February 1974, 89.

5. Morrison, *Bluest Eye*, 98.

6. Ibid.

7. Toni Morrison, *Sula* (New York: Alfred A. Knopf, 1973; Plume Books, 1982).

8. Toni Morrison, *Tar Baby* (New York: Alfred A. Knopf, 1981).

9. Morrison, *Sula*, 143.

10. Morrison, *Tar Baby*, 282.

11. Morrison, quoted in "Intimate Things in Place: A Conversation with Toni Morrison with Robert Stepto," *Massachusetts Review* 18 (473–489): 477.

12. Morrison, *Sula*, 140, 173.

13. Morrison, quoted in Judith Wilson, "A Conversation with Toni Morrison," *Essence*, July 1981, 81.

14. Ibid., 133.

15. Morrison, quoted in Thomas LeClair, "The Language Must Not Sweat," *New Republic*, March 1981, 27.

16. Wilson, "A Conversation," 81.

17. Morrison, *Bluest Eye*, 110.

18. Morrison, *Sula*, 68.

19. Toni Morrison, *Song of Solomon* (New York: Alfred A. Knopf, 1977).

20. Morrison, *Tar Baby*, 281.

The Dramatic Voice in
Toni Morrison's Novels   Margaret B. Wilkerson°

In the 1970s when Toni Morrison spoke at Mills College in California, she was asked whether she was writing any plays. She replied, "No, I am trying to perfect the novel form." Her enthusiastic readers and critics could have argued that she had already achieved that goal and should feel no impediment to pursuing the drama, if she wished. Not until 1985 did Morrison announce that she was writing a play, *Dreaming Emmett*, to be produced by the Capital Repertory Company early in 1986.[1] The idea had been taking shape in her mind for some time; she had set it to paper, without dialogue, two years earlier. *Dreaming Emmett* opened its world premiere on 4 January 1986.

Morrison's initial reluctance to attempt playwriting is understandable. Crossover writers have not enjoyed much success in recent years. Novelist E. L. Doctorow's play *Drinks with Dinner* was too static to hold the audience's attention, according to critics, although his *Ragtime*, was very popular and became a successful film. Other novelists such as E. E. Cummings and Charles Dickens have met with similar difficulties in writing for the theatre.

The very nature of theatre presents its own set of challenges for the novelist. Action, in theatre, is most often and most effectively propelled through spoken and visual forms such as actors, setting, and dialogue. Narration, a primary technique used brilliantly by writers like Morrison, has very limited use in dramatic texts. The language of the theatre is both visual and metaphorical. Drama depends as much on subtext or what is not stated as what is, with gesture adding its interpretative role. Thus, the novelist is not able to depend on eloquent, descriptive passages. What replaces her total command of action and scenario is the collaborative process of theatre. The novelist is accustomed to "running the shop by herself," as Morrison told an interviewer. "No one is allowed into the process, as she has conversations with her characters, and determines what has to happen. She is supremely confident in her abilities as a novelist, and so guards her work very closely until it is finished, and only then does she give it up to other people: her audience."[2] In theatre, however, early in the process she must sign on with a creative partner, the director—and shortly

---

°This essay was especially written for this book and is published here for the first time by permission of the author.

thereafter, the actors and designers whose involvement inevitably leads to revisions, sometimes even reconceptualizations of the work. The solitary, creative individual control of all the imaginative elements is impossible in the theatre, yet it is the stock-in-trade of the novelist. So Morrison would quite naturally approach writing for the theatre with some trepidation.

Yet, it was inevitable that she would eventually succumb to the temptation. The dramatic voice is strong in her novels. Her characters are complex and well-developed; conflict is sharply defined; dialogue is crisp, revealing, and concise; climactic scenes are often handled through dialogue. This essay will identify examples of some of these and other dramatic characteristics in her novels, and will speculate on their transferability to the stage. What is characteristic of Morrison's dramatic voice and how might it sound in the theatre?

Morrison is an engaging storyteller with an instinct for the significant human action. A dramatist must be a good storyteller who knows precisely where to begin her tale so that the precious onstage time is used effectively. Morrison always begins her narrative with an arresting event: the presentation (casual in its tone) of a child having her father's baby (*The Bluest Eye*); an insurance agent attempting to fly off a roof (*Song of Solomon*); Shadrack announcing National Suicide Day (*Sula*); or a sailor jumping ship and braving a treacherous overtow that sweeps him out to sea (*Tar Baby*). In each novel, Morrison immediately plunges the reader into the midst of tangled lives made complex by their personal histories and made interesting by their mystery. Each life skirts the edge of madness born of human will and eccentricity. Morrison has an eye for the fantastic in human behavior, that which seems eccentric only because of the telling but which is, in fact, quite familiar and even normal. The Shadracks, Pecolas, and Milkmans are all too familiar in the lore of black folk culture; only in the objectification or transformation into word do they become somehow "strange." Morrison has the instinct of the dramatist for selecting and heightening that which is hidden and ignored in human experience, but which bears the imprint of authenticity and truth.

The centrality of the storytelling instinct, however, must not obscure the importance of character in a dramatic text. As the visible enactors of the play's action, character is not only "the most interesting phenomenon anywhere,"[3] but drives the plot in many of the theatre's greatest works. That "complex of intellectual, emotional and nervous habit" that defines character,[4] engages the audience as it reveals itself through the play's action. Morrison, as novelist, presents a pastiche of characters fascinating enough in their own right, but whose traits are bound to their individual and collective histories. There is, for example, Milkman of *Song of Solomon* whose search for his father's gold leads him on a unique journey through self where he learns the meaning of his name and finally liberates himself from the bondage of ignorance and materialism. At each turn in his adventure, secrets about himself and his family surface, charting his growth into maturity. Guitar grows in another direction, into the fanatical obsessions of the Seven Days whose madness has the cold, rational logic of Old Testament morality. Guitar's tenderness is distorted by the hard edge of anger and revenge. Milkman and Guitar speak for themselves. Morrison does not "feminize" them—they neither speak her sentiments nor her biases. She presents her characters, especially her male characters, in all their contradictions—a necessary attribute of a good dramatist.

Morrison exhibits a profound grasp of masculine characters, and the society and rituals they create. She is observant and selects, in descriptive narrative, only those details that help to create the fictional setting. One of her most impressive moments occurs in *The Bluest Eye* when Cholly Breedlove seeks out the father who abandoned him before birth. He finds him in Macon, Georgia.

> At the end of the alley he could see men clustered like grapes. One large whooping voice spiraled over the heads of the bended forms. The kneeling forms, the leaning forms, all intent on one ground spot. As he came closer, he inhaled a rife and stimulating man smell. The men were gathered, just as the man in the pool hall had said, for and about dice and money. Each figure was decorated some way with the slight pieces of green. Some of them had separated their money, folded the bills around their fingers, clenched the fingers into fists, so the neat ends of the money stuck out in a blend of daintiness and violence. Others had stacked their bills, creased them down the middle, and held the wad as though they were about to deal cards. Still others had left their money in loosely crumpled balls. One man had money sticking out from under his cap. Another stroked his bills with a thumb and forefinger. . . . Then with a whoop the cubes flew from his hands to a chorus of amazements and disappointments. Then the thrower scooped up money, and someone shouted, "Take it and crawl, you water dog, you, the best I know." There was laughter, and a noticeable release of tension, during which some men exchanged money.[5]

This passage could easily be written as stage directions. Enough physical detail is given to visualize the scene and to stimulate actors to create appropriate characters. That it is a scene to which women are rarely privy is testimony to Morrison's imagination.

With the scene set, she then casts the young Cholly Breedlove and his long lost father in bas relief against this human background. The father's rejection of Cholly, without ever recognizing his son, is all the more dramatic when framed by that most inclusive of black male rituals (the dice game). The aborted encounter traumatizes the young boy and as he strains to "stop the fall of water from his eyes . . . his bowels suddenly opened up, and before he could realize what he knew, liquid stools were running down his legs. At the mouth of the alley where his father was, on an orange crate in the sun, on a street full of grown men and women, he had soiled himself like a baby."[6]

The reader/audience already knows that this same Cholly will, in several years, come to resent his own children and will repeat the cycle in another form by raping his daughter. At this point, however, Morrison is slowly piecing together the jigsaw puzzle of his character, revealing the face behind the mask of fury and anger that eventually devastates his family.

Then in a very moving passage she draws on the nature of black music to chart the path to Cholly's "freedom"—a freedom that allows him to be the damaged, selfish character who can violate his own daughter.

> The pieces of Cholly's life could become coherent only in the head of a musician. Only those who talk their talk through the gold of curved metal, or in the touch of black-and-white rectangles and taut skins and strings echoing from wooden corridors, could give true form to his life. Only they would know how to connect the heart of a red watermelon to the asafetida bag to the muscadine to the flashlight on his behind to the fists of money to the lemonade in a Mason jar to a man called Blue and come up with what all of that meant in joy, in pain, in anger, in love, and give it its final and pervading ache of freedom. Only a musician could sense, know, without even knowing that he knew, that Cholly was free. Dangerously free. Free to feel whatever he felt—fear, guilt, shame, love, grief, pity. Free to be tender or violent, to whistle or weep. . . . Free to take a woman's insults, for his body had already conquered hers. Free even to knock her in the head, for he had already cradled that head in his arms. Free to be gentle when she was sick, or mop her floor, for she knew what and where his maleness was. . . . In those days, Cholly was truly free. . . . He was alone with his own perceptions and appetites, and they alone interested him.[7]

Morrison's ability to step out of her own gender into the complex of attitudes, experiences, and rituals of another gender is fundamental to the creation of characters who are well-defined, complex, and engaging.

She is equally adept at shaping female characters who speak with distinct voices. The best examples occur in *Sula,* her only novel built around the friendship of two women, Sula and Nel. Despite their shared girlhood and love for each other, these friends make separate and very different compromises with life, decisions that lead eventually to the breakup of their relationship. Early in the novel, Morrison creates a common context for her two major characters in "the delirium of their noon dreams,"[8] sketching the caste that they share and that provides the foundation for their friendship.

> So when they met, first in those chocolate halls and next through the ropes of the swing, they felt the ease and comfort of old friends. Because each had discovered years before that they were neither white nor male, and that all freedom and triumph was forbidden to them, they had set about creating something else to be. Their meeting was fortunate, for it let them use each other to grow on. Daughters of distant mothers and in-

comprehensible fathers (Sula's because he was dead; Nel's because he wasn't), they found in each other's eyes the intimacy they were looking for.[9]

However close they are, Morrison develops in Sula and Nel quite separate adult personalities that drive their personal choices. Forged out of the "throbbing disorder"[10] of her home life, Sula's independent nature propels her out of the little town of Medallion. Nel, on the other hand, "had no aggression. Her parents had succeeded in rubbing down to a dull glow any sparkle or splutter she had."[11] And so she marries and becomes a complement to Jude, her husband. Only with each other do the women's thoughts and personalities expand.

Morrison successfully mines the natural ore of human experience, creating believable characters who challenge ordinary notions about human behavior and who are shaped as much by their own mysterious psyches as by circumstances. Her characters' raison d'etre is revealed most often through poignant descriptive passages. In the theatre, of course, these passages may be incorporated into dialogue, but are more likely to become stage directions, descriptions of character analysis and motivation left to the final interpretation of the performer and director. Thus, the medium of theatre adds another element to the equation of character development, the living human being in the form of the actor who is perhaps the final, most complex laboratory for the artistic imagination. Although Morrison is not alarmed that she must relinquish total control over character to the collaborative process of theatre, she is keenly aware of the challenge. In a 1986 interview, she commented that it has "a quality of excitement that charges you, keeps you alert. But at the same time, having to relinquish, abandon, give up all the things one worked so hard on, the mood . . . to relinquish that has a certain tension."[12] Crossing over to the theatre means, for example, that the eloquent passage describing Cholly Breedlove's "liberation" might be expressed onstage by a piece of music whose dissonant strains pick up earlier themes associated with Cholly's experiences or may become simply part of the actor's preparation for the role. The portraits of Nel and Sula may become psychological motivation for actors to create visually what the dramatic text merely suggests. Unlike the novelist, the playwright must relinquish control after supplying the foundation and framework for characters that are finally shaped and presented by live performers.

One of Morrison's most valuable dramatic assets is the richness and scope of her vision. It is also one of her most challenging characteristics to transform into theatre production. The black people who form her subject matter live on the periphery of large, productive towns and are marginal to the lives of white people. Yet Morrison's focus on their lives reveals a tapestry of attitudes, beliefs, delusions, and fears that tie them to a fertile and sometimes confusing past. In each novel, retrospective (character's memory and perspective) provides more than exposition, and is often deliberately withheld in order to create mystery and suspense which slowly build the tension in the story or plot line. Thus the past is given a crucial role to play—context and motivation for action in present time. The character's actions cannot be fully comprehended without it. This literary choice is more than a stylistic preference; it is integral to Morrison's depiction of the black people in her novels. The past is ever-present as folklore and attitudes perpetuated by the community and as scars on the mind and spirit.

Memory becomes the means of recapturing personal and social history as well as a pivotal factor in the character's course of action. For example, in *Tar Baby*, Son's recollection of his eight homeless years begins to explain his eccentric behavior early in the novel and sets him on a course that climaxes in his love affair with Jadine. In *Song of Solomon* Milkman travels "down home" to discover the secrets of his family and himself, a journey that is also a trip backwards in time—for the people he finds in Danville and Shalimar (the backwoods of Virginia) are indeed frozen in time. They recount the stories he has come to hear as if they had happened yesterday. Thus the past exists permanently in the present, in the minds of these people.

The chapter headings in *Sula* suggest that it simply moves chronologically from 1919 to 1965. Memory, however, plays an important role even here. The people of Medallion keep alive, through attitude and behavior, the bizarre history of Sula's family and the town. Shadrack, Sula, and Nel, are bound together by their memory of and silence about the circumstances of Chicken Little's death. It is this secret, harbored and interpreted by each according to his or her needs, that rushes in at the end of the novel to clarify the character of each as well as the real nature of their connection. The last chapter of the novel moves fluidly from Nel's memories of Chicken Little's death and Sula's funeral to Shadrack's memories as it brings into sharp focus the final revelations: the nature and meaning of Sula for Nel, Shadrack and the people of Medallion.

In *The Bluest Eye*, the fact of Pecola's baby and its origin is simply and quickly told in one page near the beginning of the novel. "There is really nothing more to say—except why," states the narrative voice at the end of this passage. "But since why is difficult to handle, one must take refuge in how."[13] Much of the novel is a retrospective justified by the question "How" and the implied query "Why" Cholly Breedlove would impregnate Pecola, his daughter. Told through the voices and perspectives of children much of the time, the story moves forward until it is "interrupted" by two short chapters that reveal the personal histories of Pecola's mother and father, Pauline and Cholly Breedlove. With Morrison's swift narrative strokes, the chapter on Cholly climaxes with his rape of Pecola—the various details of his troubled life and soured relationship with Pauline shrouding from him the real nature of his horrible act.

The creative use of memory is integral to Morrison's work and will surely play a significant role in any dramas that she writes. How one translates this characteristic to the stage is another matter. Realism is not a likely option—a chronological depiction of daily reality or sequential plot development, even with occasional flashbacks, would be cumbersome and would fail to convey the total integration of the past and present which is so critical to Morrison's vision. A theatrical form or style that allows for a fluid use of memory and time and expresses subjective perspective will come much closer to capturing the unique qualities of her writing.

Thus, it is not surprising that Morrison's first produced play, *Dreaming Emmett*, uses a dream metaphor—a form that allows the distortion of time as well as bizarre acts which carry their own peculiar rationality. It is also understandable why her play would focus on the lynching of Emmett Till, or rather the meaning attached to that historical event. Emmett Till was a 14 year old black youth from Chicago who was lynched in Mississippi (1955) after whistling at a white woman. The men accused of his murder were found not guilty. The incident received national publicity. An all-too-typical case, it has become permanently etched in the memory of blacks who lived through that period, and a classic example of the brutality and oppression directed at the black community. The lynching of black men is ever present as fact or threat in Morrison's novels. "Everybody wants the life of a black man,"[14] states Guitar. The death of Milkman's grandfather at the hands of white men is testimony to that assertion. Sula repeats Guitar's idea in her ironic comment to Jude.

> I mean everything in the world loves you. White men love you. They spend so much time worrying about your penis they forget their own. The only thing they want to do is cut off a nigger's privates. And if that ain't love and respect I don't know what it is. And white women? They chase you all to every corner of the earth, feel for you under every bed. I knew a white woman wouldn't leave the house after 6 o'clock for fear one of you would snatch her. Now ain't that love? They think rape soon's they see you, and if they don't get the rape they looking for, they scream it anyway just so the search won't be in vain. . . .[15]

The murder of Emmett Till possesses the historicity that Morrison requires. It is at once a poignant metaphor for the history of black-white relationships and a profoundly disturbing historical moment in the national consciousness. It is, for Morrison, the perfect event to connect the imperatives of her vision with the collective memory of her audience and to present that awareness in the public medium of theatre. The dream format allows Morrison's unbridled imagination full play. The young black man dreams his revenge on his murderers only to have his creation challenged by a woman of the 1980s who emerges from the audience. The characters on trial appear in elaborate masks that are stripped off only to reveal more layers hiding the real face. Although some critics claimed that the play featured two different styles, the choice of a kind of surrealism, projecting the subconscious onstage has the potential to capture for the theatre some of Morrison's finest literary qualities.

Finally, however, characters onstage must speak. Dialogue is the primary means of revealing character and moving the drama, regardless of theatrical style. The dialogue in Morrison's novels reveals her to be a master with confident control of language. She has a sharp ear for the nuances of human utterance. Her description of the Maginot Line's laugh in *The Bluest Eye* would be welcome notes for any actor playing the role:

> The Maginot Line put a fat hand on one of the folds of her stomach and laughed. At first just a deep humming with her mouth closed, then a larger, warmer sound. Laughter at once beautiful and frightening. She let her head tilt sideways, closed her eyes, and shook her massive trunk, letting the laughter fall like a wash of red leaves all around us. Scraps and curls of the laughter followed us as we ran.[16]

Note her description of adult conversation as heard by Frieda and Claudia, the young narrators of *The Bluest Eye*.

> Their conversation is like a gently wicked dance: sound meets sound, curtsies, shimmies, and retires. Another sound enters but is upstaged by still another; the two circle each other and stop. Sometimes their words move in lofty spirals; other times they take strident leaps, and all of it is punctuated with warm-pulsed laughter—like the throb of a heart made of jelly. The edge, the curl, the thrust of their emotions is always clear to Frieda and me. We do not, cannot, know the meanings of all their words, for we are nine and ten years old. So we watch their faces, their hands, their feet, and listen for truth in timbre.[17]

Actors train for many years to develop as accurate a sense for the messages communicated by nonverbal aspects of speech—the rise and fall of the human voice, the punctuation of grunt and laughter, tone and timbre, facial expression and gesture.

Morrison is equally capable of reproducing those sounds in actual dialogue. Again, through the ears of a child, the young Cholly, the reader hears the implied lilt and rhythm in the speech and idiom of the adults in *The Bluest Eye* as they discuss Aunt Jimmy's death.

> "What'd she die from?"
> "Essie's pie."
> "Don't say?"
> "Uh-huh. She was doing fine, I saw her the very day before. Said she wanted me to bring her some black thread to patch some things for the boy. I should of known just from her wanting black thread that was a sign."
> "Sure was."
> . . .
>
> "Well, I had no more got my clothes on when Sally bust in the door hollering about how Cholly here had been over to Miss Alice saying she

was dead. You could have knocked me over, I tell you."
"Guess Essie feels mighty bad."
"Oh, Lord, yes. But I told her the Lord giveth and the Lord taketh away."
. . .

"Did she leave anything?"
"Not even a pocket handkerchief. The house belongs to some white folks in Clarksville."
"Oh, yeah? I thought she owned it."
"May have at one time. But not no more. I hear the insurance folks been down talking to her brother."
"How much do it come to?"
"Eighty-five dollars, I hear."
"That all?"
"Can she get in the ground on that?"
"Don't see how."
. . .

"Jimmy's people may all have to chip in. That undertaker that lays out black folks ain't none too cheap."
"Seems a shame. She been paying on that insurance all her life."
"Don't I know?"[18]

The conversation pokes almost irreverently at Aunt Jimmy's private matters while lovingly mourning her death. The text itself implies the rise and fall of the women's voices and the nuances of their dialogue. The tone of their speech suggests the ritual of the wake and provides a muted prelude to the joy of the funeral banquet that follows.

Morrison not only knows the human vocal instrument but creates with painstaking precision the dialect of her characters. Although the previous passage offers some examples, the following excerpt from one of Pauline Breedlove's monologues about her early life with Cholly captures fully the syntax and rhythms of a black dialect.

"The onliest time I be happy seem like was when I was in the picture show. Every time I got, I went. I'd go early, before the show started. They'd cut off the lights, and everything be black. Then the screen would light up, and I'd move right on in them pictures. White men taking such good care of they women, and they all dressed up in big clean houses with the bathtubs right in the same room with the toilet. Them pictures gave me a lot of pleasure, but it made coming home hard, and looking at Cholly hard. I don't know. I 'member one time I went to see Clark Gable and Jean Harlow. I fixed my hair up like I'd seen hers on a magazine. A part on the side, with one little curl on my forehead. It looked just like her. Well, almost just like. Anyway, I sat in that show with my hair done up that way and had a good time. I thought I'd see it through to the end again, and I got up to get me some candy. I was sitting back in my seat, and I taken a big bite of that candy, and it pulled a tooth right out of my mouth. I could of cried. I had good teeth, not a rotten one in my head. I don't believe I ever

did get over that. There I was, five months pregnant, trying to look like
Jean Harlow, and a front tooth gone.[19]

As Pauline muses about her life, its bittersweet qualities emerge effectively
through her speech, laced with the humor and pathos characteristic of
black folk culture.

Morrison uses the monologue very effectively in *Song of Solomon.*
Lena's shocking speech to Milkman, characterizing him as a "sad, pitiful,
stupid, selfish, hateful man,"[20] is a fitting climax to Part 1 by both subject
matter and placement. It occurs shortly after Milkman's perceptions of
himself, Pilate and Macon, his father, have been shaken. He has felt the
shame of being arrested, of being caught "like a kid on a Halloween trick-
or-treat prank [stealing Pilate's sack] rather than a grown man making a
hit."[21] He has seen his father and Pilate assume accommodating postures
before the policemen. But more importantly, he has stolen from the woman
who had saved his life, and this same woman had demeaned herself in
order to save him from punishment. When Lena slaps him physically and
verbally, Milkman and the reader / audience have been carefully prepared.

Morrison knows that there are moments that must be communicated
through the speech of characters, when even her beautifully written
narrative will not suffice. Of all of her novels, *Sula* is most like a play as the
story is frequently moved through dialogue and the narrative often
restricted to moments of silence. The "scene" in which Sula and Nel meet
after ten years apart reveals changes that have occurred in these women
during their separation while it advances the story line. It could easily be
presented onstage in its present form.

> "Hey, girl . . ." [Sula]
> "Hey yourself. Come on in here." [Nel]
> "How you doin'.'" Sula moved a pile of ironed diapers from a chair and
> sat down.
> "Oh, I ain't strangled nobody yet so I guess I'm allright."
> "Well, if you change your mind call me."
> . . .
>
> "Want some cool tea?"
> "Mmmm. Lots of ice, I'm burning up."
> "Iceman don't come yet, but it's good and cold."
> . . .
>
> Nel bent to open the icebox.
> "You puttin' it on Nel. Jude must be wore out."
> "*Jude* must be wore out? You don't care nothin' 'bout my back, do you?"
> "Is that where it's at, in your back?"
> "Hah! Jude thinks its everywhere."
> "He's right, it is everywhere . . . Remember John L.? when Shirley said he
> got her down by the well and tried to stick it in her hip?" Nel giggled at the
> remembrance of that teen-time tale. "She should have been grateful. Have
> you seen her since you been back?"

"Mmm. Like a ox."

"That was one dumb nigger, John L."

"Maybe. Maybe he was just sanitary."

"Sanitary?"

"Well. Think about it. Suppose Shirley was all splayed out in front of you? Wouldn't you go for the hipbone instead?"

Nel lowered her head onto crossed arms while tears of laughter dripped into the warm diapers. Laughter that weakened her knees pressed her bladder into action. Her rapid soprano and Sula's dark sleepy chuckle made a duet that frightened the cat and made the children run in from the backyard. . .[22]

By the end of this "scene," the reader/audience knows that the qualities exhibited by Nel and Sula as girls have become more pronounced and have made them into very different people. Sula is more independent and critical of the town (and the conventional) as ever, while Nel has become a full member of the Medallion "tribe." Only their friendship and memory of shared secrets modify their sharp differences and allow them to reestablish their relationship almost immediately. Morrison consciously adopts a casual tone in what could easily be written as a tear-filled, sentimental scene of reunion. The subtext (the possibility that they will be unable to pick up where they left off) creates an almost unbearable dramatic tension that engages the reader/audience, and that is relieved only by their shared laughter at the "teen-time tale."

Toni Morrison has many literary gifts to offer the theatre. Her instinct for storytelling, her free-standing characters, her astute ear for language and observation of human gesture are critical qualities for the extraordinary dramatist. Even more important, however, is her focus on the historical and psychological complexities in the lives of "ordinary" black women and men. The richness of language and perception that she brings to this subject matter should be brought to the stage so that the theatre itself may learn from her dramatic voice.

Notes

1. *Dreaming Emmett* was commissioned by the New York State Writers Institute of the State University of New York. Toni Morrison has been appointed to the Schweitzer Chair at SUNY Albany.

2. Robert Meiksins, "Toni Morrison & Gilbert Moses: A Collaboration," *Play by Play* [Capital Rep Newsletter] 1, no. 3 (December 1985–January 1986): 1.

3. Lajos Agri, *The Art of Dramatic Writing* (New York: Simon and Schuster, 1946), 90.

4. Statement attributed to William Archer, author of *Playmaking, A Manual of Craftsmanship*, in Agri, *Art of Dramatic Writing*, 88.

5. Toni Morrison, *The Bluest Eye* (New York: Washington Square Press, 1970), 121–22.

6. Ibid., 124.

7. Ibid., 125–26.

8. Toni Morrison, *Sula* (New York: Alfred A. Knopf, 1974), 51.

9. Ibid., 52.

10. Ibid.

11. Ibid., 83.

12. Mieksins, "Morrison and Moses," 1–2.

13. Morrison, *Bluest Eye*, 9.

14. Toni Morrison, *Song of Solomon* (New York: New American Library, 1977), 224.

15. Morrison, *Sula*, 103.

16. Morrison, *Bluest Eye*, 83.

17. Ibid., 16.

18. Ibid., 111–13.

19. Ibid., 97–98.

20. Morrison, *Song of Solomon*, 218.

21. Ibid., 211.

22. Morrison, *Sula*, 96–97.

Straining to Make Out the Words to the "Lied": The German Reception of Toni Morrison

Anne Adams°

The German republics know black Americans today through a variety of sources, the best of which is probably the intellectual arena. But almost a hundred years ago W. E. B. DuBois moved in the rarefied circles of the German "privileged student rank," regarded as "just a man" of that caste "with whom they were glad to meet and talk about the world; particularly, that part of the world from whence [he] came."[1] DuBois was himself a rarity, whose intellectual background afforded him easy compatibility with the Germans he encountered. Other black American *rarae aves* like Mary Church Terrell[2] and, of course, Paul Robeson[3] have made their mark on the German intellectual scene from the early decades of this century. In Robeson's field of performance, particularly, African Americans have continued to give "color" to German opera, with, for example, certain leading roles now automatically associated with names such as Simon Estes and Jessye Norman. But there was also another Jesse fifty years ago, whose stage was the track field, and who was for most Germans the first real live American Negro they had seen, and who dominated Germans' image of his people for many years,[4] while numbers of his less extraordinary brothers came and went on the German scene.

Indeed, in the years during and after World War II, other blacks—largely jazz artists and baby-making soldiers—brought more Germans into

°This essay was written specifically for this volume and is published here for the first time by permission of the author.

direct contact with African Americans, resulting in increased, though still quite limited, familiarity. In the meantime, in the 1960s and '70s specifically, media coverage of Civil Rights activism presented blacks within the context of U.S. society to the German public. Today, the political, economic, social, and cultural intimacy that characterizes the relationship between the Federal Republic of Germany (FRG) and the United States of America is personified by the omnipresence, for forty years now, of U. S. military hardware and troops there, with their disproportionately high black membership, and by U. S. commercial and media dominance. Clearly the most visible and audible manifestation of this intimacy is the Americanization of the (West) German language. No mere general Anglicization, this phenomenon consists of an increasing invasion (linguistic borrowing) of characteristic U. S. forms, into all areas of life and in all types of communication, oral and written (including graffiti). Two generations of West Germans have lived with U. S. presence, in all racial varieties, as a normal part of their environment in their backyards and front rooms. And so, everything American from Rap Brown to rap music has come, in one form or another, to the consciousness of the average West German, especially those in the cities.

Though unable to compete with Jesse Owens, black GIs, or with "Dynasty"'s Diahann, as sources of acquaintance with the black American community, intellectual creativity in the form of literary works of a few writers have been in circulation in Germany at least since the 1941 publication of *Native Son* in translation. In the middle decades of this century Germans attempting to digest black American literature in translation were given what would become the pantheon, consisting of Wright, Ellison, Hughes, and Baldwin. The Civil Rights writings of Angela Davis, Eldridge Cleaver, Martin Luther King, Jr., and others were added to the literary translations in the seventies. However, a substantial amount of reading of black literature by Germans was, and always has been, done in the original. Because Germans, like most other peoples in the world, learn English as their first foreign language, and because of the increasing hegemony of the U. S. in the world, intellectuals, particularly academics, have been reading black American works in "American" (as U. S. English is called by Europeans). In American Studies programs—found probably at every university in the world—students usually read U.S. literature in the original. In West Germany there is significant academic attention to African Americans in literature and the social sciences. As early as 1959, and for the ensuing ten years, a distinguished black scholar was professor of North American Language and Literature at the Free University of Berlin. Even now, this quality of black literary study continues at the Free University (although now at a reduced level),[5] with Audre Lorde as visiting professor in 1984, and other black feminist literature scholars since then.

In the 1980s black women writers are appearing not only in university seminars, in "American," they are—the novelists among them, at least—

also in bookstores (and, through the help of Steven Spielberg, in the movies), in German translation. Beyond the pantheon of the four male writers mentioned above, German readers are now exposed to black women writers such as Gayle Jones,[6] Ntozake Shange,[7] Paule Marshall,[8] Maya Angelou,[9] Alice Walker,[10] and obviously, in view of the present article, Toni Morrison. In addition to those from the U. S., continental African women novelists like Buchi Emecheta,[11] and Mariama Bâ.[12] In terms of volume(s), however, among these authors, Morrison, whose entire oeuvre has been published in German, has the greatest circulation in that market. (By coincidence of timing, the film "Die Farbe Lila" (*The Color Purple*) was just opening in West German cinemas at the time of this writing, which fact will change book circulation figures). With a total of 188,000 copies of her four novels in print, Toni Morrison is the most thoroughly read, studied, and critiqued black woman writer among German reading audiences.[13]

The first three books, *The Bluest Eye*, *Sula*, and *Song of Solomon*, were all published in German within a year of each other between 1979 and 1980 (though in different chronological order) by the Hamburg-based house of Rowohlt Verlag. *Tar Baby* followed in 1982, just after its publication at home. Rowohlt's *Neue Frau* [New Woman] paperback series, in which Morrison was its first black author, includes such feminist writers as Simone de Beauvoir, Kate Chopin, Doris Lessing, Margaret Mead, Judy Chicago, and Colette, as well as most of the black women mentioned above. Through this series a readership had been already cultivated that was receptive to Morrison's work.

Doubtless, promotion within a women-focused series risks "ghetto-izing" the novels and the novelist into women's, or feminist, literature, which is not appropriate for all the Morrison books. On the other hand, given the all-male exposure to which the German reading public was accustomed for black American literature, the necessity to exploit an audience for Morrison among readers already enthusiastically reading fiction and nonfiction written by women justifies the marketing of the Morrison works in the *Neue Frau* series. In fact, in the past 20 years, since international media coverage of U. S. blacks has focused on the social and political issues and events around race relations, the Afro-American works published and read in German have been almost exclusively the socio-political writings of the 1970s. The editor of Rowohlt's *Neue Frau* series attributes initial slow sales of the hardcover German editions of the Morrison novels to "the public's fatigue with the Black Movement writing of the '70s."[14] She acknowledges the frustrating experience that promotion of the several black women writers' novels in Germany, though embraced by German feminists, still suffers under the residual effects of audience ennui that is based in an assumption of having "already heard what the Black writer has to say."[15] But for the Morrison project, the combination of a two-week promotional tour by the author in 1982, following the publication of the German edition *Tar Baby*, and the issuing of the books in paperback brought a vindicating increase in interest and sales.

From the scholarly attention given to Morrison's writings and to Morrison the writer, and from mass-market reviewers' assessments of the novels, we get the two formal voices of critical reception to her work. Within the German-language media community of the FRG, Switzerland, and Austria, some twenty-five studies including books, articles, doctoral dissertations, interviews, newspaper and magazine reviews, found for the present essay, are devoted wholly or in part to Toni Morrison's work. As can be expected, the quality of the criticism ranges from enlightened insightful interpretation to uninformed racist fabrication. Appropriately, the academic studies are based on the original English texts. On the other hand, the reviewers critique (and the public reads) the German translations, which themselves vary from competent to inadequate. As I will discuss below, Morrison's language, with all it encompasses, is difficult to accommodate in German. Because of the varying levels of acquaintance with the cultural context of Morrison's work, newspaper reviewers see the novels within the general framework of American literature, while the academic/scholarly studies treat the works within the Afro-American literary tradition and/or within the framework of women's literature, as components of the large mosaic of U. S. narrative fiction.

In the analyses of the form and content of the Morrison novels the studies basically cover the major theme, motifs, and structural devices that elucidate the social, cultural, historical, and political dimensions of the Afro-American experience. Absent is any significant attention to details of literary artistry that would extend the discussion beyond considerations merely of the black experience to an examination of underlying levels of poetic discourse that distinguish Morrison's work. The eight scholarly essays/studies examined here include five that treat the Morrison oeuvre as a whole on the basis of broad topics, and three that discuss more narrowly delimited topics in one or two novels. The single novel that receives the specialized attention in all three cases is *Song of Solomon*.

"Die Black Community," "die *Black community*," "die schwarze community," "die schwarze Gemeinde": are four variants for naming this phenomenon discussed in the German studies. Ranging from the nearly English form void of any markings to indicate a foreign phrase, to the German translation of the phrase, these variants offer an example of the state of flux, within German discourse, of terminology for U. S. cultural phenomena in general, and for Afro-American cultural phenomena in particular. But this very fluctuation, this means of terminology, also demonstrates the fact that the concept "Black community" is acquiring independent status in German academic discourse; it refers to a phenomenon for which the German phrase is not an adequate denotation. Whether it is the borrowed English phrase, italicized as a foreign expression; the blend of the German adjective with the English noun; or the literal German equivalent—the prevalence of "Black community" in one variant or another is an indication of its centrality in the critical approaches to Morrison's work. In each of the essays that use the referent, the discussion of the literature at hand is prefaced with an explication of the phenomenon of the "Black community." These explications reveal interesting differences in usage and conception of the phenomenon. For example, Klaus Ensslen, in his book that surveys Afro-American literature *Einführung in die schwarzamerikanische Literatur* [Introduction to Afro-American literature] defines the origins of the concept in the following manner: "Out of the confinements of the ghetto . . . evolved in the '60s the positive self-image of the culture-bearing Black community, casting off its [previous] attitude of self-renunciation . . . Black community is no longer understood as just common suffering but as an alternative existence with superior values."[16] Malwine Blunck, in a doctoral dissertation on Morrison, introduces the term early on in presenting Morrison's cultural background as it is reflected in her novels: ". . . in *Sula* and *Song of Solomon* the settings are fictionalized models of the typical Ohio small town with an established Black community which—clearly separated from the Whites—developed a life of its own."[17] A third writer, Anne Koenen, whose 1980 interview with Morrison appears in the anthology *History and Tradition in Afro-American Culture*, picks up on Morrison's reference to Black community (in the context of Sula's behavior), but with noteworthy semantic differences:

> Morrison: [Sula's putting her grandmother away is] more unforgivable than anything else she does, because it suggests a lack of her sense of community. Critics devoted to the Western heroic tradition—the individual alone and triumphant—see Sula as a survivor. In the Black community she is lost.
> Koenen: I especially like your description of *communities*. They give me a very good idea what it is like living in such a *neighborhood*, and it reminds me a little bit of the *neighborhood* I lived in as a child, where people used to sit in front of their houses in the evenings (my italics).[18]

In her 1985 book on four black women authors, Koenen's language suggests she has gained greater understanding of "Black community" when she discusses women writers within "the Black community" or socio-psychological issues of that community as addressed in women writers' works. "[Morrison] makes it clear that Black community is not an invention of political movements of the '60s, even though its earlier collectively understood presence has been replaced by conscious effort. The description of the Black community as presented by Morrison makes precise and clearly recognizable the picture of a characteristic common Black culture."[19] Nevertheless, whether defined on the basis of its recently articulated rhetorical character or on the basis of its socio-politico-cultural character, "Black community" has unfortunately become objectified in the German criticism of Morrison's (as well as other recent writers) work.

While there is general acknowledgement in the German criticism that Morrison's three U.S.-situated novels make little or no direct mention of white society, nevertheless, there is generally some reference to white society as the backdrop upon which the black community is to be seen in relief. Obviously this is sometimes appropriate, when, for example, Guitar is discussed. But when Utelinde Wedertz-Furtado, in "Historical Dimensions of Toni Morrison's *Song of Solomon*," moves from Guitar's "solution to black-white relationships" to an analysis of other characters in that novel, she continues to regard those characters and their intrafamilial relationships as "patterns of behavior within the black community which are ultimately a consequence of and reaction to the surrounding white society."[20] Wedertz-Furtado states further that Morrison, "who in her previous novels always chose female black protagonists, elaborates on the treatment of black women within their community in her portrayal of Milkman's mother Ruth and his older sisters Magdalene and First Corinthians."[21] Or, about Macon Dead, Wedertz-Furtado attributes his disposition at home to the same external cause that governs his relations with his tenants: "Having achieved a considerable amount of material success, holding an outwardly comfortable middle-class position, Macon maintains and increases his status by exploiting the poorer blacks who depend upon him. This shows him to be a classic example of the oppressed adopting the means of the oppressor. The prevalent atmosphere in his house is one of hatred, criticism, and bullying, nipping in the bud any sign of real life."[22] Even Hagar's madness resulting from Milkman's rejection of her is attributed to her realization that she isn't beautiful a la white woman in his eyes. But, in fact, the reader sees that Hagar is crazy and trying to kill Milkman long before she arrives at that "revelation." While we cannot ignore the crippling effect that emulation of the white middle-class model and value system has on the Dead family, this reductionist formula for explaining all behavior of Dead family members ignores Morrison's particular analysis of relationships and motivational complexities of individuals—black individuals. But even more disturbing about this reductionist formula is that it necessarily rests on the "pathology" theory of the black community. Black people's behavior is "aberrant" because they are responding to oppression by the white world.

Another example of this interpolation of the white community into studies of Morrison's work appears in an unpublished paper by Rowohlt editor Angela Praesent given at the Free University of Berlin in 1979. Following a sociological overview of the black community, Praesent discusses the three Morrison novels extant at that time on the basis of their central conflicts. Her comment on the implied presence of the white community is introduced appropriately, with reference to *The Bluest Eye*. But she generalizes the point for all three novels. "The conflict with the White environment is, in Morrison, not an outward, actual one; it is at work insofar as it impacts on the characters in crucial experiences, blocks their development or draws out all their potential strength."[23] Praesent's discussion, which is devoted to a comparative analysis of the structures of the three novels, depends partly on an assignment of relative socio-economic class status of the central characters, determined by relative social and economic proximity to the white middle class. Thus, for Praesent, the specter of the white community shapes the black community of Morrison's fiction. An even more obsessive preoccupation with the black-community-as-a-product-of-white-oppression perspective is demonstrated in Klaus Ensslen's brief survey of Morrison's novels in his above-mentioned book. Besides giving a confused chronology (naming *Sula* as the first novel but nevertheless citing correct publication dates for all four novels[24]), Ensslen criticizes, or at least laments, Morrison's failure to achieve, after the first two books, the degree of naturalistic gloom that he regards as the value of Morrison's earlier work: "Morrison has not, in other novels like *Song of Solomon* and *Tar Baby* again achieved the sparely lyrical but socio-psychologically extraordinary penetrating illumination that offers a complete understanding of the wretched existence of the everyday milieu of *The Bluest Eye*.[25] Ensslen therefore dismisses the last two novels for their tendency toward the fantastic and the exotic. Such prescriptive criticism, allowing only naturalism or social realism as the legitimate vehicle for black literary discourse not only misses the form of Morrison's political engagement but also denies her the right to alternative creative forms for examining the questions of the African American experience as part of the larger human experience.

Of the subject matter in Morrison's fiction, obviously "the Black woman" gets a large share of attention from German scholarship, as from any other circles of criticism. Ranging in quantity of treatment from brief overview to booklength study (of Morrison and three other black female novelists), the analyses of Morrison's black women discuss these characters from perspectives of their position within the black community and family, as well as from feminist perspectives of self-realizing human beings. It is unfortunate that, of the essays/monographs that give attention to the women, none includes *Tar Baby* in the discussion, either due to the date of the essay or because of a single-novel topic based on another novel.

The passing mention that Klaus Ensslen makes of the subject of women is in his description of *Sula*, which for him demonstrates that women's relationships with each other, are more important and certainly more enduring than relationships with "men who restlessly drift in and out."[26] A more insightful treatment of the black woman's situation is given by Peter Bruck who, in discussing the motif of flying in *Song of Solomon*, points up the differences in what "flying" means and portends for a man and for a woman, as presented in this novel and in *Sula*. "If mobility, both in a geographical and sexual sense, is seen as a male metaphor, it follows the feminine experience demands an original expression of its own."[27] Bruck cites the case of Sula, the "pariah," and of Pilate the blues singer, as female metaphoric counterparts to flying. But at this point he ignores Pilate's entire characterization as the quintessence of flight in Morrison's use of the metaphor. Although Bruck quotes Milkman's self-revelation at the end of the novel that Pilate "without ever leaving the ground . . . coud fly,"[28] the critic here seems to see Pilate's ability to "fly" only as it contributes to Milkman's enlightenment. But when he discusses Morrison's alternative forms for female flight, for Pilate he sees only the blues-singing. And, what's worse, he only brings Pilate and her blues-singing into female-flight discussion to compare her with Hagar, Ryna, and Corinthians, who, unable to sing the blues, succumb instead to the pain of love.

Malwine Blunck's 1984 doctoral dissertation on Morrison, which covers the first three novels, devotes a section of the discussion on *Sula* to "perspectives on the role of the Black woman." Basing her perspectives on Mary Helen Washington's themes identified in the introduction to *Blackeyed Susans*, Blunck reviews the treatment of those themes (mother-daughter relationships, growing up black and female, black male-female relationships, and the destructive effects of the white beauty standard) in the novels under consideration. She proceeds to discuss the themes of woman-friendship, possessive love, and personal independence in *Sula*, concluding with an interpretation of the character Sula through the symbolism of water. The most engaging part of her discussion here comes in these latter two topics, where she introduces connections between Morrison's ideas and those of writers from other cultures. Acknowledging that Friedrich Nietzsche probably did not have women (God knows, not black women!) in mind in his formulation of the fate of the individual who pursues independence. Blunck applies that Nietzschean formula to Morrison's protagonist.[29] She demonstrates a parallel on this subject also with German novelist Alfred Döblin's *Berlin Alexanderplatz*.[30] Citing Morrison's frequent use of the water motif to refer to Sula, Blunck analyzes the character according to water symbolism, and makes a comparison with water characterization in Chinese philosophy,[31] and in the work of the Rumanian philosopher Mircea Eliade.[32] In going beyond the consideration of Morrison's character as an Afro-American woman specifically, Blunck suggests here some very interesting grounds for further comparative literature research between Morrison and other Western and Eastern thought. The most intensive, though admittedly sociological study of "the Black woman" within the parameters of contemporary black female authors' fiction is Anne Koenen's book *Zeitgenössische Afro-amerikanische Frauenliteratur: Selbstild und Identität bei Toni Morrison, Alice Walker, Toni Cade Bambara und Gayl Jones* [Contemporary Afro-American women's literature: Self-image and identity in Toni Morrison, et al.]. Acknowledging in her introduction, the evils of sociological analysis of black literature, Koenen quotes Morrison's own displeasure with such assessments of her work, expressed in an interview with Koenen:

> I'm always a little disturbed by the sociological evaluations white people
> make of Black literature. Unless they are used as servants of aesthetics. I
> don't think it is possible to discuss a literature without taking into
> consideration what is sociologically or historically accurate, but most of
> the criticism in this country stops here. It's demoralizing for me to be
> required to explain Black life once again for the benefit of white people.
> Or to feel that I have to write about people who are "typically Black."[33]

Koenen, however, proceeds to give a sociological analysis anyway. Her
stated intention, to include some consideration of aesthetic and formal
criteria in her discussion, is disposed of in a brief section on background
material, in which she makes the general point that the metaphors and
imagery in black women writers' work are based on phenomena in nature.
Grounding her analysis in a synthesis of theoretical criteria of black
feminist criticism, incorporating a set of directional questions articulated
by Morrison, and of general feminist criticism, Koenen sets down the intent
and method of her study:

> This approach is legitimized by the oppression of women in patriarchal
> societies and views literature in connection with woman's position in the
> society. Hence arises the necessity for examining literature in the context
> of its economic and social conditions and thus an interdisciplinary
> approach, which, in this case, comprehends the situation of the Black
> woman in the U.S.[34]

Her materialist critical perspective thus announced, Koenen's well-
researched analysis draws on a thorough background of the primary and
secondary sources of Afro-American women's writing, extending from
Our Nig to *Our Mothers' Gardens,* as well as the literature on the sociology
of the Afro-American experience. While positing the search-for-identity
model of black literary analysis as her premise ("the search for identity
stands at the center of Black women's literature"),[35] Koenen actually
demonstrates the more self-determined "process of the development of
positive self-images"[36] in the works of the black women writers. So that,
instead of the "Who-am-I?" perspective, connoted by the search-for-
identity model of analysis, Koenen in fact—unwittingly—applies a "This-
is-who-I-am" perspective through her self-image development model.

Koenen analyzes the complexities of the black woman's experience
according to topics that define, on the one hand, her relations within the
intimate spheres of her life and, on the other hand, internal and external
phenomena that bear upon her life and contribute to her self-definition.
Although Koenen's topics (childhood; the white beauty standard; education and vocation; politics and culture; sexuality; motherhood; relationships with black men, black women, and white women; survivors and
victims) have been established to discuss the works of all four women
novelists she studies, a greater number of the subtopics are centered around
Morrison characters than around those of any other single writer. And,

since Koenen's book was prepared before *Tar Baby* could be incorporated into the analysis, (it is given a few brief mentions) this last text would have provided even more Morrison material for some of the topics. Nevertheless, the greater, more insightful attention given to Morrison over the other three writers is probably due to Koenen's having interviewed her (1980; revised by Morrison, 1983).

Koenen's treatment of Morrison's topics of black female-headed households and black women's relationships with other black women and with black men serve as good examples. In these cases, as in most others, Koenen emphasizes the "self-inventing" of these women as the factor that does or should underlie their characters as whole, surviving human beings. Reviewing first, as she does with all her topics, the sociological literature on the subject, of black female-headed households, in this case the mythology and the reality of the "Black matriarchy," Koenen concentrates on the phenomenon, in *Sula* and *Song of Solomon*, of the family of three generations of women, or, as Morrison says in the interview with Koenen, "a woman producing a woman producing a woman in a kind of non-male environment, and each generation has a different problem."[37] Koenen notes that Eva Peace and Pilate Dead, who both could fill the strong-grandmother stereotype, actually give some new dimensions to the stereotype: they don't manifest the proverbial, cliched love for children, and, with their respective physical deformities—Eva's missing leg, Pilate's missing navel—they both have a mythical aura about them. But the two are different from each other in the emotional quality of their matriarchal character, Koenen notes. "The strength that assures survival for Eva and her children is presented as questionable by Morrison. Eva is a demonstration of survival at any cost, the cost of affection to her daughters, of the capacity to love in general. Eva hasn't . . . survived whole, but is deformed in her personality by the survival struggle."[38] Pilate, on the other hand, Koenen continues, in spite of a similar survival struggle, is capable of generous love, having received the same from loving males, her father and brother, during her childhood.

Beyond the stereotyping of the grandmothers, Koenen analyzes the generational problems mentioned by Morrison above as a progressive degeneration of personalities: the farther down the generations of women in these families go, the weaker their personalities become. This thesis is accompanied by the question: to what does Morrison attribute this generational degeneration? Her analysis demonstrates that the extraordinary power and presence of the matriarchs Eva and Pilate removes any hurdles / struggles / ordeals as tests for their daughters and granddaughters. Thus they have no reason to assert themselves, nor have they, with Eva or Pilate, a model or the necessity to mold themselves according to the traditional role of woman / mother. But of the second and third generations, it is, oddly enough, the daughters who are weaker than the granddaughters. Hannah Peace and Reba Dead, Koenen points out, live entirely from and for their sexuality. While Hannah is depicted as exercising a strangely beneficent influence on the men she makes love to and, by extension, on their wives, Reba is portrayed as essentially vacuous.[39] By comparison, the third generation, Sula and Hagar, although different from each other in the attention they receive in the family, grow up without any restrictions, and chart their own devastating courses, particularly in their relationships with lovers. Koenen's conclusion about the factors that lead to this generational degeneration is that, rather than being a function of the female-based household per se, it is due to the individual characters of the women Morrison draws.

Among the several aspects of women-friendships that Koenen takes up, her discussion of the symbolic difference between Sula and Nel is the most engaging. Despite Morrison's labeling of Sula as "evil," Koenen contends that not only are the author's sympathies with Sula, but that clearly Morrison's own position on the question of identity is reflected through her. The antipathy toward the Nels of the world, spiders afraid of the free fall which "required—demanded—invention"[40] and "surrender to the downward flight"[41]—this antipathy Koenen reads as a repudiation, on Morrison's part, of conventionality, particularly in the woman's traditional, oppressed, role. Holding such role-bound women partially responsible for remaining in this condition, Morrison expresses her impatience with those who won't even make the attempt to free themselves. But Koenen notes, as in Sula's case, Morrison shows that the effort is not necessarily rewarded; she gives no facile solution.

Similarly, regarding the pessimistic outlook on love relationships between women and men, Koenen acknowledges that Morrison offers no resolution. Although the causes can be stated simply enough—the man's desire to be free and unencumbered vs. the woman's desire to hold on to the man—the remedy is not forthcoming in Morrison's stories. Koenen remarks upon Morrison's failure to address the question of whether the man's desire for freedom is not really an expression of fear of attachment, an inability to deal with this issue. Nor does she delve into the reasons for Sula's and Hagar's turn to possessive behavior. Indeed, Koenen suggests that the women's feelings appear to be "biologically conditioned."[42]

The accusation against Morrison of biological determinism is more openly asserted at the end of Koenen's book where she draws her conclusions about the four authors' perceptions of sex roles and characteristics. She finds that, unlike Alice Walker and Toni Cade Bambara, Morrison holds certain characteristics such as the desire to be free and the aversion to attachment to be male qualities, and the nesting and nurturing behavior to be female qualities, sexually determined rather than socially. Morrison is demanding, however, that these acknowledged female roles and characteristics be accorded new valuation, thereby eradicating the definition of female qualities as inferior. But Koenen's feminist reading does not accept this new valuation as a realistic distinction from female roles under a patriarchal society. How can one tell the difference between those roles embraced by women themselves and imposed by the patriarchy? How do you achieve a new valuation of old phenomena? For Koenen, Morrison's position approaches a renewal of the glorification of the biological role.[43]

Besides the sociological studies of the black community and of the black woman in particular, the folklore/history/culture also receives significant attention in German scholarship on Morrison. While Anne Koenen makes only contextual references to the role of Afro-American cultural heritage in the lives of Morrison's characters, her criticism bears noting before proceeding to the more concentrated attention of other critics. In her insistence on materialist relevance, Koenen is unable to reconcile Morrison's portraiture of the wellsprings of Afro-American culture with the bases of the contemporary black woman's and man's self-definition. Referring to a thesis common to the work of Morrison and Hurston, Koenen points out that the two writers share the conviction that the black woman's emancipation can be realized only from within the context of black culture.[44] Yet Koenen faults Morrison for presenting an anachronistic black community, nostalgic, dying out, or even "as in *Song of Solomon*—backward, underdeveloped"[45] (referring to the southern communities of Milkman's odyssey). And so the critic demands that the novelist transfer the cultural community to the reality of the big city and contemporary times. (Doubtless, if Koenen had been able to include a more exhaustive treatment of *Tar Baby*, it would have only provided more fuel for her argument on this issue). But in making this demand Koenen is ignoring Morrison's avowed purpose in reviving the history through the lore of black folk as the wellspring of the culture. If the critic's reading cannot yield a transposition of the spirit of the lore—containing the values, standards, perspectives, motivations of the Afro-American community— to any community of African Americans in other quadrants of space and time, then she has not listened closely to what Morrison is talking about.

One critic who focuses on the subject of Morrison's development of Afro-American folk heritage and history does indeed appreciate the novelist's motive in the method, taking a position which refutes Koenen's criticism. Using as her point of departure two Morrison essays "Rediscovering Black History" and "The Black Experience: A Slow Walk of Trees (as Grandmother would say). Hopeless (as Grandmother would say)," in her article on history in *Song of Solomon*, Utelinde Wedertz-Furtado refers to Morrison's own articulation of her motives in the "Rediscovering" article:

> There is no need to be nostalgic about "the good old days" because they weren't . . . but to recognize and rescue those qualities of resistance, excellence and integrity that were so much a part of our past and so useful to us and to the generations of blacks now growing up.[46]

With detailed attention to the tableau of historical references incorporated into the novel, the critic delineates the process by which Milkman develops a historical consciousness which reveals his own family's history embedded in his people's history. Besides reconstructing the historical framework of the first part of the novel, Wedertz-Furtado analyzes the central role of Pilate as the embodiment of the history and culture of which Milkman becomes conscious. "Embracing the vital elements of black culture, Pilate keeps alive the past. At the same time she transcends it by her love and will power, not allowing its negative elements to restrict her . . . confronted with a series of test situations during his various encounters with people in the South, Milkman finds that Pilate shares the values of the Southern community. His aunt's instructions . . . become essential for his survival."[47] In Pilate's example for Milkman, Wedertz-Furtado sees a similarity with the instructions of Ellison's grandfather character to the grandson in *Invisible Man* in dealing with white folks and other obstacles in his life. Wedertz-Furtado finds more general concordance between Ellison and Morrison in their treatment and understanding of history and in the universality of the individual's struggle.

Another Milkman-Invisible Man connection is drawn in Walter Gobel's article "Identitat and Mythos in Toni Morrison's '*Song of Solomon*' (Identity and myth in Toni Morrison's *Song of Solomon*).[48] Viewing Morrison's folklore vehicle in this novel and in *Tar Baby* as a retreat into mythic blackness, Gobel classifies it as a third stage in the (mandatory) Afro-American literary search for identity, following the rebellion against white society in *Native Son* and the frustration and ambivalence toward that society in *Invisible Man*. In a slightly patronizing tone, Gobel acknowledges that, in comparison with Wright and Ellison, Morrison's invoking of black-community values and the rejection of those of white society might indicate a sign of growing self-assuredness of black American literature. But, he recognizes that Morrison, in her artistic recasting of black mythology and folklore as a vehicle for self-definition, stands in a tradition that includes Charles Chestnutt, Zora Hurston, Ishmael Reed, and others. Cavalierly grouping African Americans with all other immigrant groups, he poses the question, What good does it do black folks in America to go searching for their roots in the original motherland, when, like all other American immigrants their identity in the 20th century is in America? It might, Gobel allows, conceivably do some good for continental Africans to indulge in mythic blackness; but will it do the job of waking Ellison's invisible men and women out of their hibernation? Or, is it instead, just a retreat from reality? But Gobel's attitude can be perhaps appreciated in the context of his seeming impatience with the "current intensive preoccupation with the past in the search for cultural and historical continuity" as exemplified by "only its most well known literary testament today: Arthur Hailey's (!) *Roots*."[49] One recognizes Dr. Gobel's problem.

With all of the published Morrison studies by Germans concentrating on matters of content, there is relatively little material that gives attention to language and structure. As for language, there is appropriate acknowledgement, in some essays, of the poetic quality of the writing, citing the obvious metaphors. Further discussion of Morrison's Afro-American language follows below in the section on the translations. Regarding structure, the identification of *Song of Solomon* as *Bildungsroman* appears in the articles by Wedertz-Furtado and Peter Bruck (as well as in a book by the U. S. scholar Vanessa White comparing works of Morrison and other Afro-American novelists with novels of two East German writers).[50] The two unpublished studies included here, Angela Praesent's paper and Malwine Blunck's dissertation, devote some attention to structure. The former, which appears to be the earliest West German study on Morrison, attempts to demonstrate that, in the first three Morrison works (to 1979) the primary and secondary characters come from the black middle class (white-influenced), and black lower class (traditonal African-American), respectively. From this Praesent analyzes the narratives to show that "in critical situations the protagonists seek the key to their individual situations and behavior in the emotional history of their forbears."[51] This structural sketch underlies Praesent's conclusion of the regenerative social-psychological value that the old wisdom of the Afro-American culture holds for its contemporary members. As a first brief examination of Morrison by the West German critics community, Praesent's paper, though simplistic in its sketchy analysis of three texts, points in the direction later German critics' would take, as evidenced in the present inventory.

Malwine Blunck's dissertation on Morrison characteristically discusses structure for the three (ante-*Tar Baby*) works she studies. Most interesting is her treatment of the *Song of Solomon* text, which she analyzes as a folktale itself with a mythic hero, referring to classic folktale criteria of Vladimir Propp[52] and mythologic archetypes of Joseph Campbell,[53] Carl Jung,[54] and Otto Rank.[55] Blunck's analysis of the structure, as that of a classic folktale, is based on Propp's thirty-one functions or basic elements described in his *Morphology of the Folktale*, common in the folktales of the most diverse cultural societies and from the remotest of times. As the archetypal mythical hero, Milkman's odyssey is equated to the individuation process described by Jung, involving Pilate as the embodiment of the misunderstood past, herself having passed, according to Jung's prescription, through similar stages as the hero for whom she is the bringer of healing. The possibilities suggested by Blunck's work for comparative literature studies involving Morrison offer particularly fertile research ground for European literary scholarship. Such comparative work would appropriately bring Morrison's novels into contact with those of other world writers of equal caliber.

Newspaper reviews of Morrison's novels in German translation are a mix of sensitive intellectual critique, dangerously superficial and naive social commentary, and hausfrau-baiting exoticism. Although twenty newspaper and magazine reviews and interview articles were found for this essay, the availability of reviews is not consistent for all the novels. There are, for example, none for *Sula*, a situation due in part to the publication history of the translations, discussed below. The reviews available, however, represent a cross-section of daily and weekly papers of relatively broad national circulation in West Germany, including a Swiss and an Austrian paper. They range from the very conservative to the progressive, from metropolitan tabloid daily to national intellectual weekly, and include the West German counterpart in prestige to the *New York Times*. And, from the perceptions as recorded in the reviews and in the interviews, we get a reflection of the substance that the reading public—or that part of it that would be attracted to literature by an American Black female—is given to expect in this literature.

The Rowohlt promotion statement—and therefore some of the reviews and interviews generated by it—calls Toni Morrison one of the most important voices of black America. And so, this mass market public, reading the literary journalists, is therewith introduced to this version of the Voice of (black) America. If the Morrison version of the African American experience is only incompletely accessible to a nonblack untutored American readership, it eludes the West German readership almost altogether. It is not simply that the reviews are mostly negative; nor are they written from an unfamiliarity with Afro-American literature. But, as with other signs of black life in America, the German journalistic community first met Afro-American literature as a literary arm of the 1960s–70s protest movement, and classified this branch of American literature accordingly. Therefore, when a Toni Morrison comes to their attention at the end of the 70s with her literary fist unballed, the journalists have to adjust their focus. Accustomed to looking at black America from within the framework of white America, the German literary journalists have difficulty looking at a full frame of black America. If black America is engaging in literary screaming at white America, the reviewers can hear and comprehend that. But Morrison denies them a white handle to grab hold of; she omits a white passe-partout upon which to mount the black picture; and her black picture shows humane superiority rather than human inferiority. This requires some adjustment for the German reviewers. Not finding the familiar form of protest, they focused on other surface phenomena they could recognize and apply to the social realism literature of the oppressed black community, and missed the new form that the protest takes. Consequently, the reviews of Toni Morrison's works are, at best, affirmation of the exoticism of black people, at worst, affirmation of the pathology of the black community.

Song of Solomon was German readers' introduction to Toni Morrison. Published in hardcover in 1979, the translation was done by Angela Praesent, herself responsible for Rowohlt's publication of this, and subsequently, the other Morrison works. For the most part, the reviewers didn't know what to make of *Song of Solomon*, as some actually expressed in their reviews. But what they did make of it gave a dangerously skewed message to the West German reading public of what this most important voice of black America was saying. The reviews were given titles such as "On the Trail of the Past," "On the Trail of the Family," but also "They Create Their Own Hell," "Hatred of the Family," and even "The Hole in the Tire of the Dodge" (referring to the shootout when Macon pursued Porter for his rent). Such were the attention-grabbing terms in which this new brand of Afro-American fiction was introduced. As the first novel by an Afro-American woman to be published in Germany, it is not surprising that comparative links were drawn between it and previously known black male and white writers, for various reasons. These included the already mentioned black pantheon as well as Eudora Welty and William March. Interestingly, the frequent assertion is that *Song of Solomon* (1979) is a follower of Haley's *Roots* which is referred to consistently as a novel. Since the TV film of *Roots* was aired in West Germany before *Song of Solomon* was published in German (*Solomons Lied*, 1974), the misleading idea that Morrison's novel followed the "wave" begun by Haley's "novel" (this latter described by one critic as a melodramatic trivialization of black history)[56] was perpetuated by reviewers of *Solomons Lied*.

While the genealogy connection with *Roots* seems to be an issue of accord among the reviews, the confrontation with the Afro-American cultural phenomena of *Song of Solomon* triggered quite diverse responses. For example, the review that appeared in the (Swiss) *Neue Zurcher Zeitung* gives a balanced synthesis of plot, structure, and themes, with adequate attention to the function of the historical and folkloric elements. The reviewer praises the book for qualities often sought in vain in bestsellers: concentration on material of which the writer is intimately knowledgeable, the ability to express the universal through the particular, and "the skill with symbolic language to transfer subconscious reality into mythological images." In comparison with the Baldwins and the Wrights of Afro-American literature, Morrison "writes from the consciousness of a vital and life-affirming humanity."[57] The review in the *Deutsche Zeitung* is similarly sensitive, recognizing the integrity of the Afro-American cultural heritage (albeit exotic) and its function in the self-realization of its people. Other reviewers, however, couldn't handle Morrison's cultural presentation. One writer, refuting the publisher's promotion assertion that Morrison's novel sheds "light on a self-contained Black culture," expressed an opinion shared by other reviews, calling the novel structurally jumbled with elements of the supernatural adding to the confusion. For example, Pilate is referred to, in the majority of cases, as a witch or sorceress. Impatient with those fantastic aspects of the novel, this reviewer, in *Die Welt*, finds Morrison's "true talent" in her "realistic depiction of the world of the Black American." He speculates that it is obviously a form of racial self hate that causes Morrison to depict all her character's relations as violent and antagonistic, and that if such a depiction of black life had been written by a white writer, he or she would surely—and justifiably—be charged with racism.[58] For a final example of the pathology view of *Song of Solomon* I offer a brief writeup in a librarians' publication, *Die neue Bucherei* noting that the book "provides glimpses into the Black psyche, whose nature appears strange and threatening to us . . . [The book] seems absolutely important to an understanding of the behavior of Blacks in America."[59] These represent the range of reviews of West Germany's introduction to Toni Morrison, the new "important voice of Black America." Of the eight reviews located for this novel, five are of the type that "couldn't handle" the book. Within a few months after the publication of *Solomons Lied*, Rowohlt brought out *Sehr blaue Augen* [The Bluest Eye], but in paperback and, unlike the former, in the *Neue Frau* series. The reviews were fewer and briefer, all citing the abysmal, violence-ridden lives of blacks. Even so, two of the three available reviews speak of the "charm" of the story as the haunting desire of a little girl for blue eyes. The significance of Morrison's symbol is lost on these reviewers, and doubtless also on the German female readership to whom the reviews are directed. *Sula*, in translation, followed in a few months, in 1980, also in the paperback *Neue Frau* series, marketed with a new printing of *The Bluest Eye*, but without individual promotion.

For the publication of *Teer Baby* [Tar Baby] Rowohlt brought Morrison to Germany for a promotional tour, which generated public appearances and interviews as well as reviews of this fourth book. Nine such articles were located in this research. This time there is greater tolerance in the newspaper reviews for the mythic and magical elements, because they are compatible with the exotic context of the Caribbean setting and its African cultural sources. While the conflicts between white and black are pointed out (one review bearing the title "Story about People of Different Colors," another, "The Butler's Honey-Brown Niece"), only one suggests a conflict among the blacks. That one pits a "primitive, wife-murdering sailor" against an emancipated, white-oriented girl. In all the reviews the point of attraction of the book is its exotic Caribbean atmosphere, complete with sex and intrigue.

In this assessment of the reviews of Toni Morrison's novels in the West German press it is instructive to consider the coverage in the *Frankfurter Allgemeine Zeitung*, the one paper in which reviews for all three promoted novels were found. Relatively conservative, the FAZ is the most widely distributed West German daily, appearing also in 144 foreign countries, and can be considered domestically a counterpart to the *New York Times*. As the first review of a Morrison work to appear in the FAZ, the article on *Song of Solomon* is not only a travesty of the novelist's work but, worse than that, irresponsible journalism. After acknowledging Morrison's poetic language as a discursive form new to Afro-American fiction, the reviewer proceeds to abuse *Song of Solomon*, giving as its content every pathological motif found in all Morrison's novels and inventing some of his own: "*Song of Solomon* is about Blacks who do violence to each other, physical and psychic violence; it's about fathers who rape their daughters who are minors, and girls seduced by their mothers' boyfriends. Women are beaten, mothers let their sons burn, daughters abandon their mothers."[60] After setting up this list of fabrications as the action of *Song of Solomon*, the reviewer concludes that it is blacks themselves who create their own hell. Then, in an attempt to intellectualize, he continues that he doesn't know what a white reader should make of a novel by a black writer, in which the black characters are made responsible for their self-destructive behavior. And so on for two columns. Thus, clearly having not read the novel under review, nor apparently any of the others he has confused with it, the reviewer wrote this damaging diatribe introducing Morrison to Germany's widest readership. The FAZ, in its position of prestigious credibility, is perpetuating the blatantly racist impression of hopeless pathology of Afro-Americans through this shamelessly irresponsible review of the first Morrison work available to German audiences.

The reviews of *The Bluest Eye* and *Tar Baby*, both written by the same person, are only more benign in degree. The description of *The Bluest Eye* is once again an account of the wretched life in the black community with some of the same kinds of violence mentioned above as part of normal everyday life, the fantasy of a child for blue eyes offering a tender diversion from the ugliness of her life. This reviewer's article on *Tar Baby*, informed by biographical facts about the visiting author, gives a summary of Morrison's other three novels in a discussion of her Afrocentric perspective and writing style. But the discussion of *Tar Baby*, after an appropriate plot synopsis and reference to the underlying folktale, ends on a note of doubt about the possibility of reconciliation between such people as the Jadines and the Sons, since each individual is motivated by the vicissitudes of his or her own past. This conclusion might reflect an unavoidable barrier to Europeans to recognize the full dilemma in the conflict between black individuals represented by these two characters.

The good news, though, is really good, and it comes in the two magazine articles that appeared as a result of Morrison's 1982 promotional tour. An interview in West Berlin's biweekly city-life magazine *Zitty* features Morrison's views on the politics in black women's writing. Much of the discussion focuses on Morrison's theme of the challenge, faced by the contemporary black person, to reconcile his or her black past with requirements for pursuing the "good life" in America (particularly as this issue is alluded to at the conclusion of the above-mentioned FAZ review of *Tar Baby*). The interview also addresses Morrison's themes that are not limited to the black experience, such as the dual standard of behavior for men and women, and the critical importance of the individual's integrity in love relationships. The feminist women's magazine *Emma* carried an article co-authored by Anne Koenen and Germany-based American feminist critic Tobe Levin, which focuses on the complexities of Morrison's female images. Acknowledging the importance of mothers and grand-mothers as role models for Morrison's and other black female authors, the article points out the strengths and versatility of the novelists' women characters and the role of women friendships among blacks. In reference to Morrison's statement on the difference between literary characterizations of black women and white women, the article suggests that such strengths as represented in Morrison's black women might be preferable for European women as literary images over the delicate, fragile image that has heretofore characterized them.

In the foregoing we have assessed the reception of Toni Morrison's work on two separate fronts, representing two different levels of West German readers, the academic critics/scholars/university professors, on the one hand, who read the work in the original language, "American," that is Morrison's own text; and, on the other hand, the literary journalistic critics, who mostly read the novels in their German translations. Given the crucial role that Morrison's Black discourse plays in her work, particularly in dialogue, the absence of any attention to this subject in the essays from the academic critics (except for a few misinterpreted references in Blunck's dissertation) is striking. There are acknowledgements of poetic language, metaphors, and the richness of the Afro-American language but no attempts to analyze the discourse itself, at least not so far. When the question of Morrisonian discourse is extended to the German translations of her work, however, it becomes clear that this is a subject of such socio-linguistic complexity that it may be, at this point a topic more appropriate for German scholars of English linguistics than for those engaged in literary criticism.

The translations, done by four different translators (or, in one case, by a pair of translators) vary greatly in quality and fidelity to the original texts. This is not unusual. In spite of such expected variation, however, the common outcome in all the translations reveals what seems to be incompatibility between the black American and German languages. What does this mean: the syntax and the distinct word usage of black discourse seem to defy transferral into the medium of German. Translations of dialects can indeed be rendered successfully, given approximately similar socio-linguistic contexts between language communities, as, for example, with rural speech, uneducated speech, children's speech, proletarian speech, and so forth. But none of these is the issue with regard to Afro-American language, as has been by now convincingly established by U. S. linguists, sociologists, psychologists, educators, jurists, and, most impor-tantly, by writers. Because of its creolized form, Afro-American language presents a German translator with a linguistic phenomenon that exceeds the framework of American English.

This case can be illuminated by a brief comparison with translations of

Afro-American literature in French. Because of the long-standing existence of French creoles, that is, languages with African-based structures and French lexicon, that developed in the French Antilles and are spoken in various forms also in West Africa, these creole languages provide a formal medium for rendering the Afro-American creolized English into French. This has been done with the works of several Afro-American writers, including Morrison, with more satisfactory results than are yielded by the German translations of Morrisons' works.

But of the four Morrison translations the first, *Solomons Lied*, by Angela Praesent, is by far the best in transferring the language of both the author and her characters. Praesent does a skillful job with Morrison's poetic language of invented images, for example, in the description of Macon Dead's stultifying effects on his daughters and wife's personalities, or Guitar's "Wanna fly, you got to give up the shit that weighs you down," or the description "Hagar, killing, ice-pick-wielding Hagar," which is actually perfectly suited to the compounding of attributives in German. Other images, particularly those in which Morrison strings actions together with dramatic effect, such as: "[Macon] dropped [the fork] on the table while his hand was on its way across the bread plate becoming the fist he smashed into [Ruth's] jaw" suffer in the translation, because German syntax cannot accommodate such verb sequences, thus forfeiting the effect. Then there are Morrisonian images and constructions that the translator simply wasn't able to satisfy entirely, such as "buttery complexions" or "Bryn Mawr had done what a . . . liberal education was designed to do: unfit her for . . . useful work" or "[Pilate's] lips moved as she played an orange seed around her mouth" or "[Hagar] toyed sometimes with her unsucked breasts" (translated as "unused breasts"). But these are normal translation matters between English and German or of the translator's creative skill.

It is the characters' dialogue, however, that presents the greatest problems in this as well as the other German translations of the Morrison novels. Locutions that involve the grammar and syntax of Afro-American speech, its word usage, including slang, forms of address, and the use of profane terms whose casualness and frequency mollify their effect to the level of colloquial emphasis—are characteristic features of the oral language that evade graceful transfer into the German language. Angela Praesent's translation, while approaching the original quite closely, comes off in the final analysis as a socially lower version of the standard, rather than a characteristically informal, differently structured language. In other words, the German rendering of the Afro-American oral language forces it into a vertical socio-linguistic valuation scale rather than allowing for a linear variant scale. Praesent, recognizing the validity of the language and at the same time attempting to give the flavor of its informality and nature-based intimacy, was compelled to devise means to accommodate its features. So, rather than attempt an "ungrammatical" German, Praesent simply reduced enunciation, producing the unfortunately unavoidable effect of low-class speech. Other types of locutions, eloquent in the mouths of Pilate ("You all must be the dumbest unhung Negroes on earth"), Macon ("There is probably a potato dish that's supposed to have lumps in it. Mashed ain't the dish."), and Guitar ("You got a life? Live it! Live the motherfuckin' life! Live it!")—wilt in the German. With respect to Guitar's and others' use of profanity, Praesent judiciously gives the German equivalents in some cases, where it is tolerable to German sensibilities, substituting, in other cases (such as the above) milder emphatic terms. Even so, the degree to which profanity and casual sexual references make up part of the male discourse in the German text are an additional feature that contributes to the low-class status effect. Thus, in remaining relatively loyal to the original text, Praesent's *Solomons Lied*, a competent translation informed by her apparent familiarity with and sensitivity for the integrity of Afro-American language as a cultural form, demonstrates the complex problem of translating culture with text.

By comparison with *Song of Solomon*, however, the translations of *The Bluest Eye* and *Sula*, equally laden with the language and cultural institutions of the Afro-American community fall considerably shorter in capturing Morrison's discourse. Unlike Angela Praesent's *Solomons Lied*, *Sehr blaue Augen* and *Sula* read like watered down Germanizations of the originals. Apparently the result of the translator's conscious decision not to attempt to render the language of the author, *The Bluest Eye* reflects Morrison's style least of all, conveying basically the narrative in rather watered-down language, that not only doesn't approximate Morrison's poetic language but also carelessly treats many details that affect meaning or degree of meaning. *Sula*, a somewhat better translation job than *Sehr Blaue Augen* conveys Morrison's style a bit more, particularly in rendering the images. Both of these translations suffer from a lack of the sensitivity to the nuances in dialogue, however, and of socio-cultural phenomena that contribute irony and subtle humor to the narratives: for example, the misidentification of referent between "the churchwomen," in *Sula*, and its translation as "the women who attend church"; the fact that "lightening up the family complexion and thinning out the family features" as Soaphead's West Indian family advocated, in *The Bluest Eye* doesn't mean "watering down the family features"; or the altered meaning of Eva's response to Hannah "you settin' here with your healthy-ass self and ax me did I love you!" when translated to say "you settin' here on your healthy ass and ax me . . ."

The translation of *Tar Baby*, a smaller challenge in dialogue and inner monologue is certainly an adequate job. With the characters' language practically entirely of the standard variety, the quality of translation lies primarily in the imagery of the setting and the mythic phenomena. For me the most interesting single point in this translation is an external extension of a motif in the narrative itself. The issue of a name for the character called Yardman is a minor but not insignificant point in establishing the differences in perspective on identity between Son and Jadine, Son, having met him as an equal and thus naturally referring to him by his name, Gideon; Jadine, like everyone else in the household, regarding and referring to him as simply Yardman. A similar attitude of the character's station that accords him no name by his employers is reflected in the translators' choice of the appellation "Boy"—the internationalized English term from colonialism alive and well today in many places and borrowed into other languages. Passing up the German equivalent of yardman or gardener, but instead focusing on the character's multi-purpose functions as a hired hand, the two-person translator team reached into the absolute master-servant milieu to come up with not a French term, that might come from the French Antilles of the setting, not a German term, but the international word for black manservant: "Boy." The two-fold irony is that the term violates both the author's concept, literally reducing the character's status, and it violates the standard usage of the term as a manservant whose duties are customarily inside the house. Can the translators' choice be rationalized because they retained the English term "butler" for Sidney and wanted to keep all the servants' names within the British system? What's in a name? The reduction in status—and dignity—that "Boy" does to "Yardman" gives the character a decidedly different image, which in turn causes him to be viewed in a different way by the reader. As the primary representative, along with Marie-Therese, of the island's indigenous population, that entire population is regarded not as men and women whose lives are only qualitatively different from the lives of the masters who created the island's condition, but as boys and girls who are neither desirous nor capable of changing their condition.

Although the weight of this assessment of the reception and criticism of Toni Morrison in the West German literary community would appear to be negative, this impression is mitigated through reflection on the following points: 1) For better or for worse, Morrison is the most widely published Afro-American woman author in German translation; 2) She is also the most studied, in the original texts, at German, Swiss, and Austrian universities, as evidenced by the numbers of dissertations, articles, and other publications on Afro-American and women's literature in which she is included.[61] Comparative literature studies are now appearing in thesis indexes that bring Morrison into encounter with the diverse women writers of the *Neue Frau* series. Thus, both the academic and the commercial publishing communities acknowledge Morrison's place in and contribution to American literature; 3) If her novels are read as superficial anthropology as the press reviews reflect, then indeed the readership loses the essential Morrison and her presentation of the black experience via a black aesthetic. If, however, even through translations of greatly varying quality the readership expends the effort to appreciate the works as literature in a voice with an accent to which they may need to pay closer attention than to one more familiar, they will receive the essential Morrison, as a writer who addresses intelligent German readers as she does any other intelligent readers.

Notes

1. W. E. B. Dubois, *The Autobiography of W. E. B. DuBois* (New York: International Publishers, 1968), 157. This early encounter between DuBois and Germans during his graduate student years in Europe, 1892–94, was not the source of the celebrity and honors he would later earn among Germans, particularly in the German Democratic Republic, as a social scientist and socialist thinker.

2. Terrell, representing African American women at the 1904 International Congress of Women in Berlin gave her address in fluent German (Rayford W. Logan and Michael R. Winston, eds., *Dictionary of American Negro Biography* [New York: Norton, 1982], 584).

3. Robeson, admired in Germany not only as a performer but also as a socialist activist, was awarded, in 1960, the (East) German Peace Medal and an honorary doctorate from the Humboldt University. (Dorothy Butler Gillian, *Paul Robeson: All American* [Washington, D.C.: New Republic Book Co., 1976], 180–82).

4. By sheer coincidence, Jesse Owens's name again appeared in 1986 in the German press in commemoration of the 50th anniversary of the Berlin Olympics. Now, the black athlete is featured in stories which give a revised, more humane perspective on the image of this man who had been a popular curiosity to the German public during the era of National Socialism.

5. Recent plans threaten abolishment of the faculty position in Afro-American literature at the Free University.

6. Jones's *The Birdcatcher* was published in German by Rowohlt, 1986.

7. Shange's *For Colored Girls Who Consider Suicide When the Rainbow Is Enuf* was published in German by Rowohlt, 1985.

8. Marshall's *Praise Song for the Widow* was published by Rowohlt, 1986.

9. Angelou's *I Know Why the Caged Bird Sings* was published by Roter Stern in Frankfurt, 1980, and by Fischer in Frankfurt, 1985.

10. Alice Walker's *The Color Purple* was published by Rowohlt, 1984; *Meridian* by Frauenbuchverlag, 1984.

11. Emecheta's *The Joys of Motherhood* was published by Frauenbuchverlag in Munich, 1983.

12. Bâ's *Une si longue lettre* (So long a letter) and *Le chant écarlate* (The scarlet song) were published in Bergh, Switzerland by Unter Ageri, 1980 and 1982 respectively. They were later published in Germany, the former by Ullstein in Frankfurt, 1983, the latter by Fischer in Frankfurt, 1985.

13. The figure includes 18,000 copies published in East Germany.

14. Personal conversation with Angela Praesent, editor of Rowohlt Verlag's *Neue Frau* series.

15. Praesent to Adams.

16. Klaus Ensslen, *Einführung in die Schwarzamerikanische Literatur* (Stuttgart: Verlag W. Kohlhammer Gmbh, 1982), 157–58.

17. Malwine Blunck, "Toni Morrison: Eine Studie über die afroamerikanischautorin und ihr Werk (Ph.D. diss., University of Hamburg, 1984), 5. Other dissertations on Morrison in progress at various West German universities at the time of this research should be completed by the time of publication of this book.

18. Anne Koenen, "The One Out of Sequence: An Interview with Toni Morrison," in Günter H. Lenz, ed., *History and Tradition in Afro-American Culture* (New York: Campus Verlag, 1984), 208.

19. Anne Koenen, *Zeitgenössische Afro-amerikanische Frauenliteratur: Selbstbild und Identität bei Toni Morrison, Alice Walker, Tone Cade Bambara and Gayle Jones* (New York: Campus Verlag, 1985), 30.

20. Utelinde Wedertz-Furtado, "Historical Dimensions in Toni Morrison's *Song of Solomon*, in Günter H. Lenz, ed., *History and Tradition in Afro-American Culture* (New York: Campus Verlag, 1984), 228.

21. Ibid., 228.

22. Ibid.

23. Angela Praesent, "Eine afro-amerikanische Autorin: *Toni Morrison*," paper presented at the John F. Kennedy Institut of the Free University of Berlin, West Berlin, May 1979.

24. Unfortunately, this is typical of the level of accuracy of the material in Ensslen's book, intended to serve as an overview of Afro-American literature from its beginnings until the mid-1970s.

25. Ensslen, *Einführung*, 177.

26. Ibid., 176.

27. Peter Bruck, "Returning to One's Roots: The Motif of Searching and Flying in Toni Morrison's *Song of Solomon*," in Peter Bruck and Wolfgang Karrer, eds., *The Afro-American Novel Since 1960* (Amsterdam: B. R. Guner, 1982), 302.

28. Ibid., 300.

29. Blunck, "Eine Studie," 80.

30. Ibid., 81.

31. Ibid., 84.

32. Ibid., 83.

33. Koenen, *Zeitgenössische Afro-Amerikanische Frauenliteratur*, 4.

34. Ibid., 4.

35. Ibid., 19.

36. Ibid., 220.

37. Ibid., 151.

38. Ibid., 151–52.

39. Ibid., 153.

40. Ibid., 190.

41. Ibid.

42. Ibid., 179.

43. Ibid., 217.

44. Ibid., 25.

45. Ibid., 30.

46. Wedertz-Furtado, "Historical Dimensions," 223.

47. Ibid., 233–34.

48. Walter Göbel, "Identität und Mythos in Toni Morrison's 'Song of Solomon,' in *Englisch Amerikanische Studien* 5 (September 1983): 424–30.

49. Ibid., 424.

50. Vanessa C. White, *Afro-American and East German Fiction: A Comparative Study of Alienation Identity and Development of Self* (New York: Peter Lang, 1983).

51. Praesent, "Eine afro-amerikanische Autorin," 5.

52. Blunck, "Returning to One's Roots," 95.

53. Ibid., 95.

54. Ibid.

55. Ibid.

56. "Sieschaffen sich ihre eigene Hölle," *Frankfurter Allgemeine Zeitung*, 7 May 1979, 24.

57. "Auf den Spuren der Vergangenheit," *Neue Zurcher Zeitung*, 23 March 1979, 37.

58. "Auf der Suche nach Gold und Wahrheit," *Die Welt*, 5 May 1979, Section: "Die Geistige Welt," 5.

59. Review of *Salomons(sic)Lied*, *Die neue Bucherei* 5 (December 1979).

60. "Sie schaffen sich ihre eigene Hölle," *Frankfurter Allgemeine Zeitung*, 7 May 1979, 24.

61. Also in East Germany two Morrison novels, *Sula* and *Song of Solomon*, are read, having been published there by Volk und Welt in East Berlin. A review of *Song of Solomon* by Olga Wiebe appears in *Zeitschrift für Anglistik und Amerikanistik* 33 (1985): 29–39.

INDEX